S0-BXK-620

FLAVOURS OF THE WORLD

240 RECIPES
FROM ALL OVER THE WORLD

Canadian Cataloguing in Publication Data

Main entry under title:

Flavours of the world

Translation of: Un monde de saveurs.

Includes index.

ISBN 2-89535-048-5

1. Cookery, International. 1. Girard, Frédéric, 1974-

TX725.A1M6513 2001 641.59 C2001-941401-3

Design and layout: Cyclone Design Communications Inc.
Photographs: François Croteau

1 2 3 4 5 TOTAL 05 04 03 02 01

Éditions TOTAL Publishing
Outremont (Québec) Canada

Contents

Introduction

Nutrition is indispensable to human beings. It allows children to develop healthy bodies, adults to remain vigorous and ward off disease, and seniors to enjoy a full life. But first and foremost, nutrition is essential because, as stated by Molière's Harpagon, "we must eat to live." But over the centuries, human beings advanced this notion by developing the culinary arts, thereby transforming the need to eat into true gastronomic pleasures. Throughout the world, people identified edible products from their respective regions and integrated them into their cuisine. As travelers and explorers discovered that herbs and spices found in various parts of the world gave foods their own unique taste, they learned to appreciate the various flavours and aromas offered from country to country.

Today, culinary and gastronomic enthusiasts no longer have to cross the globe in order to sample its hidden treasures, as exotic foods can now be found in major grocers and specialized retailers. The intent of this cookbook is to give readers the opportunity to discover such foods and learn how to use them. More familiar foods will also be included in these pages in the form of both celebrated and original recipes.

Assembling the best recipes the world over, this cookbook presents a practical and pleasing panorama of international cuisine, all in one convenient volume. Our intent was to meet the expectations of readers who value a healthy and varied diet and are intrigued by specialties from the four corners of the globe. World travelers will also discover and fondly recall savoury dishes they may have sampled along their journeys.

The recipes presented in this cookbook have been divided into four chapters, following the traditional 5-course meal service: appetizers and salads, soups, main courses and desserts. Cooking enthusiasts can therefore create complete menus by combining recipes from different countries or even concoct a "world tour" extravaganza menu.

In fact, today's most daring chefs never hesitate to combine exotic flavours borrowed from several cultures within the same meal to impress their guests with contrasting tastes and colours. By exploring this cookbook, such gastronomic cosmopolitanism is also available to you. So forget the strict rules, follow your personal tastes and proclivities, and create some your own stunning culinary combinations!

Of course, interest in international cuisine is far from new. In fact, each country has taken elements from others to hone their culinary arts or imported products for cultivation in their native land. It was the need to procure spices that led Christopher Columbus to charter the flotilla on which he would discover America, even though his first intention was simply to go to India to bring back a cargo of spices without having to pay taxes or rights of passage. Italians imported the first tomato plants from America (specifically, from Peru, where it grew as a weed), and ever since, we associate tomatoes with Italian cuisine. Corn with which Italians make polenta also hails from America, and ever-popular Italian pasta is not Italian at all, but rather Chinese, brought to us from the Orient in the 13th century courtesy of another pioneer, Marco Polo.

Indeed, the Orient is famous for the profusion of its spices, whose combinations form curry, a condiment used from Asia to the Antilles. Every country, region, locality and family uses its own blend of curry, each boasting its own colour and aroma.

Dietary habits also vary from continent to continent depending on the availability of foods. In Asia, meat accompanies rice — not the other way around. In India, higher castes are vegetarian and thus, the wealthiest people do not eat meat. This staple is reserved only to the poor, an ironic custom considering how expensive it is!

In Hong Kong, most restaurants house vivariums and aquariums; meat is kept fresh by keeping the animal alive! This original solution allows chefs to cook quality meat that can be enhanced with herbs and spices without altering the taste. Very spicy dishes came into being to cover the gamy taste of meat. A more refined cuisine would later develop, although the penchant for peppers still varies from culture to culture.

In China, the custom of wok cooking spread following a wood shortage. The Chinese needed a way to cook foods rapidly to conserve wood, and the wok turned into the perfect cooking instrument. A similar constraint may have led South Americans to cook their fish and seafood in lime or lemon juice, having realized that the acidity of these citrus fruits reacted with the protein, producing a kind of cold curing. In Indonesia, meat is tenderized with papaya or pineapple leaves — an effect that can also be achieved with kiwi. Once again, the acidity of this fruit reacts with the meat to make it tender.

So if culinary practices vary from continent to continent, it is, in part, due to specific constraints, but also as a means of using the most economical local resources. Every country has borrowed techniques or foods from its neighbours or distant countries, transforming their national cuisine into a potpourri of sorts. It is mainly the savoir-faire and ingenuity of the chefs themselves that has allowed nations to develop and establish their culinary identity. But culinary practices suffer when closed to methods and innovations from elsewhere. Indeed, only by taking advantage of flavours and aromas from the four corners of the globe can gastronomy truly reach its greatest potential.

Basic recipes

This chapter contains important basic recipes found around the world. Using these recipes you can create and develop new dishes. Take the time to read and try these recipes, which will surely appeal to you and your guests alike. These recipes bring an original touch to your dishes. Remember: a sauce must never disguise the taste of the main dish; instead, it should enhance the flavour.

Making Stock

A richly flavoured stock is the key to success when making many soups and broths. It is very important to use cold water when preparing stock. While hot tap water may save time, it seals off the surface of the ingredients, which prevents flavours and nutrients from being released. In addition, hot tap water contains residues that can alter the taste of the soup. Use only enough water to cover the ingredients by about 2.5 cm (1 inch).

Stocks and soups must be cooked over very low heat in order to extract the maximum flavour from the ingredients. It is preferable to wait until the soup is ready before adding salt and pepper. This way, the soup will not be too salty should the liquid be considerably reduced during cooking. Nor will it be too peppery, as pepper becomes hotter the longer it is simmered.

Before using the stock to make soup, you must remove the layer of fat congealed on the surface after a few hours in the refrigerator. This can also be done at room temperature by dipping paper towels into the soup to absorb the fat.

Instant Bouillon in a Pinch

When time is at a premium, you can use canned bouillon or concentrated bouillon cubes to make soups. But rather than following the manufacturer's instructions, use only two-thirds of the recommended amount of concentrate to one part water. A tiny amount of bouillon concentrate can enhance a soup that needs a flavour boost.

Conserving Soups

Most stocks and soups will keep for 4 or 5 days in the fridge. Stock can be frozen for up to a year, and most soups for 6 months.

To be used as a stock for various poultry recipes, soups and sauces.

White chicken stock

INGREDIENTS

1.5 kg carcasses, giblets, neck, wings, legs **3 1/2 pounds**
500 mL mirepoix (1.5 cm cubes) **2 cups**
15 mL butter **1 tbsp**
2 to 3 L cold water **8 to 12 cups**

2 to 3 L
(8 to 12 cups)

METHOD

1 Rinse the carcasses and giblets well in cold water.

2 Cook the mirepoix gently without colouring. Set aside.

3 Place the carcasses and giblets in a large saucepan and cover with cold water. Bring slowly to a boil and then boil for 10 minutes, skimming constantly in order to clarify the stock.

4 Add the mirepoix, thyme and bay leaf. Lower the heat and let simmer for 2 to 3 hours. Add water to compensate for evaporation. Strain the stock through a fine sieve or cheesecloth. Allow to cool, then refrigerate and degrease. Freezes well, divided into smaller portions.

Note: If there are no carcasses available, replace with chicken legs, one of the least expensive cuts. Remove legs 45 minutes after cooking, and reserve the meat for another recipe. Return the bones to the saucepan until the stock has finished cooking.

To be used as a stock for various poultry recipes, soups and sauces.

Brown chicken stock

2 to 3 L
(8 to 12 cups)

INGREDIENTS

1.5 kg carcasses, giblets (neck, wings, legs) **3 pounds**
500 mL mirepoix, cut in 1.5 cm cubes **2 cups**

45 mL Vegetable oil **3 tbsp**
2 to 3 L cold water **8 to 12 cups**
2 fresh quartered tomatoes 2
30 mL flour **2 tbsp**
15 mL tomato paste **1 tbsp**

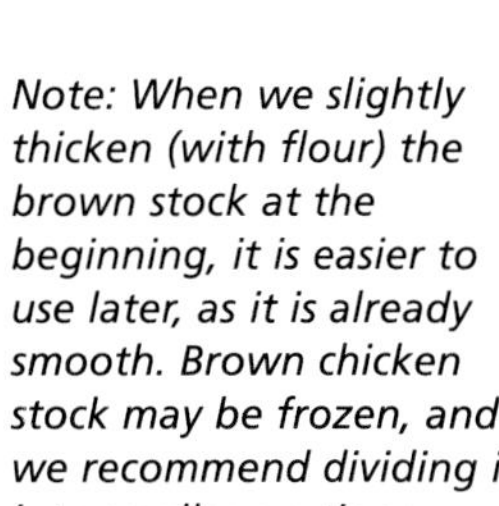

METHOD

1 Preheat the oven to 260°C (500°F).

2 Oil a roasting pan, and add the carcasses and giblets. Roast the carcasses (brown), turning periodically, for 20 to 30 minutes.

3 Add the mirepoix, mix in and continue browning for approximately 15 minutes.

4 Remove from oven and, using a slotted spoon or skimmer, place everything in a saucepan.

5 Drain the grease from the roasting pan without cleaning the pan, and add the tomato paste and flour.

6 Mix well over medium heat for 2 minutes, scraping the bottom of the roasting pan. Add a bit of the water to free the juices stuck to the bottom.

7 Pour over the roasted carcasses set aside in the saucepan. Cover with the rest of the water and simmer for approximately 2 hours.

8 Strain the stock through a fine sieve or cheesecloth. Allow to cool, then refrigerate and degrease.

Note: When we slightly thicken (with flour) the brown stock at the beginning, it is easier to use later, as it is already smooth. Brown chicken stock may be frozen, and we recommend dividing it into smaller portions.

Beef Stock

1 L (4 cups)

For clear poultry stock, do not oven roast the trimmings.

INGREDIENTS

1 kg poultry *or* beef trimmings **2 lb**
1 medium onion, coarsely chopped 1
1 celery stalk, coarsely chopped 1
1/2 celeriac, coarsely chopped 1/2
1 leek, white part, coarsely chopped 1
4 sprigs thyme 4
125 mL chopped parsley **1/2 cup**
2 bay leaves 2
2 mL whole black pepper **1/2 tsp**
250 mL white wine **1 cup**
2 L cold water **8 cups**

METHOD

1. Preheat the oven to 200°C (400°F).
2. Cut the trimmings into medium-sized pieces.
3. Place in a roasting pan and brown in the oven.
4. Once trimmings are browned, add the vegetables and return to the oven for 8 to 10 minutes.
5. Remove the roasting pan from the oven and transfer the contents to a medium-sized pot.
6. Degrease the roasting pan, deglaze with a little water and pour it into the pot.
7. Add the wine, herbs and pepper and reduce, uncovered, over medium heat.
8. Add the cold water and bring to a boil, skimming frequently.
9. Reduce the heat and simmer for 2 to 3 hours, skimming and removing fat as often as possible.
10. Strain and refrigerate.

Fish or Shrimp Stock

2 L (8 cups)

Aromatic herbs and vegetables may be added to enhance the flavour.

INGREDIENTS

- **700 g** shrimp *or* white fish trimmings **24 oz**
- **30 mL** butter **2 tbsp**
- **1** medium onion, coarsely chopped **1**
- **80 mL** coarsely chopped celeriac **1/3 cup**
- **6** green onions, coarsely chopped **6**
- **1** leek, white part, coarsely chopped **1**
- **80 mL** mushroom stems **1/3 cup**
- **1** sprig thyme **1**
- **80 mL** chopped parsley **1/3 cup**
- **1** bay leaf **1**
- **125 mL** chopped chives **1/2 cup**
- **10 mL** whole black peppercorns **2 tsp**
- **500 mL** dry white wine **2 cups**
- **3 L** cold water **12 cups**

METHOD

1. In a large pot, cook the vegetables in the butter, without browning, over medium heat.
2. Add the fish trimmings and cook for another 3 to 5 minutes.
3. Add the wine, herbs and pepper; reduce, uncovered, by one-half.
4. Add the cold water and bring to a boil.
5. Cook for 45 minutes, skimming frequently.
6. Strain, cool and set aside.

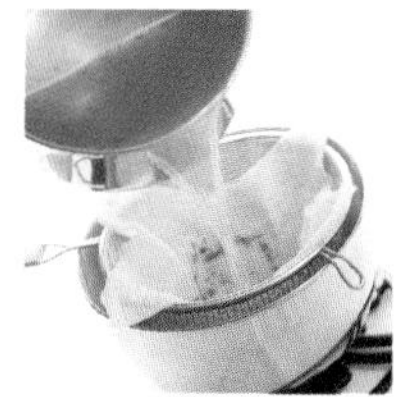

Vegetable Court Bouillon

Aromatic herbs and vegetables may be added to enhance the flavour.

2 L (8 cups)

INGREDIENTS

30 mL butter **2 tbsp**
1 onion, coarsely chopped **1**
1 large carrot, coarsely chopped **1**
1/2 celeriac, coarsely chopped **1/2**
4 green onions, coarsely chopped **4**
1 leek, white part, coarsely chopped **1**
125 mL mushroom stems **1/2 cup**
1 sprig thyme **1**
80 mL chopped parsley **1/3 cup**
1 bay leaf **1**
10 mL black peppercorns **2 tsp**
500 mL dry white wine **2 cups**
3 L cold water **12 cups**

METHOD

1. In a large pot, cook the vegetables in the butter, without browning, over medium heat.
2. Add wine, herbs and pepper. Reduce by one-half, uncovered.
3. Add the cold water and bring to a boil.
4. Cook for 45 minutes.
5. Strain, cool and set aside.

Dashi

Dashi is the basic stock used in Japanese soups and many other Japanese dishes. It is prepared with flakes of dried bonito (a type of tuna) and a piece of kombu (seaweed).

1 L water **4 cups**
2 mL salt **1/2 tsp**
1 10 cm (4-inch) piece kombu (optional) **1**
125 mL dried bonito flakes **1/2 cup**

Bring water to a boil. Add the salt, kombu (if using) and bonito flakes. Stir for a few seconds and immediately strain the stock.

Seasonings and Garnishes

Bouquet garni

Bouquet garni consists of a celery stalk, preferably with leaves, a bay leaf, a sprig of thyme or a pinch of dried thyme, and a sprig of parsley. To make it easier to remove the bouquet garni once the soup is done, tie the ingredients in a bundle. Cut the celery stalk in two, place the thyme and parsley sprigs in the hollow of one of the celery pieces, cover with the bay leaf and the second piece of celery. Tie together with cotton string. When making stock, it is not necessary to tie the bouquet garni, since all ingredients will be strained out once the stock is done.

Salted Herbs

Salted herbs will keep for about a year in the fridge. It is preferable to rinse them before using to remove excess salt. While the choice of herbs can vary according to personal preferences and availability of ingredients, it is important to respect the proportion of salt to herbs.

250 mL chives **1 cup**
250 mL parsley **1 cup**
250 mL leek, green part **1 cup**
250 mL green onion leaves **1 cup**
500 mL celery leaves **2 cups**
75 mL savory, marjoram or oregano **1/3 cup**
500 mL coarse salt **2 cups**

Wash and dry the herbs. Chop finely and mix in a large bowl. Take one or more glass jars, add a layer of coarse salt and then a layer of herbs (about 2 cm or 1 inch), continuing until the jar is full. Finish with a layer of salt. Rinse under cold water in a sieve or strainer before using.

Curry Powder

Curry is a blend of spices used to season many dishes around the world. It is usually made with 7 different spices selected according to the cook's or the manufacturer's secret recipe. Curry can be mild, medium or hot, and the piquant aroma of a good curry will excite the taste buds. It should be replaced frequently or made in small batches. The following recipe can be used to replace a commercially prepared curry. If you are fond of spicy foods, increase the amount of cayenne.

15 mL ground coriander **1 tbsp**

5 mL ground cumin **1 tsp**

2 mL dry mustard **1/2 tsp**

2 to 5 mL cayenne pepper **1/2 to 1 tsp**

10 mL turmeric **2 tsp**

2 mL ground black pepper **1/2 tsp**

2 mL ground ginger **1/2 tsp**

Blend all ingredients well and store in an airtight container to conserve freshness. Use while flavour is at its peak, within 3 months.

Puff Pastry Twists

Use homemade or store-bought puff pastry dough. Stretch into strips 1 cm wide and 30 cm long (1/2 in. x 12 in.). Form each strip into a twist, holding both ends. Sprinkle with salt crystals (preferably sea salt) and bake at 425°F (220°C) until the twists are crusty and golden.

Garlic Croutons

These croutons may be served as is or in small cubes as a garnish for salad or soup. Soft-textured bread gives the best results.

4 slices lightly crusted bread, 2 cm (1/2-in.) thick **4**

30 mL butter, at room temperature **2 tbsp**

30 mL olive oil **2 tbsp**

1 clove garlic, finely chopped **1**

15 mL fresh parsley, chopped **1 tbsp**

3 mL fresh lemon juice **1/2 tsp**

Fresh ground pepper

In a small bowl, blend the butter, oil, garlic, lemon juice, parsley and pepper. Brush onto both sides of the bread and place on a baking sheet.

Broil at a distance of 10 to 15 cm (4 to 6 in.) from the element, until both sides of the bread are golden. Turn off the broiler and let cool in the oven before serving or cutting into cubes.

Note: To prepare the butter in a food processor: With the machine running, drop in the garlic and then the parsley; turn off the machine. Add the butter, oil, lemon juice and pepper, and run machine until the mixture is smooth.

4 servings

Port Sauce

250 mL (1 cup)

I N G R E D I E N T S

30 mL butter **2 tbsp**

60 mL finely chopped green onion **1/4 cup**

500 mL port **2 cups**

500 mL fish stock (see recipe on p. 13) **2 cups**

1 bay leaf **1**

45 mL chopped lemongrass **3 tbsp**

5 mL fresh thyme **1 tsp**

M E T H O D

1 In a 3 L (2.5-quart) pot, cook the green onion in butter over low heat.

2 Add the port and reduce by one-fifth.

3 Add the fish stock and flavourings and reduce by one-quarter over medium heat.

4 Strain the sauce and serve.

For a thicker sauce, add a mixture of 15 mL (1 tbsp) cornstarch and 30 mL (2 tbsp) water; heat for 1 or 2 minutes until sauce thickens and serve.

Meat Glaze

250 mL (1 cup)

I N G R E D I E N T S

60 mL butter **1/4 cup**

1 small carrot, coarsely chopped **1**

1 small onion, coarsely chopped **1**

1 celery stalk, coarsely chopped **1**

1/2 white part of leek, coarsely chopped **1/2**

30 mL parsley **2 tbsp**

300 g beef bones **10 oz**

250 mL port **1 cup**

250 mL red wine **1 cup**

2 1/2 L brown beef stock (see recipe on p. 12) **10 cups**

M E T H O D

1 In a medium-sized saucepan, cook vegetables and herbs in the butter, without browning.

2 Add the bones and cook for 3 to 5 more minutes.

3 Add the port and reduce by one-half. Add the red wine and reduce, uncovered, until one-quarter of the liquid remains.

4 Add the brown beef stock and bring to a boil; reduce the heat and simmer, uncovered.

5 Reduce by 90% over very low heat; strain through a chinois. Cool and set aside.

This meat glaze can be diluted with water and used as a base for a sauce.

Spanish Sauce

600 mL (2 1/3 cups)

INGREDIENTS

1 L brown beef stock (see recipe on p. 12) **4 cups**
30 mL coarsely chopped carrot **2 tbsp**
30 mL sliced onion **2 tbsp**
30 mL sliced celery **2 tbsp**
30 mL diced tomato **2 tbsp**
30 mL chopped mushroom **2 tbsp**
60 mL brown roux **1/4 cup**
1 sprig thyme **1**
6 sprigs parsley **6**
pinch whole black pepper
25 g salted bacon **1 oz**

- *To make a brown roux, melt one part butter and add one part flour. Cook, stirring constantly, until the roux turns brown. Ideal for thickening brown sauces.*
- *For a blond roux, cook only until the mixture is amber in colour.*
- *For a white roux, stop cooking before any colour change.*

METHOD

1. In a small saucepan, bring the brown stock to a boil.
2. Place the cold roux in a medium-sized saucepan and pour in the heated brown beef stock.
3. Simmer and add the vegetables, herbs and pepper.
4. Cook for 1 1/2 to 1 3/4 hours, uncovered, over low heat.
5. Strain, cool and set aside.

Demi-glace

1 L (4 cups)

INGREDIENTS

2 L spanish sauce **6 cups**

METHOD

1. Reduce by one-half over low heat.
2. Strain and set aside.

This demi-glace can be diluted with water and used as a base for a sauce.

Sweet and sour pineapple sauce

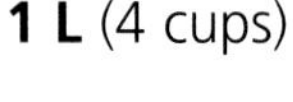

1 L (4 cups)

INGREDIENTS

15 mL vegetable oil **1 tbsp**
30 mL minced garlic **2 tbsp**
250 mL pineapple juice **1 cup**
400 mL water **1 2/3 cups**
125 mL cider vinegar **1/2 cup**
80 mL soy sauce **1/3 cup**
125 mL molasses **1/2 cup**
15 mL fresh ginger **1 tbsp**
5 mL ground coriander **1 tsp**
30 mL brown sugar **2 tbsp**
5 mL salt **1 tsp**
2.5 mL white pepper **1/2 tsp**
2 or 3 drops Tabasco sauce **2 or 3 drops**
30 mL cornstarch **2 tbsp**

METHOD

1 In a medium saucepan, sauté the minced garlic in the oil, without browning.

2 Add all other ingredients, except the cornstarch, and bring to a boil and immediately lower the heat.

3 Let simmer 10 minutes, then thicken with the cornstarch mixed with water.

4 Cook another 4 to 5 minutes, and verify seasoning.

5 Strain (optional).

This sauce is used primarily to glaze small pieces of chicken during cooking. It can also be used as a marinade; the raw chicken pieces are coated and left to marinate refrigerated for 1 or 2 hours before cooking.

Note: Pineapple chunks can be added as garnish.

Peanut, ginger and orange sauce

1 L (4 cups)

INGREDIENTS

30 mL canola oil **2 tbsp**
15 mL minced garlic **1 tbsp**
125 mL chopped onion **1/2 cup**
1 L water **4 cups**
125 mL medium orange (with peel), cubed **1/2 cup**
250 mL peanut butter **1 cup**
15 mL ginger **1 tbsp**
5 mL ground coriander **1 tsp**
5 mL cumin **1 tsp**
125 mL grated coconut, unsweetened **1/2 cup**
5 mL curry **1 tsp**
5 mL ground chili **1 tsp**
pinch cayenne pepper or a few drops of Tabasco sauce
salt to taste
10 mL cornstarch (as required) **2 tsp**

METHOD

1. In a heavy saucepan, heat the oil and sauté the garlic and onion without colouring.
2. Add the water and all other ingredients except the cornstarch. Mix well.
3. Bring to a boil, reduce the heat and let simmer approximately 45 minutes, stirring occasionally. Remember, this sauce can stick easily!
4. Thicken with the cornstarch mixed with water, if necessary. Blend in a food processor for 4 or 5 minutes, then strain through a fine sieve. Verify consistency and seasoning.

This sauce can be served with chicken brochettes, satay, or small sautéed or grilled chicken pieces (drumsticks).

Gourmet barbecue sauce (hot sauce)

1 L (4 cups)

INGREDIENTS

125 mL Worcestershire sauce **1/2 cup**
250 mL chili sauce **1 cup**
30 mL white vinegar **2 tbsp**
500 mL brown chicken stock **2 cups**
2 cloves thinly sliced garlic **2 cloves**
15 mL Dijon mustard **1 tbsp**
45 mL brown sugar **3 tbsp**
15 mL ground coriander **1 tbsp**
2 bay leaves **2**
15 mL mild paprika **1 tbsp**
15 mL powdered chili **1 tbsp**
30 mL vegetable oil **2 tbsp**
15 mL flour **1 tbsp**
15 mL freshly minced ginger **1 tbsp**
ground white pepper and salt to taste
15 mL cornstarch mixed in a bit of water **1 tbsp**

METHOD

Garnish:

125 mL carrot **1/2 cup**
125 mL celery **1/2 cup**
125 mL onion **1/2 cup**
Finely minced by hand or with a food processor.

1. In a saucepan, sauté the vegetable garnish in the oil, add the flour and mix well.
2. Add all the other ingredients, finishing with the brown stock. Mix well and bring to a boil. Let simmer for 5 or 6 minutes, and verify seasoning.
3. Thicken with cornstarch if necessary. Serve with grilled or roasted chicken, etc. Keeps well refrigerated in an airtight container. This sauce can also be frozen.

Mustard vinaigrette with sun-dried tomatoes

375 mL (1 1/2 cups)

INGREDIENTS

250 mL olive oil **1 cup**

30 mL Dijon mustard **2 tbsp**

1 egg yolk **1**

30 mL balsamic vinegar **2 tbsp**

30 mL cider vinegar **2 tbsp**

30 ml chopped shallots **2 tbsp**

30 ml chopped fresh parsley **2 tbsp**

salt and ground pepper to taste

4 dried tomato halves (soaked in lukewarm water for 2 hours, makes 30 mL – 2 tbsp) **4**

METHOD

1 Beat the olive oil, mustard and egg yolk as for a mayonnaise.

2 Add the vinegar, salt and pepper, shallots, parsley and dried tomatoes.

3 Mix well. The vinaigrette must have a smooth texture.

Note: You may replace the parsley with other herbs, such as tarragon, chives, chervil, etc. Cubes of very firm fresh tomatoes may be used in place of the dried tomatoes.

Serve with cold chicken, accompanied by lettuce, asparagus or mango squash.

Sweet pepper coulis

750 mL (3 cups)

INGREDIENTS

500 mL sliced red peppers **2 cups**

125 mL sliced onion **1/2 cup**

5 mL minced garlic **1 tsp**

30 mL vegetable oil **2 tbsp**

15 mL flour **1 tbsp**

15 mL tomato paste **1 tbsp**

500 mL chicken stock or water **2 cups**

5 mL sugar **1 tsp**

2 bay leaves **2**

2 mL salt **1/2 tsp**

1.5 mL white pepper **1/3 tsp**

15 mL cornstarch **1 tbsp**

METHOD

1 In a saucepan, heat the oil and sauté (without colouring) the peppers, onions and garlic.

2 Add the flour, bay leaves and tomato paste.

3 Add the chicken stock or water.

4 Bring to a boil, let simmer for approximately 45 minutes, and season to taste.

5 Blend in a food processor, and strain through a fine sieve. Return to the saucepan, bring to a boil, and thicken with the cornstarch mixed with water, if necessary.

6 Verify seasoning. The coulis must be smooth in texture.

May be served hot or cold with terrines or small pieces of poached fowl (chicken or turkey).

Chicken velouté with white wine

1 L (4 cups)

I N G R E D I E N T S

30 mL sweet butter (for the shallots) **2 tbsp**

30 mL minced shallots **2 tbsp**

125 mL white wine **1/2 cup**

60 mL sweet butter (for the white roux) **1/4 cup**

60 mL flour (for the white roux) **1/4 cup**

625 mL white chicken stock **2 1/2 cups**

180 mL 35% whipping cream **3/4 cup**

1. In a heavy saucepan, sauté the shallots in the butter, without colouring.
2. Deglaze with the white wine, and reduce until there is no liquid left.
3. Add the roux butter, melt and add the flour. Mix well and cook for 2 to 3 minutes over very low heat, taking care not to brown the roux.
4. Add the cold white stock, bring to a boil and add the cream.
5. Cook over low heat for 6 to 8 minutes, stirring constantly. Strain through a sieve to remove the shallots.

This velouté can be used to accompany all chicken or turkey recipes that call for a moderately seasoned white sauce.

Note: If you find that the sauce is too thick, just add a bit of white stock or cream.

Béchamel sauce

650 mL (2 1/2 cups)

This is an essential basic sauce, especially with poultry. The milk and butter flavour are the perfect enhancement to turkey and chicken, poached and cut into cubes or in strips.

I N G R E D I E N T S

White roux:

60 ml flour **1/4 cup**

60 mL soft butter **1/4 cup**

500 mL cold milk **2 cups**

salt, pepper, nutmeg (optional)

1. Melt the butter in a heavy saucepan.
2. Add the flour and mix well with a wooden spoon. Cook 1 to 2 minutes, stirring constantly.
3. Add the cold milk, and whisk until boiling. Reduce the heat, season with salt, pepper and nutmeg. Cook over low heat for 4 to 5 minutes, stirring. Make sure the sauce does not stick to the bottom of the saucepan.

Note: The consistency of the béchamel sauce depends on the quantity of milk added.

Variations

Add a bit of grated Swiss Gruyère cheese.

Add a bit of 35% cream for more smoothness.

Add crushed tomatoes, then strain through a sieve to obtain a rose-coloured sauce.

Add 2 coarsely chopped hardboiled eggs.

Madras fruit sauce

1 1/2 L (6 cups)

INGREDIENTS

250 mL apple chunks with skin **1 cup**
125 mL ripe banana **1/2 cup**
250 mL red pepper **1 cup**
250 mL green pepper **1 cup**
125 mL celery **1/2 cup**
125 mL onion **1/2 cup**
(All above ingredients cut into mirepoix)
30 mL canola oil **2 tbsp**
15 mL flour **1 tbsp**
15 mL minced garlic **1 tbsp**
30 mL Madras curry powder **2 tbsp**
5 mL ground coriander **1 tsp**
2 mL cumin **1/2 tsp**
5 mL paprika **1 tsp**
2 mL salt **1/2 tsp**
1 L white chicken stock (or water) **4 cups**
5 mL cornstarch mixed in a little water **1 tsp**

METHOD

1 Sauté all the fruit and vegetables without letting brown.

2 Add the flour and seasoning, and mix well.

3 Add the white stock or water and cook over low heat for approximately one hour.

4 Add the cornstarch mixed with a bit of water and verify seasoning to taste.

5 Bring the sauce to a boil and cook for 2 to 3 minutes, stirring carefully.

Note: The well-cooked fruit and vegetables, once blended in the food processor, act as the main thickening agent for this sauce.

Flavoured Oil

600 mL (2 1/3 cups)

Remove from the refrigerator and let stand at room temperature about 30 minutes before using.

INGREDIENTS

500 mL olive oil **2 cups**
225 mL diced tomato **1 cup**
2 garlic bulbs **2**
5 mL paprika **1 tsp**
2.5 mL crushed chili pepper **1/2 tsp**
salt to taste
ground black pepper to taste

METHOD

1. Preheat the oven to 190°C (375°F).
2. Split the garlic bulbs into cloves and place in a small ovenproof earthenware dish.
3. Drizzle the garlic with 30 mL (2 tbsp) olive oil and bake for 40 minutes.
4. Cool and peel the garlic cloves.
5. Blend all ingredients and the oil in a blender and store in an airtight container in the refrigerator.

Portuguese Herbs and Spices

250 mL (1 cup)

This recipe can be used as a dry marinade for meats; rub the meat with the mixture, wrap in plastic and refrigerate for a few hours.

INGREDIENTS

125 mL paprika **1/2 cup**
45 mL cayenne pepper **3 tbsp**
75 mL freshly ground black pepper **5 tbsp**
90 mL garlic powder **6 tbsp**
45 mL onion powder **3 tbsp**
75 mL salt **5 tbsp**
45 mL dried oregano **3 tbsp**
45 mL dried thyme **3 tbsp**

1. Combine all the ingredients in a bowl and mix well.
2. The mixture should be stored in an airtight container in a dry place.

Pili-pili

330 mL (1 1/3 cups)

This recipe can be used as a dry marinade for meats; rub the meat with the mixture, wrap in plastic and refrigerate for a few hours.

INGREDIENTS

250 mL extra virgin olive oil **1 cup**
80 mL red chili pepper **1/3 cup**

1. Lightly crush the chili pepper and place in a glass jar.
2. Add the oil and seal with an airtight lid.
3. Let stand for 1 week before using.
4. Store at room temperature or refrigerate. Remove from the refrigerator 1 hour before use so that the oil can warm up.

Appetizers and salads

Appetizers often serve as an introduction to a refined meal. A good chef will imbue it with his personal savoir-faire and thoroughly impress his guests, who will then be inspired to create equally fabulous appetizers for their own dinner parties. And therein lies the key to a successful appetizer: going for the gusto and setting the tone for the entire meal, just as the first notes of a symphony capture the imagination of spectators and keep them glued to their seats. It is important to remember, however, that creating such a positive impression lies in the subtlety and preparation of the appetizer, one that is chosen so as not to overwhelm the dishes to follow.

In addition to sophisticated appetizers, which require more preparation, a good host can also consider simple appetizers to keep his guests busy until the main course. These can accompany a cocktail and be served on a simple presentation plate. Since they can be prepared in advance, they are easy for both seasoned and novice cooks to concoct.

An appetizer should never be too heavy or served in abundance in order not to spoil the rest of the meal. Presented in the form of small bites, some appetizers make an ideal substitute for potato chips, serving as more elegant finger foods.

In the following pages, you will discover many easy recipes with light or exotic flavours that are sure to impress your guests and seal your reputation as a first-rate chef.

Since salads are both nourishing and refreshing, they can often substitute as a meal. They represent an ideal choice on hot summer days, or, prepared in advance, can easily be packed in the lunch box or picnic basket. When a salad contains a lot of lettuce, dressing should only be added at the time of serving in order not to wilt the leaves. A salad can accompany the main course, presented in a separate bowl or on the main serving dish (providing there is no sauce to drown it) to add a splash of colour. And of course, nothing beats a salad containing colourful tropical fruits. While salad dressings don't go well with wine (unless it too is made from wine), there is no need to deny yourself or your guests a delicious salad; simply refrain from sipping the wine after a bite of salad, taking a sip after a morsel of meat or bread instead.

When presented as part of an extended meal, salad is typically served before or after the main course. Either way, the salad should be chosen for its light and refreshing taste and digestibility; for instance, a green salad – primarily a mix of lettuce – will gently whet the appetite. Salads allow diners to take a break between two courses and promote digestion. In such cases, wine should not be served during the salad course.

In addition to being an excellent source of nutrients, salads make an ideal choice for enhancing any meal thanks to their lively colours and delicate flavours.

Smoked Salmon Rosettes with Puy Lentils

4 to 6 servings

Julienned endive can be substituted for the mesclun.

INGREDIENTS

400 g cooked green Puy lentils **2 cups**
60 mL chopped green onion **1/4 cup**
60 mL chopped fresh parsley **1/4 cup**
Lemon marinade
350 g smoked salmon, sliced **12 oz**
250 g mesclun **9 oz**

Lemon Marinade

60 mL lemon juice **1/4 cup**
60 mL olive oil **1/4 cup**
125 mL vegetable oil **1/2 cup**
1 mL Dijon mustard **1/4 tsp**
1/2 garlic clove, chopped **1/2**
pinch cayenne pepper
pinch salt
freshly ground pepper

MARINADE

In a bowl, blend all ingredients and refrigerate.

ROSETTES

1. In a large bowl, combine the lentils, green onion and parsley with half the marinade. Marinate for 1 hour in the refrigerator.
2. To form rosettes with the salmon and mesclun, place salmon slices flat and roll them around a bouquet of mesclun. The salmon should form the shape of a flower.
3. Place the rosettes in the centre of the plates, drizzle with remaining marinade and place the marinated lentils around the rim.

Gravlax with Old-Fashioned Mustard

serves **4 to 6**

INGREDIENTS

750 g salmon fillet with skin **1 1/2 lb**
60 mL coarse salt **1/4 cup**
60 mL sugar **1/4 cup**
30 mL crushed black peppercorns **2 tbsp**
250 mL chopped fresh dill **1 cup**
1 medium lemon, sliced **1**
250 mL Old-Fashioned Mustard **1 cup**

Old-Fashioned Mustard
(makes 500 mL or 2 cups)

1 medium onion, chopped **1**
1 clove garlic **1**
30 mL balsamic vinegar **2 tbsp**
125 mL old-fashioned mustard (Meaux) **1/2 cup**
15 mL lemon juice **1 tbsp**
15 mL Worcestershire sauce **1 tbsp**
1 mL ground black pepper **1/4 tsp**
5 mL dried tarragon **1 tsp**
250 mL olive oil **1 cup**

Gravlax

1. Place the salmon fillet in the centre of a sheet of aluminum foil, skin side down. Sprinkle with salt, sugar and pepper. Cover with dill and lemon slices. Wrap carefully and place in a deep dish.
2. Cover with a board. Place a weight (1 kg/2 lb maximum) on the board. Refrigerate 24 hours.
3. Remove the dill and the lemon slices.
4. Wipe the salmon carefully and serve in thin slices with Old-Fashioned Mustard.

Old-Fashioned Mustard

1. Blend all the ingredients in a food processor or blender until creamy.
2. Refrigerate until ready to serve.

SPAIN

Tomatoes Stuffed with Romano Beans

4 to 6 servings

INGREDIENTS

125 mL pine nuts **1/2 cup**

60 mL sliced green onions **1/4 cup**

60 mL sliced carrots **1/4 cup**

60 mL sliced celery **1/4 cup**

60 mL sliced red pepper **1/4 cup**

250 g portobello or oyster mushrooms **1 cup**

15 mL olive oil **1 tbsp**

400 g cooked romano beans or one 540 mL (19-oz) can romano beans, rinsed and drained **2 cups**

60 mL chopped fresh parsley **1/4 cup**

1 kg tomatoes (4 to 6 medium-sized) **2 lb**

Walnut Oil Dressing

60 mL red wine vinegar **1/4 cup**

175 mL walnut oil **3/4 cup**

pinch salt

pinch ground white pepper

METHOD

Dressing

In a small bowl, whisk together all the ingredients and refrigerate.

Stuffed Tomatoes

1. In a nonstick skillet, toast the pine nuts for 5 minutes over medium heat until they start to turn golden. Remove from heat and reserve.
2. Wash the mushrooms and cut into bean-sized pieces.
3. In a large pot, heat the olive oil over medium heat and cook the vegetables for 2 to 3 minutes. Add the mushrooms and beans. Add salt and pepper to taste and cook for 2 to 3 more minutes. Remove from heat and allow to cool completely.
4. Place in a salad bowl and mix in the pine nuts and two-thirds of the dressing.
5. Cut off the tops of the tomatoes and save to be used as "lids" once the tomatoes are stuffed.
6. Scoop out the contents of the tomatoes and fill with the mushroom/bean mixture, replace the "lids" and drizzle with the remaining dressing.

Serve the tomatoes on a bed of salad greens.

Scallops with Black Bean Salsa

4 to 6 servings

INGREDIENTS

500 g large scallops 1 lb

180 mL lime juice (4 or 5 limes) 3/4 cup

1 mL salt 1/4 tsp

5 mL jalapeño pepper (optional) 1 tsp

Freshly ground pepper

Black Bean Salsa

400 g cooked black beans or one 540 mL (19-oz) can black beans, rinsed and drained 2 cups

125 mL finely diced mango 1/2 cup

125 mL chopped red onion 1/2 cup

1 clove garlic, chopped 1

60 mL chopped fresh coriander 1/4 cup
or 5 mL dried coriander 1 tsp

30 mL red wine vinegar 2 tbsp

15 mL olive oil 1 tbsp

5 mL brown sugar 1 tsp

1 mL salt 1/4 tsp

pinch cayenne pepper

freshly ground pepper

Scallops

1. Slice the scallops in half lengthwise and marinate in the lime juice with the seasonings for 20 to 30 minutes or until the scallops are slightly blanched. Remove from the marinade and refrigerate. Save the marinade in a separate container and refrigerate.
2. On a plate, form a crown of scallops and place the salsa in the centre. Drizzle the scallops with a little marinade.

Black Bean Salsa

In a large bowl, mix all the ingredients and refrigerate for at least 1 hour before serving.

A classic created at the end of the 1800s by a chef at Antoine's, one of the most famous restaurants in New Orleans. Owing to the richness of the sauce, the recipe was named after the Rockefellers, the wealthiest family in the United States at that time.

UNITED STATES

Oysters Rockefeller

4 servings

INGREDIENTS

90 mL butter **6 tbsp**
250 mL cleaned and finely chopped fresh spinach **1 cup**
90 mL finely chopped watercress **6 tbsp**
45 mL finely chopped fresh parsley **3 tbsp**
125 mL finely chopped green onions **1/2 cup**
10 mL finely chopped green pepper **2 tsp**
2 mL ground black pepper **1/2 tsp**
2 mL dried marjoram **1/2 tsp**
2 mL dried basil **1/2 tsp**
0.5 mL cayenne **1/8 tsp**
2 mL salt **1/2 tsp**
15 mL Herbsaint or Pernod **1 tbsp**
125 mL 35% cream **1/2 cup**
coarse salt or crumpled aluminum foil
as a bed for the oysters
24 oysters **24**

METHOD

1. Melt the butter in a large pan without letting it brown. Cook the spinach, cress, parsley, green onions and green pepper over low heat for 5 minutes, stirring constantly. Add the black pepper, marjoram, basil, cayenne, salt and Herbsaint or Pernod, and cook for 1 minute.
2. Stir in the cream, bring to a boil, reduce the heat and simmer for 5 to 7 minutes until the mixture is slightly thicker than a sauce. Adjust the seasoning and set aside.
3. Spread a layer of about 2.5 cm (1 in.) coarse salt in a large rectangular dish. Preheat the oven to 200°C (400°F).
4. Brush the oysters with cold water, open and shuck them. Place the shucked oyster on the bottom shell and place it on the bed of salt. Sponge off any excess liquid on the oysters with a paper towel.
5. Top each oyster with a spoonful of sauce and broil on the lower rack of the oven for about 10 minutes until the sauce begins to bubble around the edges of the shell. Use a tong to lift the shells from the baking dish and serve immediately. Individual portions can also be prepared by putting a layer of salt in each serving dish; the baked oysters can then be served in their dishes.

PORTUGAL

Chicken-liver Terrine with Sherry

This paté may also be served warm.

4 servings

INGREDIENTS

350 g chicken livers **12 oz**
250 mL butter **1 cup**
2 cloves garlic, crushed **2**
30 mL sherry *or* wine vinegar **2 tbsp**
5 mL finely chopped fresh sage **1 tsp**
salt to taste
black pepper to taste
8 fresh whole sage leaves **8**
8 small slices toasted bread **8**

METHOD

1. Rinse and dry the chicken livers.
2. In a saucepan, melt 30 mL (2 tbsp) butter and brown the livers, along with the garlic, for about 5 minutes (livers should be pink inside).
3. Place the livers in a food processor container and add sherry and sage.
4. Melt 150 mL (2/3 cup) of the remaining butter and add to the mixture in the food processor.
5. Season and purée until smooth.
6. Place the mixture into individual moulds and smooth the surface with a small spatula.
7. Melt the rest of the butter and pour over the paté. Garnish with the fresh whole sage leaves and refrigerate for 3 hours.
8. Unmould and serve with toasted bread.

FRANCE

Escargot Bundles with Garlic Cream

Makes **18**

It is easier to work with filo if the unfolded sheets are placed on a piece of plastic wrap, covered with a second sheet of plastic wrap and a dampened dish towel. Remove only one sheet of filo at a time.

INGREDIENTS

Filling

30 mL olive oil 2 tbsp

48 escargots, rinsed and drained 48

15 mL chopped green onion 1 tbsp

1/2 clove garlic, chopped 1/2

400 g cooked flageolets or one 540 mL (19-oz) can flageolets, rinsed and drained 2 cups

2 mL dried basil 1/2 tsp

2 mL paprika 1/2 tsp

1 mL dried thyme 1/4 tsp

1 mL salt 1/4 tsp

pinch cayenne pepper

200 g blue or goat cheese, crumbled 7 oz

Garlic Cream

6 cloves garlic 6

250 mL milk 1 cup

500 mL 35% cream 2 cups

60 mL soy sauce 1/4 cup

pinch salt

pinch ground white pepper

Bundles

18 leaves filo dough 18

125 mL melted butter 1/2 cup

METHOD

GARNISH

1 In a large skillet, heat the oil over high heat and sauté the escargots, green onion and garlic for 2 minutes.

2 Add the flageolets, basil, paprika, thyme, salt and cayenne, and cook over medium heat for 5 more minutes.

3 Remove from heat and let cool completely. Refrigerate.

GARLIC CREAM

1 In a small pot, blanch the garlic in 250 mL (1 cup) milk, that is, bring to a boil and remove from heat. Rinse the garlic under cold water and discard the milk. Repeat the operation a second time.

2 Place the blanched garlic in a small pot and pour in the cream and soy sauce. Season and bring to a boil, uncovered. Simmer over medium heat for 5 minutes or until the sauce has been reduced by one-third. Remove from heat and allow to cool for 10 to 15 minutes.

3 In a blender or food processor, blend the sauce for about 3 minutes. Strain and set aside. Keep warm.

BUNDLES

1 Heat the oven to 190°C (375°F).

2 To form a bundle, cut 1 sheet of filo dough into 4 equal sections; brush each one with melted butter and place one on top of another so that the corners do not line up.

3 Place 60 mL (4 tbsp) of escargot-flageolet filling in the middle and sprinkle with cheese. Bring the corners of the filo together over the filling and twist to form a small bundle. Repeat with the remaining dough and filling.

4 Place the bundles on a cookie sheet and bake at 190°C (375°F) for 10 minutes or until they are golden.

5 Pour a small amount of garlic cream over the bundles. Serve as an appetizer on a plate garnished with lettuce leaves, 2 to 3 bundles per serving.

Confit of Duck on a Bed of Bean Sprouts

4 to 6 servings

INGREDIENTS

30 mL olive oil 2 tbsp
1 kg duck legs (4 to 6) 2 lb
30 mL chopped green onion 2 tbsp
pinch salt
freshly ground pepper
15 mL rice vinegar 1 tbsp
400 g carrots, julienned 14 oz
400 g bean sprouts 14 oz
sesame dressing
45 mL sesame seeds 3 tbsp

Sesame Dressing

125 mL vegetable oil 1/2 cup
60 mL rice vinegar 1/4 cup
30 mL sesame oil 2 tbsp
pinch salt
10 mL brown sugar 2 tsp

METHOD

Dressing

1 In a small pot, whisk together all the ingredients and cook over low heat. Set aside. Keep warm.

Duck Legs

1 In a large skillet, heat the olive oil over medium heat, arrange the duck legs skin side down and cook for 5 to 8 minutes.

2 Add the green onion, salt and pepper, and cook for 2 to 3 more minutes over low heat. Turn the duck legs over and deglaze with rice vinegar. Remove from heat and keep warm.

3 In a bowl, mix the carrots and bean sprouts and arrange in the middle of the plates. Add the duck legs and drizzle with warm dressing. Sprinkle with sesame seeds.

Smoked Sturgeon Millefeuilles

serves **4 to 6**

INGREDIENTS

20 sheets phyllo pastry **20**
125 mL melted butter **1/2 cup**
250 mL sour cream **1 cup**
60 mL chopped fresh parsley **1/4 cup**
60 mL chopped fresh tarragon **1/4 cup**
60 mL chopped fresh chervil **1/4 cup**
60 mL chopped fresh chives **1/4 cup**
pinch cayenne pepper
125 mL 35% cream **1/2 cup**
15 mL lemon juice **1 tbsp**
2 mL Dijon mustard **1/2 tsp**
salt and freshly ground pepper
500 g smoked sturgeon, sliced **1 lb**

METHOD

1. Preheat the oven to 190°C (375°F).
2. Cut the sheets of phyllo pastry in four. Brush each sheet with melted butter and layer them.
3. Cut an 8-cm (3-in.) circle from the layered sheets of pastry. Repeat with remaining sheets.
4. Place the circles of pastry on a baking sheet and bake 10 to 15 minutes, or until golden.
5. Remove from oven and let cool at room temperature.
6. In a large bowl, mix the sour cream, herbs and cayenne pepper. Refrigerate until ready to use.
7. For the sauce, beat together the cream, lemon juice and mustard. Adjust the seasoning. Refrigerate until ready to serve.
8. Place a circle of pastry on a work surface. Spread with sour cream mixture, cover with slices of sturgeon and top with another circle of pastry. Repeat twice more.
9. Arrange the millefeuilles on individual plates and surround with sauce.

Gratin of Chickpeas and Goat Cheese

4 to 6 servings

INGREDIENTS

- **15 mL** olive oil **1 tbsp**
- **60 mL** chopped green onion **1/4 cup**
- **1** clove garlic, chopped **1**
- **400 g** cooked chickpeas or one 540 mL (19-oz) can chickpeas, rinsed and drained **2 cups**
- **2 mL** chili powder **1/2 tsp**
- **1 mL** ground cumin **1/4 tsp**
- **1 mL** dried oregano **1/4 tsp**
- pinch dried thyme
- pinch cayenne pepper
- pinch salt
- freshly ground pepper
- **250 g** chorizo (a dry Spanish sausage), thinly sliced **9 oz**
- **60 mL** chopped fresh parsley **1/4 cup**
- **180 mL** crushed tomatoes **3/4 cup**
- **250 g** goat cheese **9 oz**

METHOD

1. In a large skillet, heat the olive oil over medium heat. Cook the green onion and garlic for 2 minutes.
2. Add the chickpeas, seasonings and sliced chorizo; cook for 3 minutes.
3. Add the crushed tomatoes and parsley. Stir and reheat thoroughly. Remove from heat.
4. Place the mixture in the middle of the plates and cover with goat cheese. Place under the grill of the oven briefly until the goat cheese has softened a little.

Chicken Livers with Pinto Beans

4 to 6 servings

INGREDIENTS

30 mL olive oil **2 tbsp**

1 kg chicken livers, cleaned **2 lb**

225 g Shiitake or oyster mushrooms, minced **8 oz**

60 mL chopped green onion **1/4 cup**

1 clove garlic, chopped **1**

2 mL fresh ginger **1/2 tsp**

400 g cooked pinto beans or one 540 mL (19-oz) can pinto beans, rinsed and drained **2 cups**

30 mL soy sauce **2 tbsp**

180 mL 35% cream **3/4 cup**

60 mL butter **1/4 cup**

60 mL chopped fresh parsley **1/4 cup**

METHOD

1. In a large skillet, heat half the olive oil over high heat. Sear the livers for 2 minutes. Lower the heat and continue cooking for 3 minutes. Remove from heat, place the livers in a bowl and keep warm.
2. In the same skillet, add the rest of the olive oil and sauté the mushrooms, green onion, garlic and ginger for 3 minutes at medium heat. Add the beans and cook for another 3 minutes.
3. Deglaze with the soy sauce and add the 35% cream. Bring to a boil over high heat for 1 minute to reduce.
4. Remove from heat and gradually add the butter, stirring gently. Sprinkle with chopped parsley.
5. Place the bean-mushroom mixture in the middle of the plates; surround with chicken livers and cover with sauce.

Shrimp Quesadillas

serves **4 to 6**

INGREDIENTS

12 20-cm (8-in.) wheat tortillas 12

500 g shredded mozzarella cheese 1 lb

500 g small shrimp, cooked and shelled 1 lb

250 mL thinly sliced peppers (red, green, orange, etc.) 1 cup

125 mL thinly sliced green onion 1/2 cup

500 mL Salsa 2 cups

250 mL sour cream 1 cup

Salsa (makes 1 L or 4 cups)

1 can plum tomatoes (796 mL/28 oz) 1

3 cloves garlic 3

1 small jalapeño pepper, chopped (optional) 1

15 mL Worcestershire sauce 1 tbsp

30 mL lime juice 2 tbsp

125 mL chopped cilantro 1/2 cup

125 mL chopped onion 1/2 cup

125 mL chopped green pepper 1/2 cup

10 mL ground cumin 2 tsp

5 mL chili powder 1 tsp

pinch sugar

salt and freshly ground pepper

METHOD

QUESADILLAS

1. Place half the tortillas flat on a work surface. Cover with half of the mozzarella cheese.
2. Mix the shrimp, peppers and green onions in a large bowl. Divide the mixture evenly among the tortillas.
3. Sprinkle the tortillas with the remaining mozzarella cheese and cover with the remaining tortillas. Refrigerate until ready to serve.
4. To serve, heat a non-stick frying pan over low heat. Cook the tortillas, one at a time, 2 to 3 minutes on each side. Remove from pan and cut into 6 pieces.
5. Serve hot with Salsa and sour cream.

SALSA

1. Purée all the ingredients in a food processor 3 to 5 minutes. Refrigerate until ready to serve.

Aiguillettes of Duck with Bean Sprouts

4 to 6 servings

INGREDIENTS

30 mL olive oil **2 tbsp**
500 g duck fillets **1 lb**
120 g julienned carrot **4 oz**
120 g julienned leek (white part only) **4 oz**
120 g julienned red pepper **4 oz**
500 g bean sprouts **1 lb**
125 mL canned whole corn kernels **1/2 cup**
1 clove garlic, chopped **1**
pinch cayenne pepper
salt and pepper
180 mL cashew pieces **3/4 cup**

Raspberry Dressing

60 mL raspberry vinegar **1/4 cup**
60 mL olive oil **1/4 cup**
60 mL walnut oil **1/4 cup**
60 mL vegetable oil **1/4 cup**
pinch salt
pinch ground white pepper
2 mL Dijon mustard **1/2 tsp**

DRESSING

1 In a bowl, whisk together all the ingredients until a smooth mixture is obtained. Refrigerate until serving.

AIGUILLETTES

1 In a heavy skillet, heat half the olive oil over high heat and sauté the duck fillets for 2 to 3 minutes (or according to preference). Remove from heat and keep warm.

2 In the same hot skillet, add the remaining olive oil and sauté the julienned carrot, leek and red pepper for 2 minutes.

3 Add the bean sprouts, corn and chopped garlic to the skillet and cook for 3 more minutes. Season. Lower the heat, add the cashews and half the dressing; cook for 1 more minute.

4 Divide the bean sprouts and vegetables into servings on the plates. Top with the aiguillettes and drizzle with the remaining dressing.

Lupini and Chipolata Gratin

To give this dish a Moroccan flavour, substitute chickpeas and merguez for the chipolatas and lupini.

4 to 6 servings

INGREDIENTS

15 mL olive oil **1 tbsp**

250 g chipolata sausages, cut into 1 cm (1/2-inch) rounds **1/2 lb**

125 mL chopped onion **1/2 cup**

375 mL fresh tomatoes, seeded and chopped **1 1/2 cups**

400 g lupini, cooked and skinned, or one 540 mL (19-oz) can lupini, rinsed, skinned and drained **2 cups**

1 clove garlic, chopped **1**

60 mL dried tomatoes rehydrated in oil, drained and chopped **1/4 cup**

1 mL salt **1/4 tsp**

freshly ground pepper

pinch sugar

60 mL chopped fresh basil **1/4 cup**
or **5 mL** dried basil **1 tsp**

180 mL freshly grated Parmesan **3/4 cup**

METHOD

1. In a skillet, heat the olive oil over medium heat and sauté the sausages for 3 to 5 minutes or until cooked.
2. Remove from the skillet and keep warm.
3. In the same skillet, caramelize the onion for 3 or 4 minutes. Add the chopped tomatoes, lupini, garlic and dried tomatoes. Season and cook, uncovered, for 5 minutes.
4. Return the chipolatas to the skillet and add the chopped basil. Cook for 1 minute and remove from heat.
5. Place in the middle of the plates, sprinkle with Parmesan and place under the grill of the oven for 1 minute.

Red Bean and Goat Cheese Rillettes

4 to 6 servings

INGREDIENTS

125 mL chopped green onion **1/2 cup**

1 clove garlic **1**

15 mL olive oil **1 tbsp**

200 g cooked red beans or half a 540 mL (19-oz) can red beans, rinsed and drained **1 cup**

2 mL chili powder **1/2 tsp**

1 mL salt **1/4 tsp**

freshly ground pepper

500 g goat cheese, crumbled **1 lb**

60 g diced unsalted butter **1/4 cup**

60 mL chopped fresh rosemary **1/4 cup**

or **10 mL** dried rosemary **2 tsp**

METHOD

1 In a skillet, sauté the green onion and garlic in the olive oil for 2 to 3 minutes over medium heat. Add the beans, chili powder, salt and pepper, and cook for another 3 to 5 minutes. Remove from heat and let cool completely.

2 In a double boiler, melt the goat cheese until soft. Remove from heat and gradually add the butter, chopped rosemary and bean mixture, and stir gently.

3 Line a 25 cm by 10 cm (10- by 4-in.) mould with plastic wrap and pour in the mixture. Refrigerate for 24 hours.

8 servings

Cabreiro Rolls

INGREDIENTS

90 mL olive oil **6 tbsp**

5 mL thyme **1 tsp**

5 mL cracked black pepper **1 tsp**

15 mL chopped coriander **1 tbsp**

20 marinated black olives **20**

250 g cabreiro *or* goat cheese **8 oz**

4 sheets filo dough **4**

125 mL melted butter **1/2 cup**

100 g butter **3 oz**

45 mL Portuguese herbs and spices (see recipe on p.31) **3 tbsp**

8 small slices toasted bread **8**

METHOD

1 Combine the oil, thyme, pepper, coriander and the Portuguese herb-spice mixture; add the olives and marinate for at least 24 hours.

2 Preheat the oven to 200°C (400°F).

3 Crumble the cheese.

4 Fold out a sheet of filo dough on a clean work surface and cut into 4 equal pieces, which will create 8 rectangles. Cover the filo with a clean, damp cloth to prevent it from drying.

5 Brush the two rectangles of filo with melted butter and place one on top of another.

6 Repeat the operation with the three remaining filo sheets.

7 Place one-eighth of the cheese on the section of filo closest to you, leaving a 1.5 cm (3/4-in.) border on each side.

8 Roll the cheese-filled dough one turn and then fold the edges in along the entire length. Finish rolling the dough and place on a cookie sheet.

9 Repeat the process with the rest of the dough.

10 Place the cookie sheet in the oven for 5 to 7 minutes.

11 Meanwhile, add the butter to the herb-spice mixture, and butter the bread with this mixture; toast in the oven.

12 Place 2 slices of bread on a small plate and a cheese roll on each one. Garnish with marinated olives and fresh herbs.

SPAIN

Stuffed Squid

4 servings

INGREDIENTS

8 medium squid, cleaned 8
60 mL olive oil **1/4 cup**
125 mL chopped red onion **1/2 cup**
125 mL long-grain white rice **1/2 cup**
80 mL white wine **1/3 cup**
500 mL water **2 cups**
125 mL cornmeal **1/2 cup**
1 medium tomato, finely diced 1
90 mL chopped coriander **6 tbsp**
1 medium egg, beaten 1
ground white pepper to taste
30 mL olive oil **2 tbsp**
540 mL canned ground Italian tomatoes **2 1/4 cups**
250 mL Spanish onion, chopped **1 cup**
1 clove garlic, chopped 1
salt to taste
ground black pepper to taste

METHOD

1 In a medium-sized saucepan, sauté the onion in the oil and add the rice. Pour in the wine and reduce by three-quarters. Add the water and cook the rice.

2 When the rice is three-quarters cooked, add the cornmeal, diced tomato, coriander and egg, stirring constantly, until rice is completely cooked. Remove from heat and keep warm.

3 Clean the squid under cold running water, and separate the head from the body by pulling gently. Remove the cartilage and ink gland, taking care not to pierce it. Reserve the ink gland to colour the tomato compote.

4 Cut the head lengthwise and spread out on a work surface. Using a knife, make diagonal cuts and then a second series of cuts in the other direction to form small diamond shapes.

5 Heat 30 mL (2 tbsp) olive oil in a large skillet over high heat, and brown the squid heads, cut side down, and remove from skillet.

6 Stuff the squid with rice and close with a wooden skewer.

7 In a saucepan, sauté the garlic and onion in the oil and add the canned tomatoes. Season with salt and pepper and reduce until thickened.

8 Add the squid heads and tentacles; cook, covered, over low heat for 15 minutes.

9 Remove the squid; before serving, colour the tomato mixture with a little squid ink. The rest of the ink can be frozen in an airtight container.

Oyster and Mung Bean Stew

CHINA

INGREDIENTS

15 mL olive oil **1 tbsp**
75 mL sliced carrots **1/3 cup**
75 mL sliced celery **1/3 cup**
75 mL sliced red pepper **1/3 cup**
30 mL sliced green onions **2 tbsp**
500 g cooked mung beans **2 cups**
36 fresh oysters, shucked **36**
500 mL saffron-flavoured vegetables **2 cups**
1 mL salt **1/4 tsp**
freshly ground pepper
60 mL dill, chopped **1/4 cup**
or **2 mL** dried dill **1/2 tsp**

Saffron-flavoured Vegetables (1 L - 4 cups)
125 mL chopped onion **1/2 cup**
125 mL chopped carrot **1/2 cup**
1 leek, chopped (white and green parts) **1**
60 mL chopped white mushrooms **1/4 cup**
60 mL chopped celery **1/4 cup**
60 mL chopped parsley **1/4 cup**
1 mL fennel seeds **1/4 tsp**
1 mL coriander seeds **1/4 tsp**
a few whole peppercorns
pinch dried thyme
2 bay leaves **2**
1/4 mL saffron **1/4 tsp**
15 mL olive oil **1 tbsp**
1.5 L water **6 cups**

METHOD

4 to 6 servings

Oyster Stew

1. In a medium pot, heat the olive oil over medium heat. Sauté the sliced vegetables for 3 to 5 minutes.
2. Add the mung beans, shucked oysters and the saffron-flavoured vegetables.
3. Bring to a boil, lower the heat and simmer for 2 minutes. Add salt and pepper.
4. Remove from heat. Sprinkle with chopped dill.

Vegetables

1. In a large pot, heat the olive oil over medium heat. Cook all the vegetables, with spices, for 5 to 8 minutes.
2. Add water, bring to a boil, and simmer, uncovered, for 15 to 20 minutes or until the liquid has been reduced by one-third.
3. Remove from heat and filter through a sieve. Refrigerate.

The leftover vegetables may be frozen in an airtight container.

Prosciutto and Lima Beans with Port

4 to 6 servings

This appetizer may be served as part of an antipasto plate.

INGREDIENTS

400 g cooked small lima beans or one 540 mL (19-oz) can lima beans, rinsed and drained **2 cups**

75 mL sliced red onion **1/3 cup**

500 g seedless red grapes, sliced in half **1 lb**

500 g thinly sliced prosciutto **1 lb**

Port Dressing

45 mL balsamic vinegar **3 tbsp**

45 mL port **3 tbsp**

125 mL olive oil **1/2 cup**

1 mL salt **1/4 tsp**

pinch cayenne pepper

freshly ground pepper

METHOD

1. In a bowl, whisk together all the ingredients of the dressing. Refrigerate.
2. In a salad bowl, mix the beans, onion slices and grapes with two-thirds of the dressing. Marinate for 30 minutes in the refrigerator.
3. Garnish the plates with prosciutto slices and drizzle with the remaining dressing. Place the bean and grape mixture in the centre of the plates.

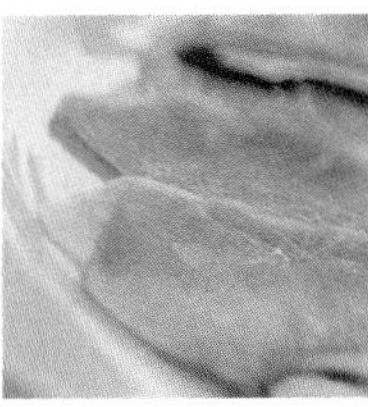

Sardines in Citrus Marinade

Serve with a chilled dry white wine.

4 servings

INGREDIENTS

16 medium-sized fresh sardines **16**
750 mL vegetable oil **3 cups**
60 mL chopped green onion **4 tbsp**
1 clove garlic, chopped **1**
5 mL chopped fresh thyme **1 tsp**
5 mL paprika **1 tsp**
15 mL orange zest **1 tbsp**
10 mL lime zest **2 tsp**
60 mL chopped parsley **4 tbsp**
125 mL olive oil **1/2 cup**
180 mL white wine vinegar **3/4 cup**
250 mL white wine **1 cup**
125 mL finely chopped black olives **1/2 cup**
salt to taste
ground white pepper to taste

METHOD

1. Scale and clean the sardines, and remove their fins. Wash and pat dry.
2. Heat the vegetable oil to 190°C (325°F) in a medium-sized saucepan, and fry the sardines, a few at a time; drain and allow to cool.
3. Heat the olive oil and sauté the green onion and garlic. Add the wine vinegar and reduce by one-quarter; add the white wine and reduce by another quarter.
4. Add the thyme, paprika, orange and lime zest, parsley and black olives. Cook for 5 minutes over low heat; allow to cool and season.
5. Place the sardines in a glass dish and cover with marinade. Refrigerate for 12 to 24 hours before serving.

PORTUGAL

Fresh Figs with Paio de Barrancos

For a variation, use prosciutto instead of Paio de Barrancos.

2 servings

INGREDIENTS

- **6** fresh figs **6**
- **15 mL** butter **1 tbsp**
- **80 mL** finely chopped green cabbage **1/3 cup**
- **60 mL** finely chopped onion **1/4 cup**
- **60 mL** vinho verde *or* white wine **1/4 cup**
- pinch almond powder
- pinch sugar
- **5 mL** chopped coriander **1 tsp**
- **90 g** Paio de Barrancos sausage **3 oz**

METHOD

1. In a small skillet, melt the butter over low heat and add the onion, cooking until translucent.
2. Add the cabbage and the wine; reduce by one-half.
3. Add the almond powder and sugar; reduce until no wine remains.
4. Remove from heat, add the coriander and allow to cool.
5. Julienne the sausage and cut the figs in half widthwise.
6. When the onion and cabbage have cooled, use the mixture to garnish the lower halves of the figs, add the julienned sausage and place the upper halves of the figs on top, slightly off centre.

This mixture can also be served as a salad or as a canapé on toasted bread.

TUNISIA

Cod with Safflower Oil and Balsamic Vinegar

4 servings

INGREDIENTS

450 g salt cod **1 lb**
125 mL safflower *or* olive oil **1/2 cup**
5 mL balsamic vinegar **1 tsp**
30 mL white wine vinegar **2 tbsp**
5 mL paprika **1 tsp**
pinch cayenne pepper
pinch nutmeg
ground white pepper to taste
2 hard-boiled eggs **2**
80 mL capers **1/3 cup**
8 lemon slices **8**
4 red onion slices **4**

1. In a glass bowl, combine the safflower oil, both vinegars, paprika, cayenne, nutmeg and pepper; mix well.
2. Cut the salt cod into thin strips and add to the bowl; marinate for 8 hours in the refrigerator.
3. Serve with half a hard-boiled egg, capers, lemon and onion slices.

Bruschetta

2 servings

INGREDIENTS

180 mL diced tomato **3/4 cup**
125 mL finely chopped onion **1/2 cup**
60 mL finely chopped garlic **1/4 cup**
125 mL finely chopped black olives **1/2 cup**
30 mL chopped fresh parsley **2 tbsp**
45 mL olive oil **3 tbsp**
salt to taste
freshly ground black pepper to taste
6 croutons (toasted) **6**
100 g cabreiro *or* goat cheese **3 1/2 oz**
60 mL olive oil **1/4 cup**
15 mL balsamic vinegar **1 tbsp**
10 mL finely chopped green onion **2 tsp**
salad greens

METHOD

1. In a medium-sized bowl, blend the tomato, onion, garlic, black olives, parsley and olive oil; season. Leave to macerate for 2 to 6 hours at room temperature.
2. Spread the cheese evenly onto the toasted broa.
3. Spread the bruschetta mixture onto the toasted broa.
4. In a small bowl, combine the oil, vinegar and green onion; mix well.
5. Serve the bruschetta toasts with a small green salad, drizzled with dressing.

Leeks in Vinaigrette

FRANCE

4 small servings

A first course that can be prepared a day or two in advance. One hour before serving, remove from the refrigerator so that the vinaigrette can liquefy.

INGREDIENTS

4 medium leeks, white part only **4**
5 mL salt **1 tsp**
15 mL white wine vinegar **1 tbsp**
2 mL dried tarragon **1/2 tsp**
2 mL mild Hungarian paprika **1/2 tsp**
1 mL Meaux mustard **1/4 tsp**
1 mL salt **1/4 tsp**
60 mL virgin olive oil **1/4 cup**

METHOD

1. Cut an X about 8 cm (3 in.) into the upper part of the leek. Wash the leeks under cold running water, opening them up to wash away any sand or soil. Place the leeks in a saucepan in which they can be laid flat, cover with cold water and add the salt. Bring to a boil over high heat, cover and cook at medium heat 15 to 25 minutes, until they are tender when tested with a fork. Remove the leeks from the saucepan, and allow to cool at room temperature.
2. While the leeks are cooking, prepare the vinaigrette by mixing the remaining ingredients in a small bowl.
3. Place the leeks in a dish just large enough to contain them; add the vinaigrette and marinate for at least 2 hours before serving.

Those with little tolerance for spices may prefer to halve the quantity of cayenne. The sauce may be made a day in advance. In this case, the oysters must be cooked for an additional 3 minutes. For a variation, replace the oysters with fillets of white-fleshed fish. Cook until the sauce bubbles and the fish is easily flaked with a fork.

UNITED STATES

Oysters Bienville

4 to **6** servings

INGREDIENTS

24 large oysters 24
60 mL butter 1/4 cup
125 mL finely chopped green onion 1/2 cup
250 mL chopped fresh mushrooms 1 cup
60 mL chopped fresh parsley 1/4 cup
2 small garlic cloves, minced 2
60 mL dry sherry 1/4 cup
60 mL flour 1/4 cup
375 mL milk 1 1/2 cups
125 mL 35% cream 1/2 cup
250 g finely chopped cooked shrimps 8 oz
4 egg yolks 4
22 mL fresh lemon juice 1 1/2 tbsp
5 mL salt 1 tsp
2 mL white ground pepper 1/2 tsp
1 mL cayenne 1/4 tsp

Garnish

80 mL grated Parmesan cheese 1/3 cup
30 mL bread crumbs 2 tbsp
1 mL mild Hungarian paprika 1/4 tsp
1 mL salt 1/4 tsp

METHOD

1 Clean and open the oysters. Shuck the oysters and place them on the lower half of the shells. Place the oysters in a large saucepan or in individual cassolettes, on a bed of coarse salt. Store in the refrigerator while you continue with the recipe. The sauce can also be made in advance and used when the oysters are prepared.

2 In a large skillet, melt the butter without browning it. Over low heat, cook the green onions and mushrooms for 5 minutes. Add the parsley and garlic and continue cooking for 1 minute. Stir in the sherry and simmer until the mixture is reduced by one-half.

3 Remove the saucepan from the heat and gradually add the flour. Whisk in the milk and cream little by little. Bring to a boil, stirring constantly, and simmer until the sauce thickens.

4 Add the shrimps to the sauce. Combine the egg yolks, lemon juice, salt, white pepper and cayenne in a small bowl and gradually add to the sauce, whisking in a thin stream of egg yolk mixture. Cook over low heat for 3 minutes, stirring constantly with a wooden spoon.

5 Mix the garnish ingredients in a small bowl.

6 Preheat the oven to 200°C (400°F). Remove the oysters from the refrigerator, sponge off the liquid with a paper towel and top each oyster with a spoonful of sauce. Sprinkle the garnish over the oysters and bake for 15 minutes in the centre of the oven, until the sauce begins to bubble around the edges of the shell. Serve immediately.

FRANCE

Eggplant Caviar with Mussels and Lentil Coulis

4 to 6 servings

INGREDIENTS

15 mL olive oil 1 tbsp
60 mL chopped celery 1/4 cup
125 mL chopped onion 1/2 cup
125 mL chopped carrot 1/2 cup
1 leek, chopped (white part only) 1
1 mL coriander seeds 1/4 tsp
1 mL fennel seeds 1/4 tsp
pinch dried thyme
2 bay leaves 2
freshly ground pepper
1 kg mussels 2 lb
45 mL water 3 tbsp

Eggplant Caviar

60 mL water 1/4 cup
15 mL olive oil 1 tbsp
1 kg eggplant, cubed 2 lb
500 g fresh tomatoes, chopped 1 lb
60 mL balsamic vinegar 1/4 cup
60 mL chopped green onion 1/4 cup
2 cloves garlic, chopped 2
60 mL chopped fresh parsley 1/4 cup
1 mL salt 1/4 tsp
pinch cayenne pepper
freshly ground pepper

Lentil Mint Coulis

400 g cooked green lentils or one 540 mL (19-oz) can lentils, rinsed and drained 2 cups
125 mL fresh mint 1/2 cup
2 cloves garlic 2
5 mL Dijon mustard 1 tsp
60 mL chopped green onion 1/4 cup
Juice of half a lemon
75 mL olive oil 1/3 cup
75 mL cold cooking liquid from mussels 1/3 cup
1 mL salt 1/4 tsp
pinch cayenne pepper
freshly ground pepper

METHOD

Mussels

1. In a large pot, heat the olive oil over medium heat. Cook the vegetables with the coriander, fennel, thyme, bay leaves and pepper, uncovered, for 3 to 5 minutes.
2. Add the mussels and water; cover and cook until the mussels open (about 3 to 5 minutes).
3. Shuck the mussels, place them in a bowl and add lemon juice. Place in refrigerator. Save a few mussels for garnish.

Caviar

1. Heat oven to 230°C (450°F).
2. Grease a baking sheet with olive oil.
3. Peel and cut the eggplant into 2.5 cm (1-in.) cubes. Place on the baking sheet, sprinkle with water, cover with aluminum foil and bake at 230°C (450°F) for 1 hour.
4. Remove the eggplant slices from the oven and leave to drain in a sieve for 30 minutes. In the meantime, chop the tomatoes, green onion, garlic and parsley, and place in a salad bowl. Add the remaining seasonings and marinate while you mash the eggplant. Mix the mashed eggplant with the other vegetables. Refrigerate.

Lentil Mint Coulis

In a food processor or blender, blend all ingredients until a smooth mixture is obtained. Strain and refrigerate.

Finishing touches

1. Mix about 10 mussels with 1 portion of caviar. From this mixture, make dumplings of 30 mL (2 tbsp) each.
2. Place 2 to 3 dumplings on each plate and drizzle with lentil mint sauce.

The eggplant caviar can be made the day before it is served.

Skewered Oysters

As a first course, serve individual oysters on toothpicks. Sprinkle with lemon juice as soon you remove them from the oven and serve on a bed of lettuce.

4 servings

INGREDIENTS

12 bacon slices **12**
24 fresh oysters **24**
fresh lemon quarters

METHOD

1. Slice the bacon in half widthwise. Cook the bacon for about 2 minutes to eliminate some of the fat; the bacon should not be allowed to become crisp.
2. Clean and open the oysters to remove the flesh.
3. Roll a piece of bacon around each oyster and thread onto skewers. Continue with the remaining oysters to make four brochettes.
4. Place on a baking sheet equipped with a rack and broil 8 cm (3 in.) from the burner for a few minutes until the bacon is crisp, turning once.
5. Serve with fresh lemon quarters.

Bouchées

Stuffed cherry tomatoes

1. Select small ripe but firm tomatoes.
2. With a sharp knife, remove the tomato's cap, and set aside.
3. Scoop out the contents of the tomatoes using a teaspoon.
4. Stuff the tomatoes with gourmet poultry salad (see recipe p. 91). Pack to overflowing.
5. Replace the tomato cap diagonally, and garnish with a sprig of parsley or fresh dill.

Chicken liver mousseline for medaillon bouchées on toast

1. The chicken liver mousseline mixture for bouchées (see recipe p. 91) is rolled in a plastic wrap, with the ends well sealed.
2. Place approximately 1 cm of hot water in the bottom of a small saucepan.
3. Arrange the mousseline rolls in the saucepan and cover. Place in the oven at 180°C (350°F) for 10 to 12 minutes. The roll must be firm to the touch.
4. Let cool and cut into rounds.
5. Serve as is or on toast. Decorate with a small sprig of fresh dill.

Choux balls or puff pastry bouchées

1. Use miniature choux.
2. Cut the tops and keep them to make covers.
3. Garnish with chicken liver mousseline for bouchées (see recipe p. 91) or gourmet poultry salad for bouchées and sandwiches (see recipe p. 91), ensuring that the garnish overflows from the choux.
4. Replace the cover in such a way as to be able to see the garnish.

Note: Unsweetened choux are available on order from all fine pastry shops. They can also be made at home, using a choux pastry recipe.

Quail eggs

Use pickled quail eggs purchased in grocery stores, or cook fresh quail eggs for 3 to 4 minutes.

1. On a cracker or small toast, pipe a small rosette of chicken liver mousseline for bouchées (see recipe p. 91).
2. Carefully place the quail egg on top of the rosette, pressing down gently.

Chicken liver mousseline for bouchées

Makes **24** bouchées

INGREDIENTS

500 g chicken liver terrine (see recipe p. 44) **1 lb**

125 mL soft unsalted butter **1/2 cup**

45 mL brandy or cognac **3 tbsp**

salt and freshly ground pepper, to taste

METHOD

1 Mix all ingredients in the food processor, including the melted fat and jelly that formed during the cooking of the terrine.

2 The mixture must be as smooth as possible so that it can be easily spread with a spatula or in a pastry bag on toasts, croûtons, etc.

VARIATION: After processing in the food processor, you can add chopped pickles, chopped red pepper that has been quickly blanched, minced chives, etc., calculating 6 tbsp (90 ml) for the above quantity of mousseline.

Poultry salad for bouchées and sandwiches

Makes **24** bouchées

INGREDIENTS

250 mL cooked poultry meat, finely chopped with a knife **1 cup**

2 finely chopped hard-boiled eggs **2**

30 mL capers, drained, chopped **2 tbsp**

15 mL fresh chopped parsley **1 tbsp**

60 mL chopped celery **1/4 cup**

60 mL home-made mayonnaise, or other **1/4 cup**

salt and freshly ground pepper

METHOD

1 Mix all ingredients together. Use salt sparingly, as there is already some in the mayonnaise.

FRANCE

Scallops with Pickled Cucumbers

serves **4 to 6**

INGREDIENTS

15 mL olive oil **1 tbsp**
15 mL unsalted butter **1 tbsp**
500 g large, fresh scallops **1 lb**
salt and freshly ground pepper
500 g Pickled Cucumbers **1 lb**

Pickled Cucumbers (makes 500 g or 1 lb)
5 medium cucumbers **5**
60 mL coarse salt **1/4 cup**
125 mL olive oil **1/2 cup**
30 mL balsamic vinegar **2 tbsp**
60 mL chopped fresh dill **1/4 cup**
salt and freshly ground pepper

METHOD

Scallops

1. In a large frying pan, heat the olive oil over high heat. Add the butter and sear the scallops 1 minute on each side. Do not overcook. Sprinkle with salt and pepper.
2. Remove the scallops from the pan and arrange them on individual plates with warm Pickled Cucumbers.

Pickled Cucumbers

1. Peel the cucumbers and cut them in half lengthwise. Using a small spoon, remove the seeds and slice into 1-cm (1/2-in.) half moons.
2. Place the cucumbers in a bowl, sprinkle with coarse salt and mix well. Let stand 30 minutes. Rinse with cold water, drain well and pat dry with paper towel.
3. Heat the olive oil over low heat in a 2-L (8-cup) saucepan. Add the cucumbers and simmer, uncovered, 10 to 15 minutes, or until pickled. Remove from heat.
4. Add the balsamic vinegar and the dill. Adjust the seasoning and let cool slightly before serving. Store in the refrigerator.

Bream Sashimi

serves **4 to 6**

INGREDIENTS

500 g bream fillets, cleaned **1 lb**
60 mL vegetable oil **1/4 cup**
15 mL sesame oil **1 tbsp**
30 mL rice vinegar **2 tbsp**
30 mL lemon juice **2 tbsp**
500 mL thinly sliced daikon radish **2 cups**
60 mL thinly sliced green onion **1/4 cup**
30 mL thinly sliced fresh ginger **2 tbsp**
salt and freshly ground pepper
30 mL black sesame seeds **2 tbsp**

METHOD

1. Cut the bream fillets into thin strips and arrange them around the edge of individual plates.
2. In a large bowl, whisk together all the liquid ingredients. Set aside one-third of the dressing.
3. Add the vegetables and ginger, adjust the seasoning and mix well.
4. Place the vegetables in the centre of the plates and drizzle the fillets with the remaining dressing. Sprinkle with sesame seeds.

Parsleyed Mussels with Cream

4 servings

A hearty vegetable stock may be substituted for the wine.

INGREDIENTS

48 mussels **48**

2 large green onions, chopped **2**

1 clove garlic, chopped **1**

15 mL olive oil **1 tbsp**

30 mL butter **2 tbsp**

250 mL Portuguese vinho verde *or* white wine **1 cup**

80 mL chopped Italian parsley **1/3 cup**

5 mL chopped fresh thyme **1 tsp**

1 bay leaf **1**

125 mL 35% cream **1/2 cup**

ground black pepper to taste

METHOD

1 Thoroughly clean the mussels under cold running water and discard any that appear damaged. If a mussel is slightly opened, tap it lightly. If it does not close, this indicates the mussel is dead and must be discarded.

2 Heat the oil and butter over high heat in a large pot and sauté the green onions, garlic and mussels. Add the wine and cook, covered, over medium heat for 10 minutes, stirring occasionally.

3 Remove the mussels and keep warm.

4 Reduce the cooking liquid by three-quarters and add the cream, thyme, bay leaf and ground pepper; reduce by one-half again.

5 Add the mussels and cook for 1 to 2 minutes before serving.

6 Arrange the mussels on deep plates, sprinkle with parsley and serve with the cream. They may be seasoned with lemon juice.

Brandade

serves **4 to 6**

INGREDIENTS

1 kg salt cod **2 lb**
60 mL olive oil **1/4 cup**
250 mL 35% cream **1 cup**
2 mL ground white pepper **1/2 tsp**
pinch cayenne pepper
salt to taste
60 mL chopped fresh dill **1/4 cup**
250 mL Aioli **1 cup**

Aioli (makes 500 mL or 2 cups)
375 mL mayonnaise **1 1/2 cups**
125 mL plain yogurt **1/2 cup**
30 mL Dijon mustard **2 tbsp**
30 mL lemon juice **2 tbsp**
3 cloves garlic, chopped **3**
pinch cayenne pepper
salt and freshly ground pepper

METHOD

1. Place cod in a large bowl and cover with cold water. Let stand 12 hours, changing the water 6 to 8 times.
2. Remove the cod from the water and cut it into medium-sized pieces. Poach in hot water over very low heat 6 to 8 minutes.
3. Drain well. Remove the skin and bones, then shred the fish. Let stand at room temperature until ready to use.
4. In a large saucepan, heat the olive oil over high heat. Add the shredded cod and reduce the heat to low. Stir with a wooden spoon until a smooth paste forms.
5. Add the cream, pepper and cayenne pepper and mix well. Simmer 2 to 3 minutes over very low heat. Remove from heat. Stir in the salt and let cool. Stir in the dill.
6. Pour the brandade into a deep dish, cover with plastic wrap and refrigerate 12 hours.

AIOLI

1. Whisk together all the ingredients in a medium-sized bowl.
2. Refrigerate until ready to serve.
3. Serve the brandade hot with Aioli and croutons fried in oil.

Frog Legs with Mushrooms

serves **4 to 6**

INGREDIENTS

30 mL olive oil 2 tbsp
48 small frog legs 48
500 g mixed mushrooms (shiitake, oyster and portobello), thinly sliced 1 lb
2 cloves garlic, chopped 2
pinch cayenne pepper
salt and freshly ground pepper
30 mL white wine 2 tbsp
180 mL 35% cream 3/4 cup
60 mL unsalted butter 1/4 cup
60 mL chopped fresh parsley 1/4 cup

Marinade

30 mL olive oil 2 tbsp
5 mL sesame oil 1 tsp
15 mL soy sauce 1 tbsp
5 mL Worcestershire sauce 1 tsp
5 mL oyster sauce 1 tsp
5 mL hoisin sauce 1 tsp
2 mL paprika 1/2 tsp
2 mL ground coriander 1/2 tsp
2 cloves garlic, chopped 2
pinch cayenne pepper
salt and freshly ground pepper

METHOD

Marinade

Whisk all the ingredients together in a bowl. Add the frog legs and toss gently. Marinate in the refrigerator 2 hours.

1 In a large fry pan, heat half the olive oil over high heat. Sauté the frog legs 2 minutes.

2 Reduce the heat to moderate and cook 3 to 4 minutes longer, or until the meat pulls away easily from the bones. Remove from pan and keep warm.

3 In the same pan, heat the remaining olive oil and sauté the mushrooms, garlic and seasonings 2 to 3 minutes.

4 Deglaze with wine and add cream. Bring to a boil over high heat. Boil 1 minute.

5 Remove from heat and add butter gradually, stirring gently.

6 Place the sautéed mushrooms in the centre of individual plates, arrange the frog legs around the edge and pour sauce over. Garnish with parsley.

FRANCE

Persillé of Mixed Beans with Apricot Chutney

4 to 6 servings

INGREDIENTS

250 g boneless chicken breast, cubed 1/2 lb

175 mL 35% cream 3/4 cup

15 mL olive oil 1 tbsp

60 mL chopped green onion 1/4 cup

1 clove garlic, chopped 1

salt and pepper to taste

400 g cooked mixed beans or one 540 mL (19-oz) can mixed beans, rinsed and drained 2 cups

60 mL chopped fresh parsley 1/4 cup

Apricot Cardamom Chutney

250 g dried apricots 1/2 lb

125 mL boiling water or hot chicken stock 1/2 cup

15 mL olive oil 1 tbsp

250 mL thinly sliced onion 1 cup

1 mL ground cardamom 1/4 tsp

10 mL brown sugar 2 tsp

1 mL salt 1/4 tsp

freshly ground pepper

15 mL balsamic vinegar 1 tbsp

METHOD

PERSILLÉ

1. Preheat oven to 180°C (350°F).
2. In a food processor, purée the chicken and 35% cream until smooth. Refrigerate.
3. In a skillet, cook the green onion, garlic and beans in the olive oil over medium heat for 3 to 5 minutes. Add salt and pepper, and allow to cool.
4. In a bowl, gently mix together the puréed chicken, green onion, garlic, beans and parsley.
5. Line a 25 cm by 10 cm (10- by 4-in.) mould with plastic wrap. Pour in the mixture, set the mould in a dish of hot water and cook at 180°C (350°F) for 45 minutes. Cool before unmoulding.

CHUTNEY

1. Soak the dried apricots in boiling water or hot chicken stock for 30 minutes. Drain the apricots, reserving the liquid.
2. In a pot, cook the onion, cardamom, brown sugar, salt and pepper in the olive oil, over medium heat, until the mixture begins to caramelize.
3. Add the apricots and cook, uncovered, for another 2 to 3 minutes.
4. Deglaze with the balsamic vinegar. Add the water or stock used to soak the apricots. Simmer for another 5 minutes. Remove from heat.

Serve the persillé chilled, with warm chutney.

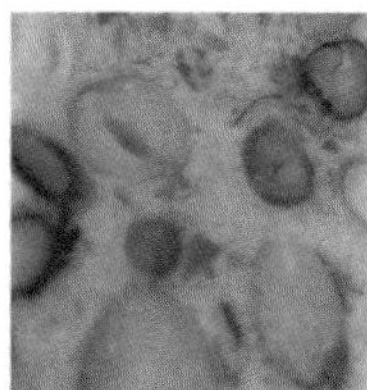

Warm Oysters with Leeks

serves **4 to 6**

INGREDIENTS

36 fresh oysters **36**

15 mL unsalted butter **1 tbsp**

3 leeks, white part only, washed and finely chopped **3**

1 clove garlic, chopped **1**

pinch dried thyme

pinch cayenne pepper

freshly ground pepper

60 mL 35% cream **1/4 cup**

60 mL chopped chives **1/4 cup**

METHOD

1. Open the oysters and place them in a saucepan with their liquor. Strain and refrigerate until ready to use. Set aside the shells.
2. In a medium frying pan, melt the butter over moderate heat and sauté the leeks, garlic and seasonings 3 to 5 minutes.
3. Add the cream and cook 2 to 3 minutes longer.
4. Purée the mixture in a food processor. Keep warm.
5. Warm the oysters over low heat about 30 seconds. Drain well.
6. Divide the leek purée among the shells and top with the oysters.
7. Sprinkle with chopped chives.

CHILE

Crab au Gratin

serves **4 to 6**

INGREDIENTS

500 mL crumbled white bread, crust removed 2 cups
250 mL milk 1 cup
30 mL olive oil 2 tbsp
1 medium onion, thinly sliced 1
2 cloves garlic, chopped 2
10 mL paprika 2 tsp
2 mL dried thyme 1/2 tsp
pinch cayenne pepper
750 g crab meat, cooked and shredded 1 1/2 lb
250 mL fish stock 1 cup
60 mL unsalted butter, cut into pieces 1/4 cup
60 mL chopped fresh parsley 1/4 cup
salt and freshly ground pepper
125 mL grated Parmesan cheese 1/2 cup

METHOD

1 Soak the bread in the milk 30 minutes. Drain and squeeze out the liquid. Refrigerate until ready to use.

2 Heat the olive oil in a large frying pan over moderate heat and add the onion, garlic and seasonings. Cook 2 to 3 minutes.

3 Add the bread, crab meat and fish stock. Bring to a boil and turn off the heat. Stir in butter and parsley.

4 Adjust the seasoning and stir gently.

5 Place the mixture on individual plates or in crab shells, sprinkle with Parmesan cheese and broil 3 to 5 minutes, or until golden brown.

6 Serve piping hot.

Frogs' Legs with Fava Beans

Variation: Large shrimps can be substituted for the frogs' legs.

4 to 6 servings

INGREDIENTS

30 mL olive oil **2 tbsp**

4 dozen frogs' legs, marinated 4

125 mL chopped green onion **1/2 cup**

1 clove garlic, chopped 1

60 mL chopped red pepper **1/4 cup**

60 mL chopped yellow pepper **1/4 cup**

400 g cooked fava beans or one 540 mL (19-oz) can fava beans, rinsed and drained **2 cups**

250 mL coconut milk **1 cup**

1 mL salt **1/4 tsp**

freshly ground pepper

60 mL chopped fresh coriander **1/4 cup**
or **2 mL** dried coriander **1/2 tsp**

Marinade for Frogs' Legs

30 mL olive oil **2 tbsp**

30 mL Pastis or Pernod **2 tbsp**

5 mL chopped lemon grass **1 tsp**

1 mL paprika **1/4 tsp**

1 mL curry powder **1/4 tsp**

1 mL salt **1/4 tsp**

1 clove garlic, chopped 1

freshly ground pepper

METHOD

Marinade

In a large bowl, whisk all ingredients together. Add the frogs' legs and stir gently. Marinate in the refrigerator for 2 hours.

Frogs' Legs

1. In a large skillet, heat the olive oil over high heat. Sear the frogs' legs for 2 minutes, turn over gently and reduce heat to medium; continue cooking for another 3 to 4 minutes or until the meat separates easily from the bone. Remove the legs from the skillet and keep warm.

2. In the same skillet, cook the green onion, garlic and peppers for 3 minutes over low heat.

3. Add the fava beans and coconut milk and bring to a boil. Lower the heat, season with salt and pepper, and simmer for 5 minutes. Remove from heat and add the coriander.

4. Arrange the beans on deep plates, add the frogs' legs and cover with the coconut milk.

FRANCE

Smoked Salmon Rolls with Endives

serves **4 to 6**

INGREDIENTS

180 mL vegetable oil **3/4 cup**
45 mL sesame oil **3 tbsp**
15 mL rice vinegar **1 tbsp**
30 mL soy sauce **2 tbsp**
salt and freshly ground pepper
500 g endives, julienned **1 lb**
500 g smoked salmon, sliced **1 lb**
30 mL sesame seeds **2 tbsp**

METHOD

1. Whisk all the liquid ingredients together in a bowl. Stir in salt and pepper. Refrigerate until ready to use.
2. In a large bowl, toss the endives with half the dressing.
3. Place the salmon slices flat on a work surface. Place endives in the centre of each slice, letting them stick out 2.5 cm (1 in.) on either side. Roll the salmon around the endives and cut in two.
4. Place the rolls on individual plates and drizzle with the remaining dressing.
5. Sprinkle with sesame seeds.

Lupini Salad with Caraway Seeds

To give the salad a different colour, replace the endives with radicchio and the red apples with a green or yellow variety.

4 to 6 servings

INGREDIENTS

500 g red apples (3 or 4) **1 lb**

400 g cooked lupini, skinned, or one 540 mL (19-oz) can lupini, rinsed, skinned and drained **2 cups**

Caraway dressing

500 g endives (6 to 8) **1 lb**

60 mL chopped chives (garnish) **1/4 cup**

Caraway Dressing

125 mL mayonnaise **1/2 cup**

75 mL plain yogurt, 0.1% m.f. **1/3 cup**

juice of 1 orange

10 mL Dijon mustard **2 tsp**

2 mL ground caraway seeds **1/2 tsp**

pinch ground white pepper

1 mL salt **1/4 tsp**

pinch cayenne pepper

METHOD

Dressing

1. Whisk together all ingredients for the dressing. Refrigerate.

Salad

1. Core but do not peel the apples and cut into small cubes.
2. Place apple cubes in a large bowl; mix with the beans and two-thirds of the dressing.
3. Julienne the endives and line the plates. Drizzle with the remaining vinaigrette.
4. Add the apple and lupini salad, and garnish with chopped chives.

Chickpea Salad with Cardamom

To give the salad a Mediterranean flavour, add feta cheese.

4 to 6 servings

INGREDIENTS

500 g cooked beets, sliced 1 lb
Cardamom dressing
45 mL chopped green onion 3 tbsp
45 mL chopped green pepper 3 tbsp
45 mL chopped red pepper 3 tbsp
45 mL chopped celery 3 tbsp
45 mL chopped carrot 3 tbsp
400 g cooked chickpeas or one 540 mL (19-oz) can chickpeas, rinsed and drained 2 cups
60 mL chopped fresh parsley (garnish) 1/4 cup

Cardamom Dressing

45 mL balsamic vinegar 3 tbsp
1 mL salt 1/4 tsp
1 mL oregano 1/4 tsp
1 mL paprika 1/4 tsp
1 mL ground cardamom 1/4 tsp
1 clove garlic 1
pinch cayenne pepper
freshly ground pepper
45 mL olive oil 3 tbsp
125 mL vegetable oil 1/2 cup

METHOD

Dressing

1. In a bowl, whisk together the balsamic vinegar and seasonings. Add both oils, whisking constantly. Refrigerate.

Salad

1. Arrange the beet slices around the plates and drizzle with the vinaigrette.
2. Place the chopped vegetables in a large bowl. Add the chickpeas and the remaining dressing; mix well.
3. Garnish individual servings with parsley before serving.

Lentil and Wild Rice Salad

4 to 6 servings

INGREDIENTS

400 g cooked lentils or one 540 mL (19-oz) can lentils, rinsed and drained 2 cups

250 mL cooked wild rice 1 cup

125 mL grated carrot 1/2 cup

60 mL chopped red pepper 1/4 cup

60 mL chopped green onion 1/4 cup

125 mL crushed peanuts (garnish) 1/2 cup

Thai Dressing

180 mL vegetable oil 3/4 cup

45 mL rice vinegar 3 tbsp

5 mL peanut butter 1 tsp

2 mL sesame oil 1/2 tsp

2 mL soya oil 1/2 tsp

pinch salt

METHOD

Dressing

1. In a large bowl, blend all the ingredients except the oil. Whisk until the mixture is smooth. Add the oil a little at a time, whisking constantly. Refrigerate.

Salad

1. Mix all the salad ingredients with the dressing. Marinate in the refrigerator for 1 hour.
2. Garnish the rims of the plates with exotic fruits such as pineapple, mango and kiwi, and arrange the salad in the centre of the plate.

Warm Escarole Salad with Lima Beans and Smoked Bacon

ITALY

4 to 6 servings

INGREDIENTS

225 g smoked bacon, julienned **1/2 lb**

45 mL chopped green onion **3 tbsp**

15 mL dried tomatoes in oil, drained and chopped **1 tbsp**

10 mL brown sugar **2 tsp**

400 g large cooked lima beans, skinned, or one 540 mL (19-oz) can lima beans, rinsed, skinned and drained **2 cups**

1 clove garlic, chopped **1**

pinch salt

pinch cayenne pepper

freshly ground pepper

15 mL balsamic vinegar **1 tbsp**

75 mL olive oil **1/3 cup**

500 g escarole **1 lb**

METHOD

1. Heat a large nonstick skillet over medium heat. Add the bacon strips and cook until golden.
2. Pour off the excess fat, leaving only about 15 mL (1 tbsp) in the skillet. Add the green onion, dried tomatoes and sugar. Cook for 2 to 3 minutes.
3. Add the beans and seasonings and heat thoroughly. Deglaze with balsamic vinegar. Add the olive oil. Mix well and allow to cool.
4. Arrange the escarole leaves on the plates. Add the bean and bacon mixture and drizzle with the warm dressing.

Bean Sprout and Snow Pea Salad

4 to 6 servings

INGREDIENTS

1 large carrot, julienned 1

60 g julienned red onion 2 oz

60 g julienned red pepper 2 oz

500 g bean sprouts 1 lb

250 g snow peas, cut in half, blanched but still crisp 8 oz

30 mL sesame seeds for garnish 2 tbsp

Sesame Oil Dressing

180 mL vegetable oil 3/4 cup

45 mL sesame oil 3 tbsp

15 mL balsamic vinegar 1 tbsp

30 mL soy sauce 2 tbsp

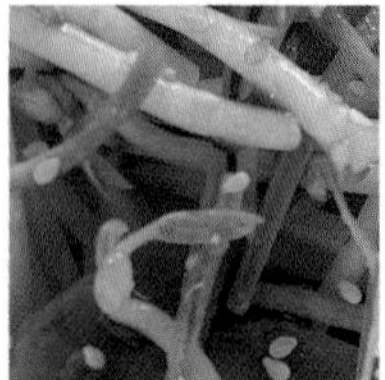

METHOD

DRESSING

1. In a bowl, whisk all the ingredients together. Refrigerate.

SALAD

1. Mix together the julienned carrot, onion and red pepper. Add the bean sprouts and snow peas.
2. Place on the plates, drizzle with the dressing and garnish with sesame seeds.

Mixed Bean Salad

Mesclun is a mixture of young lettuce shoots and leaves.

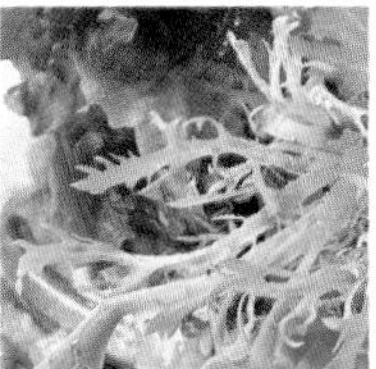

4 to 6 servings

INGREDIENTS

- **1** large tomato, seeded and chopped **1**
- **125 mL** chopped green onion **1/2 cup**
- **800 g** cooked mixed beans, or two 540 mL (19-oz) cans mixed beans, rinsed and drained **4 cups**
- Tarragon dressing
- **500 g** mesclun **1 lb**

Tarragon Dressing

- **1/2** garlic clove, chopped **1/2**
- **125 mL** chopped fresh tarragon **1/2 cup** or **10 mL** dried tarragon **2 tsp**
- **1 mL** Dijon mustard **1/4 tsp**
- pinch salt
- pinch ground white pepper
- pinch cayenne pepper
- freshly ground pepper
- **60 mL** balsamic vinegar **1/4 cup**
- **60 mL** olive oil **1/4 cup**
- **125 mL** vegetable oil **1/2 cup**

METHOD

Dressing

1. In a large bowl, whisk together all ingredients except the oils. Mix well and slowly add the oils, whisking constantly. Refrigerate.

Salad

1. In a salad bowl, combine the tomato, green onion and beans with half the dressing. Refrigerate for 1 hour.
2. Arrange the mesclun in the centre of the plates and drizzle with the remaining dressing. Place the marinated beans around the rim of the plate.

Black Bean and Citrus Salad

Variation: Add chunks of blue cheese and nuts.

4 to 6 servings

INGREDIENTS

125 mL chopped green onion **1/2 cup**
125 mL chopped mushrooms **1/2 cup**
125 mL chopped red pepper **1/2 cup**
400 g cooked black beans, or one 540 mL (19-oz) can black beans, rinsed and drained **2 cups**
Tequila dressing
2 medium-sized pink grapefruits **2**
4 medium oranges **4**
6 clementines **6**
60 mL chopped chives (garnish) **1/4 cup**
1 lime (garnish) **1**

Tequila Dressing

125 mL citrus juice **1/2 cup**
125 mL olive oil **1/2 cup**
15 mL tequila **1 tbsp**
1 mL salt **1/4 tsp**
pinch chili powder
1/2 garlic clove, chopped **1/2**
freshly ground pepper

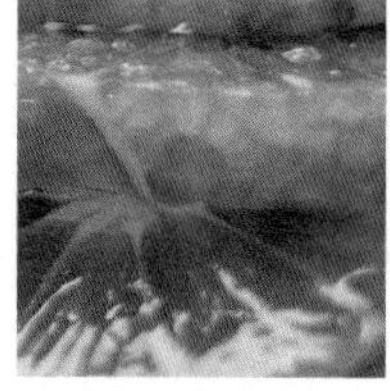

METHOD

Dressing

1. In a bowl, whisk all the ingredients together. Refrigerate.

Salad

1. In a large bowl, mix the green onion, mushrooms and pepper. Add the beans and half the dressing. Marinate for 1 hour.
2. Meanwhile, peel the citrus fruits with a sharp knife in wide strips all around from top to bottom, taking care to remove all the white membrane of the peel. Slice the fruits so that they can be used for the bottom layer of the dish.
3. Top with the bean mixture and drizzle with the rest of the dressing. Garnish with chives and lime slices.

Tex-Mex Pinto Bean Salad

4 to 6 servings

INGREDIENTS

60 mL finely chopped green pepper 1/4 cup

30 mL dried tomato in oil, drained and finely chopped 2 tbsp

60 mL finely chopped celery 1/4 cup

60 mL finely chopped fresh parsley 1/4 cup

60 mL finely chopped fresh coriander 1/4 cup

or 5 mL dried coriander leaves 1 tsp

400 g cooked pinto beans or one 540 mL (19-oz) can pinto beans, rinsed and drained 2 cups

60 mL cooked corn kernels 1/4 cup

Tex-Mex sauce

3 fresh tomatoes, sliced 3

Tex-Mex Sauce

60 mL chopped onion 1/4 cup

1 clove garlic 1

60 mL vegetable oil 1/4 cup

juice of half a lime

2 mL Worcestershire sauce 1/2 tsp

1 mL ground cumin 1/4 tsp

dash hot pepper sauce

1 mL salt 1/4 tsp

pinch brown sugar

salt and pepper

METHOD

SAUCE

1 Blend all ingredients in a blender or food processor until smooth.

SALAD

1 In a large bowl, mix all the chopped ingredients for the salad. Add the beans, the corn and two-thirds of the Tex-Mex sauce. Marinate for 1 hour in the refrigerator.

2 Garnish the plates with tomatoes and drizzle with the remaining dressing. Arrange the bean salad in the centre.

Serve with tortillas or nachos.

Italian-style Fava Bean Salad

4 to 6 servings

INGREDIENTS

400 g large fava beans, cooked and skinned, or one 540 mL (19-oz) can fava beans, rinsed, skinned and drained 2 cups

60 mL sliced green pepper 1/4 cup

60 mL sliced red pepper 1/4 cup

60 mL sliced fresh mushrooms 1/4 cup

60 mL sliced celery 1/4 cup

60 mL sliced carrots 1/4 cup

60 mL sliced zucchini 1/4 cup

1 tomato, finely chopped 1

125 mL arugula (garnish) 1/2 cup

60 mL grated Parmesan 1/4 cup

Italian Dressing

60 mL balsamic vinegar 1/4 cup

1 mL Dijon mustard 1/4 tsp

1 clove garlic, chopped 1

1 mL dried oregano 1/4 tsp

1 mL dried basil 1/4 tsp

1 mL paprika 1/4 tsp

pinch cayenne pepper

pinch thyme

pinch salt

freshly ground pepper

125 mL olive oil 1/2 cup

DRESSING

1. In a salad bowl, whisk together all the dressing ingredients except the olive oil. Add the oil in a thin stream, whisking constantly.

SALAD

1. In a salad bowl, mix all the sliced vegetables and the chopped tomato. Add the dressing and refrigerate for at least 1 hour.
2. Place the salad on the plates, garnish with arugula and sprinkle with Parmesan.

Serve with polenta for a typical Italian meal.

Rollmops and New Potatoes with Aquavit

serves **4 to 6**

INGREDIENTS

250 g salt pork, julienned **1/2 lb**
1 kg new potatoes, cooked but still firm **2 lb**
125 mL thinly sliced red onion **1/2 cup**
60 mL thinly sliced red pepper **1/4 cup**
60 mL thinly sliced green pepper **1/4 cup**
2 cloves garlic, chopped **2**
2 mL crushed fennel seed **1/2 tsp**
2 mL crushed cumin seed **1/2 tsp**
pinch cayenne pepper
salt and freshly ground pepper
250 mL Aquavit Dressing **1 cup**
750 g rollmops, drained* **1 1/2 lb**
60 mL chopped fresh parsley **1/4 cup**

Aquavit Dressing (Makes 250 mL or 1 cup)
15 mL aquavit **1 tbsp**
30 mL lemon juice **2 tbsp**
30 mL orange juice **2 tbsp**
60 mL olive oil **1/4 cup**
125 mL vegetable oil **1/2 cup**
2 mL Dijon mustard **1/2 tsp**
2 mL ground cumin **1/2 tsp**
2 mL ground fennel **1/2 tsp**
1/2 clove garlic, chopped **1/2**
pinch cayenne pepper
salt and freshly ground pepper

METHOD

1. Heat a large non-stick frying pan over moderate heat. Fry the salt pork until golden brown. Remove all but 15 mL (1 tbsp) fat from pan.
2. Cut the potatoes in half and sauté 3 to 5 minutes.
3. Add the red onion, peppers, garlic and seasonings and cook 2 to 3 minutes longer.
4. Place mixture in the centre of individual plates. Arrange the rollmops around the edge.
5. Drizzle with room-temperature dressing.
6. Sprinkle with parsley.

AQUAVIT DRESSING

1. Whisk all the ingredients together in a bowl. Refrigerate until ready to serve.

* Marinated herring fillets, rolled around a pickle or onion.

Warm Shrimp, Radish and Cucumber Salad

serves **4 to 6**

INGREDIENTS

45 mL olive oil **3 tbsp**
15 mL lemon juice **1 tbsp**
1 clove garlic, chopped **1**
1 mL dried thyme **1/4 tsp**
2 mL dried basil **1/2 tsp**
2 mL chili powder **1/2 tsp**
2 mL ground coriander **1/2 tsp**
pinch cayenne pepper
salt and freshly ground pepper
750 g large shrimp **1 1/2 lb**
3 medium English cucumbers, thinly sliced **3**
15 small radishes, thinly sliced **15**
250 mL Poppy Seed Dressing **1 cup**

Poppy Seed Dressing
(makes 250 mL or 1 cup)

125 mL olive oil **1/2 cup**
60 mL rice vinegar **1/4 cup**
15 mL sesame oil **1 tbsp**
15 mL lemon juice **1 tbsp**
15 mL poppy seeds **1 tbsp**
5 mL sugar **1 tsp**
salt and freshly ground pepper

METHOD

1 Mix together 30 mL (2 tbsp) olive oil, lemon juice, garlic and seasonings in a large bowl. Add the shrimp and marinate 1 hour in the refrigerator.

2 Heat the remaining olive oil in a large frying pan over high heat. Add the shrimp and sauté 2 to 3 minutes, or until cooked. Remove from pan and keep warm.

3 Combine the cucumber and radish slices in a salad bowl.

4 Pour half the dressing over the vegetables and mix well. Serve immediately on individual plates.

5 Top the vegetables with the warm shrimp and drizzle with the remaining dressing.

POPPY SEED DRESSING

1 Whisk all the ingredients together in a bowl. Refrigerate until ready to serve.

CANADA

Pan-Fried Scallops with Orange Fennel Remoulade

serves **4 to 6**

INGREDIENTS

30 mL olive oil **2 tbsp**
15 mL orange juice **1 tbsp**
1 clove garlic, chopped **1**
1 mL dried thyme **1/4 tsp**
2 mL paprika **1/2 tsp**
pinch cayenne pepper
500 g medium-sized scallops **1 lb**
salt and freshly ground pepper
375 mL Orange Mayonnaise **1 1/2 cups**
4 medium fennel bulbs **4**

Orange Mayonnaise
(makes 500 mL or 2 cups)
250 mL plain mayonnaise **1 cup**
125 mL plain 0.1% yogurt **1/2 cup**
80 mL orange juice **1/3 cup**
5 mL Dijon mustard **1 tsp**
30 mL old-fashioned mustard (Meaux) **2 tbsp**
1 clove garlic, chopped **1**
5 mL paprika **1 tsp**
1 mL ground white pepper **1/4 tsp**
pinch cayenne pepper
salt to taste

METHOD

1 Whisk together the olive oil, orange juice, garlic and seasonings in a bowl. Add the scallops, salt and pepper and toss gently. Refrigerate 1 hour.

2 Sear the scallops 1 to 2 minutes on each side in a large non-stick frying pan. Do not overcook. Remove from pan and keep warm.

3 Pour 250 mL (1 cup) of Orange Mayonnaise into a salad bowl.

4 Thinly slice the fennel using a mandoline or a sharp knife and place immediately in the salad bowl. Mix quickly to avoid oxidation. Serve the remoulade on individual plates.

5 Arrange the scallops around the edge and garnish with the remaining mayonnaise.

ORANGE MAYONNAISE

1 Blend all the ingredients together in a bowl. Refrigerate until ready to serve.

ITALY

Oyster, Pear and Zucchini Salad with Raspberry Dressing

serves **4 to 6**

INGREDIENTS

36 fresh oysters **36**

250 mL Raspberry Dressing **1 cup**

4 whole pears, washed **4**

4 whole medium zucchini, washed **4**

36 whole raspberries, washed **36**

30 mL black sesame seeds **2 tbsp**

Raspberry Dressing
(makes 250 mL or 1 cup)

125 mL olive oil **1/2 cup**

60 mL walnut oil **1/4 cup**

60 mL raspberry vinegar **1/4 cup**

2 mL Dijon mustard **1/2 tsp**

2 small shallots, chopped **2**

1 clove garlic, chopped **1**

2 mL dried tarragon **1/2 tsp**

pinch cayenne pepper

salt and freshly ground pepper

METHOD

1. Open the oysters and place them in a bowl with their strained liquor. Refrigerate until ready to serve.
2. Pour the Raspberry Dressing into a salad bowl.
3. Using a mandoline or a sharp knife, cut the unpeeled pears into julienne strips and place them immediately in the salad bowl. Toss quickly to avoid oxidation. Cut the unpeeled zucchini into julienne strips and add to pear mixture.
4. Drain the oysters well and place them in the salad bowl. Toss gently and place the salad on individual plates.
5. Garnish with whole raspberries and black sesame seeds.

RASPBERRY DRESSING

1. Whisk all the ingredients together in a bowl. Refrigerate until ready to serve.

Stuffed Eggplants

UNITED STATES

4 servings

INGREDIENTS

2 small eggplants, halved lengthwise 2
125 mL milk 1/2 cup
3 slices bread (no crust), torn into small pieces 3 slices
30 mL butter 2 tbsp
1/2 medium onion, finely chopped 1/2
30 mL green pepper, finely chopped 2 tbsp
500 g small shrimps, cooked 1 lb
1 large egg 1
5 mL salt 1 tsp
0.5 mL cayenne 1/8 tsp
60 mL bread crumbs 1/4 cup
30 mL melted butter 2 tbsp

METHOD

1 Place the eggplant halves, cut side down, in a large pot. Add enough cold water to cover two-thirds of the eggplants. Bring to a boil, reduce the heat to medium and cook for about 5 minutes, until the eggplant is tender when pricked with a fork. Remove the eggplants from the pot and let cool completely. Scoop out the cooked flesh with a spoon, leaving the skins intact so they can be stuffed. Coarsely chop the eggplant and leave to drain for a few minutes in a sieve.

2 Preheat the oven to 190°C (375°F). Pour milk over the bread pieces.

3 Melt the butter in a large skillet and sauté the onion and green pepper for 5 minutes, without browning. Add the shrimps and continue cooking over low heat for 5 minutes, stirring constantly. Add the cooked eggplant and continue cooking for another 5 to 10 minutes over medium heat to dry the mixture somewhat. Set aside and let cool for about 10 minutes.

4 Add the egg to the cooled mixture along with the bread and milk, salt and cayenne. Stir until the mixture is well blended. Divide the stuffing among the eggplant skins. Sprinkle with bread crumbs and drizzle with melted butter.

5 Place the eggplants in a lightly greased ovenproof dish and bake for 30 minutes. Broil for 1 to 2 minutes if the bread crumbs are not toasted enough.

Mirlitons were introduced to Louisiana by immigrants from the Caribbean. This is a main-course vegetable dish.

UNITED STATES

Mirlitons Stuffed with Shrimp

2 generous servings

INGREDIENTS

- 2 large mirlitons 2
- 2 slices bacon, cubed 2 slices
- 1 medium onion, chopped 1
- 1/4 green pepper, chopped 1/4
- 60 mL finely chopped celery 1/4 cup
- 1 small clove garlic, finely chopped 1
- 250 g uncooked shrimps, cleaned and chopped 8 oz
- 2 mL salt 1/2 tsp
- 0.5 mL cayenne 1/8 tsp
- 60 mL chopped fresh parsley 1/4 cup
- 1 mL dried thyme 1/4 tsp
- 125 mL fresh bread crumbs 1/2 cup
- 30 mL butter 2 tbsp

METHOD

1. Wash the mirlitons and cut in half lengthwise. Steam for 20 to 40 minutes until tender when pricked with a fork. Let cool while you proceed with the other steps.
2. Preheat the oven to 180°C (350°F). When the mirlitons have cooled down, remove the flesh with a large spoon, taking care not to tear the peel. Coarsely chop the mirliton flesh and set aside.
3. In a large cast-iron skillet, cook the bacon over low heat until crisp. Remove the bacon bits from the skillet and set aside. In the bacon grease, cook the onion, green pepper and celery over medium heat for about 5 minutes until transparent. Add the garlic and cook for another minute.
4. Add the shrimps and mirliton flesh and cook over low heat for a few minutes until the shrimps turn pink. Remove the saucepan from the heat.
5. Add the remaining bacon, salt, cayenne, parsley and thyme, and blend well.
6. Fill the hollowed-out mirliton skins with the shrimp stuffing and place in a buttered ovenproof dish. Sprinkle with fresh bread crumbs and small cubes of butter. Cook for 30 minutes until the bread crumbs begin to brown.

This salad can also be served as a first course. It can be refrigerated for 5 days.

UNITED STATES

6 servings

Mushroom and Olive Salad

INGREDIENTS

125 mL sliced black olives **1/2 cup**

125 mL sliced green olives **1/2 cup**

1/2 red pepper, coarsely chopped **1/2**

2 large stalks celery, chopped **2**

250 mL thickly sliced mushrooms **1 cup**

398 mL canned artichokes, drained and cut into six pieces each (1 can) **14 oz**

2 green onions, chopped **2**

30 mL Italian parsley **2 tbsp**

1 small clove garlic, minced (optional) **1**

Dressing

22 mL balsamic vinegar **1 1/2 tbsp**

15 mL marinade from the green olives **1 tbsp**

60 mL extra virgin olive oil **1/4 cup**

2 mL dried basil **1/2 tsp**

2 mL freshly ground black pepper **1/2 tsp**

0.5 mL cayenne **1/8 tsp**

METHOD

1. In a large bowl, mix the black and green olives, red pepper, celery, mushrooms, artichokes, green onions, parsley and garlic.
2. Mix the ingredients for the vinaigrette in a bowl. Pour over the salad and mix well to coat the vegetables.
3. Serve on a bed of lettuce as a side dish with grillades.

Soups

There was a time when soup was considered a meal in itself. Over a hot stove, a selection of meats, legumes and herbs would be simmered in a pot of boiling water; then, when the soup was ready, it would be served in large bowls. Soup meals are still enjoyed in some parts of the world. In fact, the expression "soup's on" arose to indicate that a meal of soup was being served. Similarly, "supper" means "evening meal." Today, small bowls of soups are served at the beginning of a meal or as an appetizer. Either way, they always make a favourable impression on guests and hint that delicious courses will follow. A good cook should thus never skirt over the soup course even if it is typically quite simple. And it goes without saying that a home-made soup is always tastier than canned soups or soup mixes made from dehydrated ingredients.

Soup has come to symbolize comfort. It warms our hearts on freezing winter days and consoles us on gloomy rainy afternoons. Some cold soups can even refresh on those dog days of summer. The ailing can rebuild their strength by consuming soups with healing properties. And of course, the aroma of simmering soups can whet the appetite on any given day. Their nutritional qualities — depending on the freshness of the ingredients — make soups a food of choice, either as an appetizer or meal.

History

An age-old technique that still fills our kitchens with mouth-watering aromas.

Preparing soup is among the oldest of cooking methods. The earliest soups were simmered in a hole in the ground, where water and ingredients were cooked using white-hot stones as an energy source. The stones were heated in a nearby fire and replaced as they cooled off. Another primitive method for making soup involved hanging an animal's stomach above a fire; the stomach served as a container for the water, ingredients and hot stones. We know that the Celts, Mesopotamians and North American native peoples all used this method.

The word "soup" comes from the same Germanic root that produced the English sup and supper. From that root came the noun suppa, which passed into Old French as "soupe," meaning both a piece of bread dipped into liquid and the broth poured onto the bread. In Roman times, the barbarians took to dipping bread into the pot to fully appreciate the taste of the soup. With time, the "pot," which, by extension, later became the French "potage," came to designate the container in which the soup was served. The Middle English word "pottage" (now rarely used) was derived from the French and meant "something cooked in a pot," that is, a soup or a stew.

Well before the advent of food preservation methods, travellers often carried with them "pocket soup," a bouillon reduced to a gelatinous consistency and then cut into cubes once cooled. Easily transported, these small cubes could be rehydrated as needed. The food industry still uses this method to make bouillon cubes, which are highly appreciated by cooks in a hurry.

Legend has it that Joan of Arc was very fond of soup, in particular wine soup. It was said that she asked to be served only soups (up to five different kinds) for the entire meal.

Serving Soup

Light soups such as consommés, vegetable soups and potages are served at the beginning of the meal or as part of a more sophisticated menu. Heartier main-course soups are usually served at the midday meal or supper, depending on tradition. In China and Japan, some soups are served at the end of the meal, as you will see when you make Mongolian Hot Pot.

At a banquet or a gourmet meal, soup is served after the hors d'oeuvres and before the main course. Cold vegetable soups such as gazpacho make a delicious first course for a picnic. Sweet chilled soups like fresh strawberry soup from Finland, served with fine biscuits, are an elegant ending for a meal.

Beverages to Serve with Soups

Some claim that wine should not be served with soup. I disagree: I feel it is highly appropriate to serve a wine with soup for a gourmet meal or with festive main-course soups such as cioppino from California and waterzooï from Belgium.

During an elegant dinner, the soup is served with the same wine that began the meal. On the other hand, if you are serving a soup that contains alcohol, serve it with the same alcoholic beverage used in the soup. For example, a sherry consommé is accompanied by a small glass of sherry. Soups that are typical of a given region or province are usually served with beverages from that region. Spicier soups from Mexico or Asian countries are best accompanied by beer.

CANADA

Here's a nourishing soup that the early Quebecers and Acadians have been making since they first settled in what would become Canada. In some regions, such as the Mauricie in Quebec, hominy (a type of corn) is added at the end to give the soup more flavour and a pleasant texture.

Pea Soup

10 servings

INGREDIENTS

450 g yellow dried peas **1 lb**

125 g salted lard **4 oz**

1 large onion, finely diced **1**

1 stalk celery, finely chopped **1**

1 bay leaf **1**

30 mL salted herbs (see page 15), rinsed in cold water **2 tbsp**

2.5 L cold water **10 cups**

500 mL hominy, rinsed in cold water and drained **2 cups**

salt and pepper to taste

1. Soak the peas in cold water overnight or for 8 hours.
2. When preparing the soup, drain the peas, rinse under cold water and place in a large pot.
3. Place the salted lard in a small saucepan, cover with cold water and bring to a boil. Immediately remove from the heat, drain and rinse in cold water.
4. Place the lard on top of the peas in the large pot. Cover with cold water and bring to a boil. Reduce the heat and skim off any foam that forms on the surface.
5. Add the onion, celery, bay leaf and salted herbs; cover and simmer for 2 to 3 hours or until the peas are tender. Stir occasionally.
6. Remove the salted lard and bay leaf. Purée half the soup in a blender or food processor. Pour the purée back into the pot with the rest of the soup. Season with salt and pepper to taste and add the hominy. Reheat and serve.

In Morocco, harira is prepared for Ramadan, the Muslim fast that lasts for one month, and during which nothing may be eaten between sunrise and sunset. Every evening, when the bell rings to announce the end of the fast, Moroccans go home to a bowl of harira accompanied by lemon quarters, couscous, dates and sweet pastries. If you find the soup too thick, add a little light chicken stock before serving. Dried chickpeas can be replaced by canned chickpeas. In this case, add 250 mL (1 cup) of rinsed, drained chickpeas 20 minutes before the soup is ready.

MOROCCO

Harira

4 servings

INGREDIENTS

125 mL chickpeas **1/2 cup**
1.5 L cold water **6 cups**
2 mL turmeric **1/2 tsp**
2 mL fresh ginger, finely grated **1/2 tsp**
2 mL saffron **1/2 tsp**
2 mL ground cinnamon **1/2 tsp**
5 mL ground pepper **1 tsp**
30 mL olive oil **2 tbsp**
500 g lamb, cut into 2 cm (1-in.) cubes **1 lb**
1 large onion, chopped **1**
125 mL brown lentils **1/2 cup**
500 mL tomatoes, peeled and coarsely chopped **2 cups**
10 mL fresh parsley, chopped **2 tsp**
10 mL fresh coriander, chopped **2 tsp**
75 mL orzo or rice **1/3 cup**
fresh lemon quarters
harissa sauce, if desired

METHOD

1. Soak the chickpeas in cold water for 8 hours. Drain well. In a small bowl, blend the turmeric, ginger, saffron, cinnamon and pepper.
2. Heat the oil in a large pot over medium heat and sauté the lamb cubes until they are browned on all sides. Remove from the pot and set aside.
3. Place the onion in the pot and sauté over low heat for 3 minutes, stirring constantly. Sprinkle with the spice mixture and sauté over low heat for 2 minutes, stirring constantly.
4. Add the chickpeas, lentils, lamb, tomatoes and water. Bring to a boil, lower the heat, cover and simmer for 1 to 2 hours or until the lamb and chickpeas are tender.
5. Add the parsley, coriander and orzo, and cook for another 10 to 15 minutes until the orzo is tender but still slightly firm. If using rice, add 25 minutes before the end of cooking.
6. Serve with lemon quarters and harissa, for extra spice. A tiny amount of harissa is usually sufficient.

Here is a soup that Africans like to eat very spicy; I have adapted it by cutting back on the spices to make it suitable for most palates. If you like your food hot, just double — or triple — the quantity of cayenne pepper or use a medium or hot curry.

NIGERIA

Curried Coconut Soup

6 servings

INGREDIENTS

750 mL canned, unsweetened coconut milk **3 cups**

750 mL chicken stock **3 cups**

10 mL mild Madras curry or curry powder (see page 16) **2 tsp**

2 mL salt **1/2 tsp**

1 mL pepper **1/4 tsp**

0.5 mL cayenne pepper **1/8 tsp**

15 mL ginger, finely grated **1 tbsp**

125 mL grated unsweetened coconut **1/2 cup**

5 mL cornstarch **1 tsp**

125 mL plain yogurt **1/2 cup**

Chopped fresh parsley for garnish

METHOD

1. Place the coconut milk and chicken stock in a pot, reserving two tablespoons, and bring to a boil over medium heat. Add the curry, salt, pepper, cayenne, ginger and half the grated coconut. Return to a boil, lower the heat and simmer for 10 to 15 minutes.
2. While the soup is simmering, spread the remaining coconut on a baking sheet and place in the oven at low heat for 2 or 3 minutes until golden. Watch it carefully, as coconut browns very quickly.
3. Mix the cornstarch and remaining chicken stock and pour into the soup in a thin stream, stirring constantly. Simmer for 5 minutes or until the stock has thickened slightly. Add the toasted coconut. When serving, put out small bowls of parsley and yogurt so that guests can garnish their soup.

CANADA

The salted herbs give a lovely flavour to the stock for this simple Acadian dish. Fricot can be prepared using chicken, beef or fish, depending on the ingredients you have on hand.

Fricot à la poule

4 servings

INGREDIENTS

1 1.5-kg chicken, cut into 8 pieces, skin removed 3 lb

15 mL butter 1 tbsp

15 mL oil 1 tbsp

1 large onion, chopped 1

15 mL flour 1 tbsp

2 L cold water 8 cups

15 mL salted herbs (see page 15) 1 tbsp

5 (625 g) potatoes, diced into 2 cm (3/4-in.) cubes 5 (1 1/4 lbs)

pinch savory *or* marjoram

salt and pepper to taste

METHOD

1 Heat the butter and oil in a large pot, without browning. Season the chicken pieces with salt and pepper; cook over medium heat until browned. Remove from the pot and set aside.

2 Place the onion in the pot and sauté until it begins to brown, stirring constantly. Sprinkle with flour and cook over low heat for 1 minute, stirring constantly.

3 Add the water, chicken pieces, rinsed salted herbs and savory. Bring to a boil, lower the heat, cover and simmer for 25 minutes.

4 Add the potatoes and continue cooking for about 15 to 20 minutes or until the potatoes are done.

This surprising combination of ingredients is sure to intrigue your guests. Fresh, high-quality curry is essential in the preparation of this soup, as are very green bananas.

TANZANIA

Curried Chicken and Banana Soup

4 servings

INGREDIENTS

1 1.5-kg chicken, cut in 8 pieces, skin removed **3 lb**
30 mL flour **2 tbsp**
45 mL peanut or olive oil **3 tbsp**
1 large onion, chopped **1**
4 (500 mL) stalks celery, sliced **4 (2 cups)**
3 cloves garlic, minced **3**
35 mL mild curry powder **2 1/2 tbsp**
5 mL crushed red chilis **1 tsp**
500 mL fresh or canned tomatoes, chopped **2 cups**
250 mL fresh or dried grated coconut **1 cup**
1.25 L chicken stock **5 cups**
2 green (unripe) bananas, peeled **2**
salt and pepper to taste

METHOD

1 Season the chicken pieces with salt and a generous amount of pepper. Dredge in flour and shake off any excess.

2 Heat the oil in a large pot and sauté the chicken pieces over medium heat until golden. Remove from the pot and set aside.

3 Place the onion and celery in the pot and sauté over medium heat for 5 minutes, stirring constantly. Add the garlic and continue cooking for 1 minute, stirring constantly. Add the curry powder and crushed red chilis; cook for 1 minute, stirring.

4 Add the tomatoes, coconut and chicken stock to the mixture. Return the chicken pieces to the pot, bring to a boil, lower the heat, cover and simmer over low heat for 90 minutes, or until the meat separates easily from the bone. Remove the chicken pieces from the pot and set aside.

5 Slice the bananas lengthwise and then into 1 cm (1/2-inch) pieces widthwise. Add to the soup and simmer 5 to 10 minutes, until they are tender but still firm.

6 Debone the chicken and cut the meat into large pieces. Add to the soup and reheat for 1 to 2 minutes before serving.

Rougemont Apple Soup

6 servings

INGREDIENTS

30 mL butter **2 tbsp**

1 medium-sized onion, coarsely chopped **1**

1 stalk celery, sliced **1**

1 leek, white part only, sliced **1**

4 medium-sized potatoes, peeled and coarsely chopped **4**

2 slightly tart apples, peeled and cubed **2**

1.5 L chicken stock **6 cups**

pinch ground cinnamon

pinch ground nutmeg

salt and pepper to taste

apple slices and ground nutmeg for garnish

METHOD

1. Melt the butter in a large pot over medium heat without browning it. Add the onion, celery and white part of the leek; sauté for 5 minutes, stirring constantly. Add the potatoes, the apples and cook for another 2 minutes.

2. Add the chicken stock and season with cinnamon and nutmeg. Add a pinch of salt and bring to a boil; lower the heat, cover and simmer for 30 to 45 minutes or until vegetables are tender.

3. Purée the vegetables in a blender or food processor, adding a little stock. Add the purée to the rest of the stock. Stir until smooth and season with salt and pepper to taste. Reheat and garnish with a small slice of apple sprinkled with a pinch of nutmeg.

This is a typical New England dish prepared with corn, an indigenous New World plant, which the early colonists, influenced by the native people, included in their cooking.

UNITED STATES

Corn Chowder

4 servings

INGREDIENTS

30 mL butter **2 tbsp**

1 small onion, finely chopped **1**

500 mL corn, fresh or frozen kernels **2 cups**

1 medium-sized potato, peeled and cut into 1 cm (1/2-in.) cubes **1**

500 mL chicken stock **2 cups**

125 mL milk **1/2 cup**

30 mL all-purpose flour **2 tbsp**

125 mL milk **1/2 cup**

250 mL 15% cream **1 cup**

pinch salt

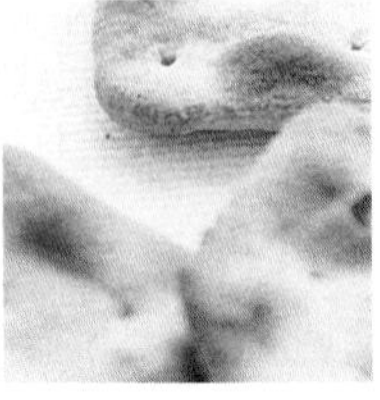

METHOD

1. Melt the butter, without browning, in a medium-sized pot. Add the onion and sauté over low heat, without browning, for about 5 minutes or until it is transparent.
2. Add the corn, potato cubes and chicken stock. Bring to a boil, lower the heat and simmer for about 15 minutes or until the potato is tender but still slightly firm.
3. Place the flour in a small bowl and gradually add the first amount of milk, while whisking the mixture. Mix well until the texture is smooth and free of lumps. Slowly pour this mixture into the soup, stirring constantly. Simmer for a few minutes, stirring occasionally.
4. Add the milk and cream, bring to a boil and immediately remove from the heat. It is important to monitor this operation, since if the chowder is allowed to boil, its taste will be greatly altered. Season with a pinch of salt.

CANADA

It is said that the first chowders in North America were made in Newfoundland. The word "chowder" comes from the French "chaudière," the name given to the pot in which French fishermen cooked their freshly caught fish.

Seafood Chowder

4 servings

INGREDIENTS

- **15 mL** butter **1 tbsp**
- **15 mL** vegetable oil **1 tbsp**
- **1** small onion, finely chopped **1**
- **1** stalk celery, finely chopped **1**
- **2 (250 g)** raw potatoes, peeled and cut into 1.5 cm (1/2-in.) cubes **2 (8 oz)**
- **375 mL** cold water **1 1/2 cups**
- **1 (250 g)** cod fillet **1 (8 oz)**
- **250 g** cooked shrimp **8 oz**
- **6** large scallops **6**
- **250 mL** milk **1 cup**
- **250 mL** 15% cream **1 cup**
- salt, pepper
- **1 mL** paprika **1/4 tsp**

METHOD

1. In a medium-sized pot, heat the oil and butter until the butter melts. Sauté the onion and celery for about 5 minutes. Add the potatoes and sauté for 2 minutes, stirring occasionally.
2. Add the water and bring to a boil; lower the heat, cover and cook for about 10 minutes, until the potatoes are semi-tender.
3. Cut the fish into cubes, taking care to remove any bones; add to the pot when the potatoes are half-cooked. Cover and simmer over low heat for 5 to 10 minutes or until the fish can be easily flaked with a fork.
4. While the fish cooks, cube the scallops and place in a small saucepan. Cover with water and simmer for about 5 minutes. Remove the scallops and reserve the liquid.
5. Add the cooking liquid to the soup, along with the shrimps and scallops.
6. Add the milk, cream and paprika. Bring to a boil and remove the pot from the heat as soon as the contents come to a boil. Season with salt and pepper.

Zucchini Soup

4 servings

INGREDIENTS

4 18 cm (6-in.) zucchinis, or equivalent, thickly sliced 4

3 medium-sized onions, sliced 3

1 small green pepper, coarsely chopped 1

2 garlic cloves, sliced 2

1 L chicken stock 4 cups

2 mL dried basil 1/2 tsp

2 mL dried tarragon 1/2 tsp

125 mL heavy or light cream 1/2 cup

salt and pepper to taste

cubes of red pepper (optional)

METHOD

1 Place the zucchini, onion, green pepper and garlic in a large pot and add chicken stock. Add the basil and tarragon. Bring to a boil and lower the heat; simmer, covered, for 20 to 30 minutes or until the vegetables are tender.

2 Purée in a blender or food processor and return to the pot. Add the cream, reheat and season to taste. Garnish each bowl with a small spoonful of red pepper cubes.

CARIBBEAN

Callaloo, a dish that originated in Africa, has become very popular in the Caribbean, with the influx of numerous African immigrants. Callaloo is made with vegetables, fish and crab.

Crab Callaloo

6 servings

INGREDIENTS

15 mL peanut or olive oil **1 tbsp**

1 slice lean bacon, cut into small pieces **1**

1 small onion, chopped **1**

500 g callaloo *or* spinach *or* swiss chard leaves, deveined and coarsely chopped **1 lb**

1 clove garlic, finely chopped **1**

2 green onions, white and green parts, chopped **2**

pinch thyme

1.5 L chicken stock **6 cups**

250 g fresh or frozen okra **8 oz**

125 mL coconut milk **1/2 cup**

250 g cooked crab **8 oz**

salt

6 drops Tabasco or other hot sauce **6**

METHOD

1. Heat the oil and bacon pieces over medium heat in a large pot until bacon is crisp and almost fully cooked.
2. Add the onion and sauté for 3 minutes. Add the callaloo leaves and garlic; sauté for 3 to 5 minutes, stirring constantly.
3. Add the chopped green onion, thyme and chicken stock and bring to a boil. Lower the heat, cover and simmer for 30 minutes.
4. While the soup is simmering, snip both ends off the okra pods and cut into 1 cm (1/2-in.) lengths.
5. After the soup has simmered for 30 minutes, add the coconut milk, okra and crab. Cover and simmer for about 10 minutes or until the okra is tender. Season with salt and Tabasco sauce to taste. This soup will keep for 2 days in the refrigerator or 3 months in the freezer.

In British Columbia, the salmon is king, and the native people of Vancouver Island make a delicious hot-smoked salmon.

CANADA

Salmon and Smoked Salmon Chowder

4 servings

INGREDIENTS

2 slices bacon, cut into 1 cm (1/4-in.) pieces **2**

1 onion, chopped into medium-sized pieces **1**

2 medium-sized potatoes, peeled and cut into 1.5 cm (1/2-in.) cubes **2**

1 L fish stock **4 cups**

1 bay leaf **1**

375 g fresh salmon, cut into 2.5 cm (1-in.) cubes **12 oz**

125 g smoked salmon chopped into small pieces **4 oz**

15 mL cognac **1 tbsp**

250 mL 15% cream **1 cup**

60 mL fresh parsley, finely chopped **1/4 cup**

salt and pepper to taste

METHOD

1. In a medium-sized pot, cook the bacon until crisp. Remove from pot and set aside. Sauté the onion in the bacon fat over low heat until it is transparent and beginning to brown, stirring constantly. Add the potatoes and cook for 1 minute over low heat while stirring.
2. Add the fish stock and bay leaf. Bring to a boil, lower the heat, cover and simmer for about 10 minutes, until potatoes are done. Add the salmon cubes and simmer for 5 minutes.
3. Add the smoked salmon and cognac; simmer for another 5 minutes.
4. Add the cream; bring to a boil over high heat and stop cooking immediately. Season with salt and pepper, and add the parsley.
5. Serve immediately.

Louisiana gumbo brings together ingredients from many different sources: roux from France, okra from Africa, spices from the Caribbean and rice from Spain.

UNITED STATES

Chicken Gumbo

4 servings

INGREDIENTS

75 mL vegetable oil **1/3 cup**

75 mL all-purpose flour **1/3 cup**

1 onion, finely chopped **1**

1 small green pepper, finely chopped **1**

500 mL fresh or canned tomatoes, chopped **2 cups**

1 L chicken stock **4 cups**

1 bay leaf **1**

pinch thyme

1 mL or more cayenne pepper, to taste **1/4 tsp**

12 fresh or frozen okra pods, sliced into 2.5 cm (1-in.) lengths, ends removed **12**

250 mL rice **1 cup**

500 mL water **2 cups**

4 boneless chicken breasts, skin removed **4**

Cajun spices (optional)

15 mL fresh parsley, chopped **1 tbsp**

250 mL parboiled rice **1 cup**

salt and pepper

METHOD

1. Heat the oil in a large pot over low heat. Gradually add the flour, stirring constantly with a wooden spoon. Continue cooking over low heat, stirring constantly for 15 to 20 minutes, or until the mixture takes on the colour of peanut butter or a filbert shell.
2. Add the onion and green pepper. Mix well and cook over low heat for 5 minutes, stirring constantly. Add the tomatoes, chicken stock, bay leaf, thyme and cayenne pepper. Bring to a boil, lower the heat, cover and simmer for 15 minutes.
3. Add the okra and continue cooking for 15 minutes or until the okra pods are tender. Season to taste.
4. While the soup is simmering, cook the rice. Bring 2 cups of salted water to a boil, add the rice, cover and simmer for 20 minutes.
5. Grill the chicken breasts while the okra is cooking. Brush the chicken breasts with oil, season with salt and pepper or Cajun seasoning and grill 10 minutes per side or until the meat is no longer pink in the centre.
6. To serve, place a serving of rice in a large soup bowl. Add the chicken breast and ladle the soup next to the rice and chicken. The gumbo may be frozen.

CUBA

It was in Cuba that Christopher Columbus discovered the beans of the Americas. He introduced them to Europe when he brought some back from his travels.

Black Bean Soup

6 servings

INGREDIENTS

500 g dried black beans or 2 cans of 540 ml (19 oz) canned black beans rinsed and drained **1 lb (2 cups)**

30 mL peanut or olive oil **2 tbsp**

15 mL annatto seeds **1 tbsp**

or **1 mL** saffron **1/4 tsp**

1 large onion, chopped **1**

1 sweet green pepper, chopped **1**

6 cloves garlic, minced **6**

250 mL tomatoes, peeled, seeded and chopped **1 cup**

125 g lean cooked ham, cubed **4 oz**

15 mL fresh coriander leaves, chopped **1 tbsp**

2 mL dried oregano **1/2 tsp**

1.75 L cold water (approx.) **7 cups**

salt and pepper to taste

Tabasco or other hot sauce

chopped coriander leaves for garnish

METHOD

1. If using dried beans, wash in cold water, cover with cold water and soak for 4 to 5 hours. Drain, rinse and cover with cold water again. Cook for 1 1/2 to 2 hours over low heat until tender. Drain and continue with the recipe. If using canned beans, drain before using.

2. Heat oil in a large pot. Add the annatto or saffron and cook over low heat for 3 minutes. Add the onion and green pepper; continue cooking for 3 minutes, stirring constantly. Add the garlic and cook for another minute. Add the tomatoes, ham, coriander and oregano. Cover and simmer for 20 minutes.

3. Wash the beans under cold water in a colander and drain well. Add to the mixture in the pot, along with the cold water. Bring to a boil, lower the heat, cover and simmer for 1 hour, stirring occasionally, until the beans are tender and the vegetables are done. Purée 500 mL (2 cups) in a food processor or blender, and return to the pot. Reheat and season to taste.

4. Add a few drops of Tabasco and garnish with coriander leaves. This soup will keep 3 days in the refrigerator or 6 months in the freezer.

Corn Soup

4 servings

INGREDIENTS

15 mL butter **1 tbsp**

1 onion, finely chopped **1**

300 g frozen corn **11 oz**

15 mL parsley **1 tbsp**

2 mL salt **1/2 tsp**

1/4 jalapeño pepper, seeded and finely chopped **1/4**

750 mL chicken stock **3 cups**

METHOD

1. In a medium-sized pot, heat the butter without browning it. Over low heat, sauté the chopped onion for about 5 minutes. Remove from heat.
2. Purée half the corn, parsley, pepper and 250 mL (1 cup) of stock in a food processor or blender. Pour this mixture into the pot along with the rest of the stock.
3. Bring to a boil, lower the heat and simmer for 20 minutes. Pour the soup through a strainer and set aside the stock.
4. Return the reserved stock to the pot with the remaining corn. Simmer for 20 minutes and serve.

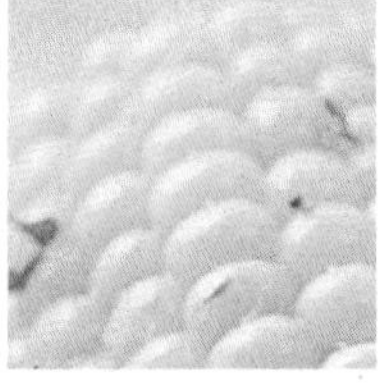

Italian immigrants from the Emilia-Romagna region have enriched the cooking of the American Southwest by adapting the ciuppin of their homeland to the ingredients of their adopted country. Use a firm fish such as red snapper or haddock.

UNITED STATES

Cioppino

6 servings

INGREDIENTS

- 6 dried mushrooms 6
- 60 mL olive oil 1/4 cup
- 1 green pepper, finely chopped 1
- 1 large onion, finely chopped 1
- 2 cloves garlic, finely chopped 2
- 500 mL dry red wine 2 cups
- 1 can (796 mL) crushed tomatoes 1 can (28 oz)
- 500 g lobster or crab, preferably live 1 lb
- 500 g fish fillets, cut into large cubes 1 lb
- 1 L mussels, scraped and washed 4 cups
- 250 g shrimps, deveined and washed 8 oz
- salt and pepper
- 1 mL dried basil 1/4 tsp
  or 15 mL fresh basil, chopped 1 tbsp
- 2 mL dried oregano 1/2 tsp
  or 15 mL fresh oregano, chopped 1 tbsp
- 60 mL (2 small sprigs) fresh parsley, chopped 1/4 cup

METHOD

1. In a small bowl, soak the mushrooms in hot water while preparing the other ingredients. When the mushrooms are soft, chop coarsely before adding them to the preparation.
2. In a large pot, heat the oil and sauté the green pepper and onion for 5 minutes over medium heat. Add garlic when done.
3. Add the wine, drained mushrooms, tomatoes and basil; cover and simmer for 15 minutes.
4. Add the lobster and fish, and simmer for 7 minutes. Add the mussels and shrimps, and cook for another 5 minutes or until all mussels have opened.
5. Season with salt, pepper and oregano. Garnish bowls with fresh chopped parsley.

This soup is usually served cold, but is also delicious warmed up.

MEXICO

Avocado Soup

4 servings

INGREDIENTS

2 perfectly ripe medium-sized avocados 2
250 mL sour cream **1 cup**
500 to 750 mL chicken stock **2 to 3 cups**
10 mL fresh coriander, finely chopped **2 tsp**
5 mL salt, or to taste **1 tsp**
15 mL fresh lime juice **1 tbsp**
pepper *or* a couple of drops of Tabasco

Garnish

Chopped green onions
Cubes of fresh tomato, peeled and seeded
Fresh chopped coriander
Tortilla chips

METHOD

1. Cut the avocados in half; remove the pits and scoop out the flesh with a tablespoon. Place in a mixing bowl, add the sour cream, part of the chicken stock, coriander, salt and lime juice. Run the mixer until the purée is smooth and creamy. As needed, add chicken stock until the desired consistency is obtained.
2. To serve chilled, refrigerate at least 1 hour before serving. Sprinkle a little garnish in each bowl and place tortilla chips on the table or around each serving bowl.
3. To serve hot, reheat over very low heat to desired temperature. Make sure the soup does not boil. The soup will keep for 1 day in the refrigerator, but must be covered with plastic wrap that touches the surface of the purée. It can be frozen for 3 months. Whisk well once thawed to restore its texture.

Cassava, a staple food in Latin American countries, is also known as manioc or yuca. The best cassavas are medium-sized and have no black dots in the white flesh. Cut into chunks before peeling.

BRAZIL

Cassava Soup

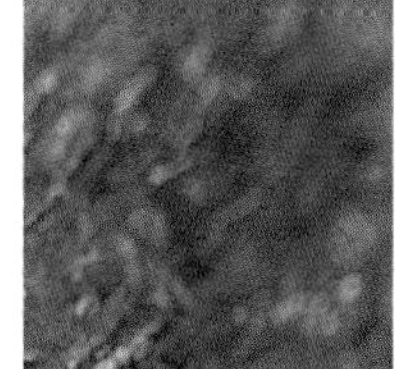

4 servings

INGREDIENTS

30 mL butter **2 tbsp**

1 medium-sized onion, chopped **1**

300 g cassava, peeled and cut into 2.5 cm (1-in.) cubes **11 oz**

1.25 L beef stock **5 cups**

salt and pepper

fresh chopped parsley *or* chives for garnish

METHOD

1. Melt the butter in a pot and sauté onion over low heat for 5 minutes, without allowing it to brown.
2. Add the cassava and beef stock, bring to a boil, cover and simmer for 30 to 40 minutes or until cassava is tender.
3. Purée in a blender or a food processor with a small quantity of stock at a time, add the purée to the rest of the stock, stir well and pass through a food mill or strainer.
4. Reheat, season with salt and pepper and serve with a garnish of parsley or chives. This soup will keep for 4 days in the refrigerator or 6 months in the freezer.

Chicken Vegetable Soup

4 servings

INGREDIENTS

1 1.5 kg chicken, cut into 8 pieces, skin removed **3 lb**

1.5 L chicken stock **6 cups**

4 medium-sized carrots, cut into 2.5 cm (1-in.) pieces **4**

3 stalks celery, cut into 2.5 cm (1-in.) pieces **3**

1 large onion, coarsely chopped **1**

1 mL ground pepper **1/4 tsp**

125 g egg noodles **4 oz**

15 mL fresh parsley, chopped **1 tbsp**

Salt to taste

METHOD

1. Place the chicken pieces in a pot large enough to hold them all in a single layer. Add the chicken stock and bring to a boil over medium heat. Lower the heat, skim as required and add the carrots, celery, onion and pepper. Cover and simmer for 30 to 45 minutes or until the chicken and vegetables are tender. The meat should separate easily from the bones. Debone the cooked chicken and cut into large pieces. Return to the pot.
2. Boil salted cold water in a large pot and cook noodles until tender. Drain the noodles and add to the soup.
3. Season with salt and pepper to taste; add the chopped parsley.

In Peru, soups are traditionally strained at the end of cooking: the stock is kept warm and the solid ingredients are served at the beginning of the meal, followed by the stock at the end. This explains why in many Peruvian soups, the ingredients are in large pieces, and the following recipe is no exception. Nowadays, the stock and the ingredients are usually served in the same bowl.

PERU

Shrimp and Corn Soup

4 servings

INGREDIENTS

750 g raw shrimps, unpeeled **1 1/2 lb**

60 mL olive oil **4 tbsp**

2 medium-sized onions, finely chopped **2**

1 small clove garlic, finely chopped **1**

1 large tomato, peeled, seeded and diced **1**

5 mL hot pepper, finely chopped **1 tsp**

2 mL dried oregano **1/2 tsp**

salt and pepper

2 L fish stock **8 cups**

2 potatoes, peeled and cut into 1 cm (1/4-in.) cubes **2**

125 mL long-grain rice **1/2 cup**

4 medium-sized potatoes, peeled and halved **4**

2 cobs corn, each cut into four pieces **2**

250 g fresh or frozen small green peas **8 oz**

250 mL milk **1 cup**

45 mL parsley, chopped **3 tbsp**

METHOD

1. Peel the shrimps and set aside the shells. Keep the shrimps chilled until use. In a large pot, heat the oil and sauté the onions and shrimp shells for 5 minutes over low heat. Add the garlic and continue cooking for 1 minute.
2. Add the tomato, hot pepper, oregano, pinch of salt and pinch of pepper and cook for another 3 minutes, stirring constantly.
3. Add the fish stock and potato cubes, bring to a boil, lower the heat, cover and simmer for 30 minutes. Pass the ingredients through a strainer to remove part of the vegetables, pressing the mixture using a wooden spoon.
4. Return liquid to the pot. Add the rice and potato halves, bring to a boil, lower the heat, cover and simmer for 20 minutes. Add the corn pieces and continue cooking for 5 minutes.
5. Add the peas and continue cooking for 10 minutes. Add the shrimps and simmer for 3 to 5 minutes over low heat until the shrimps turn pink. Add the milk, bring to a boil and remove the pot from the heat. Add the parsley, stir well, season with salt and pepper as desired and serve. Each serving should include 2 pieces each of corn and potato.

The Chinese usually serve this soup as the main course. Stuffing won ton dumplings takes time but your efforts will be rewarded when you taste this soup, which is unlike most soups served at Chinese restaurants. In addition, uncooked stuffed won tons freeze well. Just lay them out on a cookie sheet; once frozen, they can be stored in freezer bags. When preparing the soup, place the frozen won tons in a pot of boiling water as indicated below and then add to the stock. Won tons can also be pan-fried and served as appetizers.

CHINA

Won Ton Soup

6 servings

INGREDIENTS

About 36 store-bought won ton dumplings
1 egg, beaten 1

Stuffing

250 g lean ground pork **8 oz**
250 g cooked shrimps, finely chopped **8 oz**
1 egg **1**
5 mL soy sauce **1 tsp**
2 mL fresh ginger, finely grated **1/2 tsp**
a few drops of sesame oil
5 mL salt **1 tsp**
boiling water for won tons

Stock

1.5 L chicken stock **6 cups**
60 g fresh spinach leaves, torn **2 oz**
2 green onions, finely sliced **2**
soy sauce

METHOD

1. To prepare the won tons, place the pork and shrimps in a bowl and break the egg over them. Add the soy sauce, ginger, sesame oil and salt. Stir until mixture is smooth.
2. Place 5 mL (1 tsp) stuffing in the centre of a won ton wrapper 7.5 cm (3 in.) wide. Baste the edges lightly with beaten egg, fold over to form a triangle and press edges carefully so that the top and bottom stick together. Arrange the won tons side by side on a cookie sheet that has been lightly floured or lined with wax paper, leaving a little space between each one.
3. Bring the water to a boil in a pot. Add the won tons and boil uncovered over medium heat for 5 to 8 minutes or until dumplings are tender.
4. In another large pot, bring the chicken stock and spinach to a boil; simmer for a few minutes and add the cooked, well-drained won tons.
5. Reheat and serve the soup in large bowls garnished with green onion and accompanied with soy sauce.

Eggplant Soup

4 servings

INGREDIENTS

1 medium-sized eggplant, peeled and cut into 1 cm (1/2-in.) cubes 1
salt
30 mL olive oil **2 tbsp**
60 mL green onion, finely chopped **1/4 cup**
2 large cloves garlic, finely chopped 2
1 small green pepper, chopped 1
250 mL fresh or canned tomatoes, chopped **1 cup**
1 L chicken stock **4 cups**
salt and pepper to taste
croutons
grated parmesan

METHOD

1. Sprinkle the eggplant cubes with salt and leave for 30 minutes. Rinse under cold water to remove salt and blot dry with paper towel.
2. In a medium-sized pot, heat the oil and sauté the green onion over low heat for 1 minute. Add the eggplant and continue cooking for another 5 minutes. Add the garlic, stir well and cook for 1 minute, stirring constantly.
3. Add the green pepper, tomatoes and stock and bring to a boil. Lower the heat, cover and simmer for 30 to 60 minutes or until vegetables are tender.
4. Season to taste with salt and pepper and serve with croutons and Parmesan cheese.

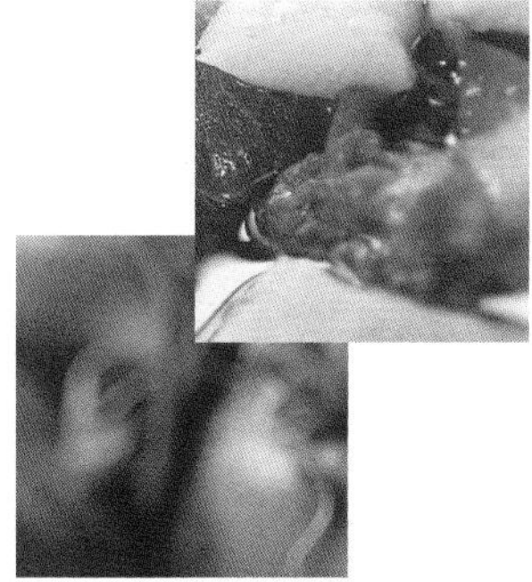

This soup dates back to when the English arrived in India at the beginning of the 19th century. They transformed India's rustic mulligatawny into a more elaborate soup served at banquets.

INDIA

Mulligatawny

4 servings

INGREDIENTS

30 mL olive oil **2 tbsp**

5 mL fresh ginger, grated **1 tsp**

1 large green apple, peeled and cut into 2 cm (1/2-in.) cubes **1**

45 mL flour **3 tbsp**

15 mL mild or medium curry powder, to taste **1 tbsp**

1 mL turmeric **1/4 tsp**

1 medium-sized onion, coarsely chopped **1**

1 medium-sized carrot, coarsely chopped **1**

2 medium-sized tomatoes, peeled, seeded and chopped **2**

1 L chicken stock **4 cups**

ground pepper to taste

125 mL cooked rice **1/2 cup**

150 g cooked chicken, cut into julienne strips **5 oz**

METHOD

1 Heat the oil in a large pot and cook the ginger over low heat for 1 minute. Add the apple and continue cooking for 1 minute.

2 In a small bowl, blend the flour, curry and turmeric.

3 Add the onion and carrot to the pot and cook over medium heat for 5 minutes. Sprinkle the flour and spice mixture over the vegetables and mix well. Cook over low heat for 1 minute while stirring.

4 Add the tomatoes and chicken stock, bring to a boil, reduce the heat, cover and simmer for 30 to 45 minutes or until the vegetables and apple are tender. Purée in a blender or food processor and return to the pot; add the rice and adjust the seasoning.

5 Serve garnished with julienned chicken.

Suimono

4 portions

JAPON

Au Japon, suimono signifie « soupe préparée avec un bouillon clair ». Au bouillon de base, on ajoute la garniture de son choix, habituellement un ou deux légumes différents plus des fruits de mer comme des pétoncles ou des crevettes. À la manière japonaise, on mange les ingrédients solides à l'aide de baguettes et on boit ensuite le bouillon à même le bol.

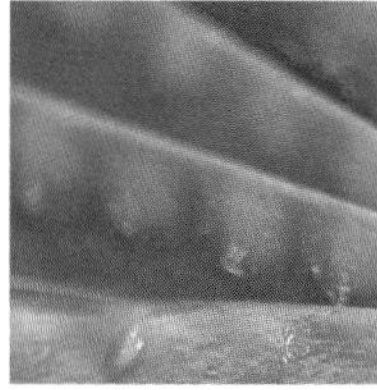

INGRÉDIENTS

500 ml dashi (voir à la page 14) **2 tasses**
15 ml mirin (vin de riz sucré) **1 c. à table**
15 ml tamari **1 c. à table**
15 ml saké **1 c. à table**

Garniture
carottes tranchées en rondelles minces
pois mange-tout
champignons shiitakés tranchés minces
tofu en petits cubes
pétoncles, crevettes ou crabe
125 g nouilles soba *ou* somen **4 oz**

MÉTHODE

1. Faire cuire les nouilles selon les instructions de l'emballage.
2. Cuire les légumes de 2 à 3 minutes dans une casserole d'eau bouillante. Égoutter et réserver. Puis, faire mijoter de 2 à 3 minutes les fruits de mer. Égoutter et réserver.
3. Chauffer le bouillon dashi à feu moyen jusqu'au point d'ébullition, ajouter le mirin, le tamari et le saké et mélanger quelques secondes en brassant.
4. Dans un petit bol creux, placer un nid de nouilles cuites. Mettre 2 ou 3 morceaux de légumes cuits et 2 morceaux de fruits de mer et de tofu autour des nouilles et verser délicatement le bouillon chaud sur le bord du bol pour éviter de déplacer les ingrédients disposés esthétiquement. Servir.

Voici une fondue chinoise couronnée d'une soupe préparée avec le bouillon qui a servi à faire cuire la viande et les légumes du repas et que l'on verse dans les bols sur des nouilles de riz cuites au préalable. Cette soupe est l'ancêtre de la fondue chinoise américaine qu'on accompagne d'une myriade de sauces modernes un peu plus riches que la sauce d'accompagnement qui suit. On trouve habituellement la pâte de fèves rouges chez les commerçants des quartiers chinois.

CHINE

Marmite mongolique

4 portions

INGRÉDIENTS

1,5 kg minces tranches de bœuf, de porc et de poulet **3 lb**

champignons frais en quartiers

un paquet d'épinards frais

pois mange-tout

nouilles de riz chinoises pour 4 portions

Sauce d'accompagnement

15 ml cassonade **1 c. à table**

15 ml eau bouillante **1 c. à table**

15 ml tahini *ou* beurre d'arachide **1 c. à table**

30 ml eau bouillante **2 c. à table**

30 ml sherry sec **2 c. à table**

125 ml sauce soja **1/2 tasse**

15 ml huile de sésame **1 c. à table**

2 ml piment de Cayenne **1/2 c. à thé**

45 ml pâte de fèves rouges chinoise **3 c. à table**

Bouillon de cuisson

2 l bouillon de poulet **8 tasses**

2 oignons verts tranchés en morceaux de 2,5 cm (1 po) **2**

1 petite gousse d'ail coupée en deux **1**

30 ml coriandre fraîche hachée **2 c. à table**

MÉTHODE

1. Dans un petit bol, mélanger la cassonade et l'eau bouillante et, dans un autre bol, mélanger le tahini et l'eau bouillante. Verser ces deux mélanges dans un bol moyen et incorporer le reste des ingrédients. Au moment de servir, verser dans de petits bols individuels.
2. Bouillon de cuisson: Mettre tous les ingrédients dans une casserole à fondue et amener à ébullition. Placer sur le réchaud au moment de servir.
3. Pour le service, disposer esthétiquement les tranches de viande sur une assiette et les légumes dans une seconde assiette.
4. Chaque convive pique des légumes et de la viande sur une fourchette à fondue, les fait cuire dans le bouillon et les déguste avec un peu de sauce.
5. À la fin du repas, chaque convive met sa portion de nouilles de riz dans son bol et le bouillon est versé sur les nouilles.

Les familles japonaises consomment cette soupe au petit déjeuner. Le miso est un aliment fermenté, composé de soja, d'orge ou de riz. On trouve une grande variété de misos sur le marché. Le miso genmai brun utilisé dans la préparation de cette soupe est fabriqué à partir de fèves de soja, de riz brun et de sel de mer et fermenté dans des barils de bois. Au Japon, on dit qu'un bol de soupe au miso par jour éloigne le médecin.

JAPON

Soupe au miso

4 portions

INGRÉDIENTS

1 l dashi (voir à la page 14) **4 tasses**

60 ml miso brun genmai de préférence **4 c. à table**

5 ml miel **1 c. à thé**

150 g cubes de poulet cuit
ou tofu *ou* petits morceaux de poisson cuit **5 oz**

2 oignons verts tranchés en biseaux **2**

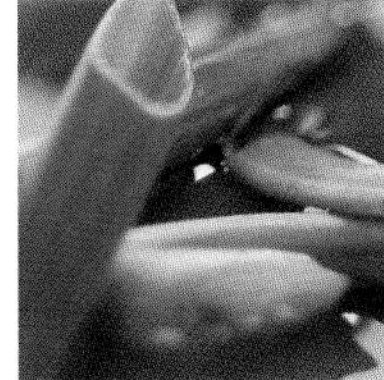

1. Verser une petite quantité de dashi dans un bol et mélanger avec le miso à l'aide d'un fouet.
2. Amener le reste du dashi à ébullition, retirer la casserole du feu et incorporer immédiatement le mélange de miso et le miel dans le bouillon.
3. Placer quelques morceaux de poulet cuit, de tofu ou de poisson cuit et d'oignons verts dans chacun des bols et verser la soupe sur les ingrédients. Servir immédiatement.

Pho tai

6 portions

INGRÉDIENTS

30 ml huile **2 c. à table**

1 petit oignon tranché **1**

1 gousse d'ail hachée finement **1**

5 tranches de gingembre frais hachées **5**

3 oignons verts tranchés **3**

2 l bouillon de bœuf **8 tasses**

125 ml oignons verts tranchés **1/2 tasse**

15 ml sauce nuoc mam *ou* sauce au poisson **1 c. à table**

225 g nouilles de riz larges **8 oz**

375 ml fèves germées **1 1/2 tasse**

225 g viande à fondue ou haut de ronde à demi congelée **8 oz**

Garniture

un bol de basilic frais déchiqueté en petits morceaux

un bol de coriandre fraîche déchiquetée en petits morceaux

un bol de feuilles de menthes déchiquetées en petits morceaux

piment fort haché finement ou sauce chili piquante

sauce nuoc mam

quartiers de limette fraîche

MÉTHODE

1 Dans une grande casserole, chauffer l'huile et faire revenir l'oignon jusqu'à ce qu'il soit transparent. Ajouter l'ail et le gingembre et faire revenir à feu doux pendant une minute en brassant sans arrêt.

2 Ajouter le bouillon de bœuf, les oignons verts et la sauce nuoc mam et laisser mijoter pendant 30 minutes. Tamiser le bouillon pour retirer les épices et les légumes.

3 Trancher la viande très mince en morceaux d'environ 2,5 cm sur 5 cm (1 po sur 2 po) et mettre de côté.

4 Pendant la cuisson du bouillon, faire cuire les nouilles selon les instructions de l'emballage. Réserver.

5 Placer les garnitures sur la table de façon que chaque convive puisse se servir à sa guise. Prendre 6 bols, y mettre un peu de nouilles cuites, des fèves germées, des oignons verts et un peu de viande sur le dessus. Couvrir de bouillon très chaud, laisser reposer de 1 à 2 minutes, le temps que la viande soit cuite, et servir.

Crème d'asperges

6 portions

INGRÉDIENTS

75 ml beurre **1/3 tasse**
la moitié d'un petit poireau haché
15 ml oignon haché **1 c. à table**
15 ml céleri haché **1 c. à table**
375 g asperges fraîches **12 oz**
75 ml farine tout usage **1/3 tasse**
1 l bouillon de poulet **4 tasses**
1 feuille de laurier **1**
une petite pincée de clou de girofle
45 ml crème à 15 ou à 35 % **3 c. à table**
sel et poivre au goût

MÉTHODE

1. Casser les asperges pour supprimer la partie coriace du pied. Pour cette opération, prendre l'asperge dans une main, retenir la tige avec le pouce et peser au centre de l'asperge. Celle-ci devrait se rompre au point le moins tendre. Couper les asperges en tronçons de 1,5 cm (1/2 po).
2. Dans une grande casserole, faire fondre le beurre et y faire revenir les asperges, l'oignon, le céleri et le poireau pendant environ 5 minutes à feu doux en brassant sans arrêt.
3. Retirer la casserole du feu, incorporer la farine au mélange de légumes, remettre la casserole sur le feu et poursuivre la cuisson en brassant sans arrêt pendant 1 minute.
4. Retirer de nouveau la casserole du feu et incorporer graduellement le bouillon de poulet. Ajouter la feuille de laurier et le clou de girofle. Remettre la casserole sur le feu, amener à ébullition en brassant sans arrêt, baisser le feu, couvrir et laisser mijoter pendant environ 45 minutes ou jusqu'à ce que les légumes soient tendres.
5. Enlever la feuille de laurier et ajouter la crème. Réchauffer et assaisonner au goût.

Waterzoï de poulet

4 portions

Ce mets traditionnel des régions côtières de la Belgique est habituellement préparé avec du poisson. Cette version de waterzoï au poulet vient des régions éloignées de la mer.

BELGIQUE

INGRÉDIENTS

1 branche de céleri 1

1 carotte moyenne 1

1 poireau de 2,5 cm (1 po) de diamètre, la partie blanche seulement 1

1 poulet de 1 1/2 kg (3 lb) environ, coupé en 8 morceaux, la peau enlevée 1

bouillon de poulet

1 bouquet garni (voir à la page 15) 1

la moitié d'un oignon piqué d'un clou de girofle

5 ml jus de citron frais **1 c. à thé**

2 jaunes d'œufs 2

190 ml crème à 35 % **3/4 tasse**

sel et poivre au goût

persil frais haché pour garnir

MÉTHODE

1 Tailler la branche de céleri, la carotte et le poireau en julienne de 0,5 cm sur 0,5 cm sur 3 cm (1/4 po sur 1/4 po sur 1 1/2 po). Placer la julienne dans le fond d'une casserole assez grande pour contenir les morceaux de poulet côte à côte.

2 Déposer les morceaux de poulet sur la julienne de légumes et les couvrir tout juste de bouillon de poulet.

3 Mettre le bouquet garni et l'oignon piqué parmi les morceaux de poulet, ajouter le jus de citron et amener à ébullition à feu moyen. Baisser le feu immédiatement, couvrir et laisser mijoter de 30 à 45 minutes ou jusqu'à ce que la chair du poulet se détache facilement des os. Retirer le poulet du bouillon et réserver au chaud.

4 Faire réduire le bouillon de cuisson pendant 5 minutes à feu moyen. Pendant ce temps, mélanger les jaunes d'œufs avec la crème.

5 Réduire le feu afin que le bouillon mijote et verser en filet le mélange de jaunes d'œufs et de crème, en brassant sans arrêt. Poursuivre la cuisson pendant quelques minutes à feu doux ; le mélange ne doit pas bouillir sinon la crème peut tourner et faire des grumeaux.

6 Assaisonner de sel et de poivre et rajouter du jus de citron au goût.

7 Pour servir, placer les morceaux de poulet dans un grand bol creux, arroser avec le bouillon de cuisson et garnir de persil haché. Accompagner de rôties beurrées.

Soupe glacée au concombre

4 à 6 portions

INGRÉDIENTS

2 concombres moyens pelés, les graines enlevées, hachés très finement **2**

10 ml sel **2 c. à thé**

500 ml yogourt nature **2 tasses**

500 ml eau froide **2 tasses**

125 ml noix de Grenoble ou autres noix, hachées **1/2 tasse**

1 gousse d'ail hachée très finement **1**

sel et poivre au goût

25 ml huile d'olive vierge **1 1/2 c. à table**

feuillage d'aneth haché pour garnir (facultatif)

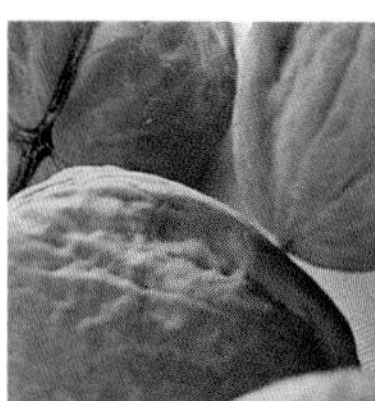

MÉTHODE

1 Placer le concombre haché dans un bol de verre. Saupoudrer des deux cuillerées de sel et bien mélanger. Laisser reposer 1 heure au réfrigérateur ou 30 minutes à la température de la pièce. Rincer à l'eau froide, égoutter et bien éponger avec un linge de coton ou des papiers absorbants pour extraire le plus d'eau possible.

2 Placer le yogourt dans un bol de verre et incorporer graduellement l'eau froide. Ajouter les noix et l'ail et bien mélanger. Ajouter les concombres bien égouttés et épongés, assaisonner de sel et de poivre, et bien mélanger pour rendre homogène. À l'aide d'un fouet, incorporer petit à petit l'huile en la versant en filet. Laisser reposer au réfrigérateur au moins une heure avant de servir. Garnir d'aneth et servir dans des bols à soupe ou des tasses. La soupe se conserve quelques jours au réfrigérateur. Mélanger de nouveau jusqu'à la rendre homogène avant de la servir.

ESPAGNE

C'est en Andalousie qu'on trouve la version la plus authentique de cette soupe. Il y a des gens qui préfèrent le gaspacho préparé sans mélangeur. Si vous utilisez cette méthode, assurez-vous de hacher les ingrédients très fins et de déchiqueter le pain en très petits morceaux. C'est avec les tomates et les concombres de saison qu'on prépare les meilleurs gaspachos.

Gaspacho

6 portions

INGRÉDIENTS

6 (750 g) tomates moyennes pelées, épépinées et coupées en dés **6 (1 1/2 lb)**

1 tranche de pain, la croûte enlevée **1**

1 grosse gousse d'ail hachée finement **1**

1 gros concombre anglais **1** *ou* **2** concombres américains pelés et coupés en dés **2**

375 ml oignon espagnol haché **1 1/2 tasse**

1 grosse branche de persil frais haché **1**

60 ml jus de citron frais **4 c. à table**

60 ml huile olive, extra vierge de préférence **4 c. à table**

30 ml pâte de tomates **2 c. à table**

10 ml sel environ **2 c. à thé**

pincée de piment de Cayenne (facultatif)

125 à 250 ml eau froide **1/2 à 1 tasse**

Garniture

dés de poivron vert

dés de poivron rouge

oignon haché

tomates en dés

croûtons à l'ail (voir à la page 16)

MÉTHODE

1 Pour peler les tomates, amener une casserole d'eau à ébullition, y plonger les tomates pendant 1 minute, retirer de l'eau et plonger dans l'eau froide. Enlever la partie dure qui retenait la queue et peler. Couper en deux dans le sens transversal et retirer les graines à l'aide d'une petite cuillère ou de vos doigts.

2 Tailler la tranche de pain en petits cubes et laisser tomber dans l'entonnoir du couvercle du robot pendant que l'appareil est en marche. Ajouter l'ail haché et mélanger quelques secondes.

3 Ajouter les tomates au mélange dans le robot et réduire en purée.

4 Ajouter les dés de concombre et réduire en purée. Incorporer les oignons et réduire en purée. Finir avec le persil. Lorsque la bonne texture est atteinte, il y a des petites particules vertes.

5 Incorporer au mélange le jus de citron, l'huile d'olive, la pâte de tomate, le sel et le piment de Cayenne et faire fonctionner l'appareil jusqu'à ce que le mélange soit homogène.

6 Ajouter l'eau froide et bien mélanger. La texture devrait avoir la consistance d'un potage épais. Réfrigérer un minimum de 2 heures avant de servir. Le gaspacho se conserve quelques jours au réfrigérateur. Servir accompagné des garnitures.

Strawberry Soup

4 servings

INGREDIENTS

320 g fresh or frozen strawberries **11 oz**
375 mL cold water **1 1/2 cups**
60 mL sugar **4 tbsp**
30 mL fresh orange juice **2 tbsp**
30 mL cornstarch **2 tbsp**
Unsweetened whipped cream for topping

METHOD

1. Crush the strawberries in a food processor or using a potato masher; small pieces of strawberry should remain. Pour into a medium-sized saucepan. Add the cold water and sugar, mix well and bring to a boil over medium heat, stirring. Lower the heat and simmer for 5 minutes. If required, skim off any white foam that forms on the surface.
2. Stir the cornstarch into the fresh orange juice and add to the strawberry mixture, stirring constantly. Simmer until the mixture thickens slightly.
3. Serve warm or chilled, topped with whipped cream.

MICROWAVE:

1. Combine the strawberries, sugar and water in a glass saucepan. Microwave on maximum power for about 7 minutes, stirring once or twice. Add the orange juice-cornstarch mixture and cook for 4 minutes at maximum power. Skim off any white foam that forms on the surface.

Madeira consommé

6 servings

INGREDIENTS

700 g stewing beef **1 1/2 lb**
1 leek, white part only **1**
1 medium-sized carrot **1**
1 stalk celery **1**
1 egg white **1**
3 L cold water **12 cups**
1 onion, studded with 2 cloves **1**
5 mL salt **1 tsp**
6 whole peppercorns **6**
1 cube instant beef bouillon **1**
60 mL madeira **1/4 cup**
pinch each of pepper and salt to taste

METHOD

1 Cut the beef in 1 cm (1/2-in.) cubes and place in a large pot.

2 Chop the leek, carrot and celery and add to beef in the pot.

3 Add the egg white and mix well.

4 Gradually add water to the mixture; bring to a boil, stirring constantly with a wooden spoon. This step is important to evenly distribute the flavours and make a successful consommé.

5 Add the onion, salt and pepper corns and simmer over very low heat for 45 minutes.

6 Dissolve the beef bouillon cube with a little stock from the pot and pour gradually over the vegetables and beef. Stir gently to ensure it is well blended.

7 Adjust the seasoning and filter the stock through a sieve lined with 2 or 3 layers of cheesecloth or muslin.

8 Add the madeira, bring to a boil and serve.

VARIATION

Consommé jardinier

4 servings

1.25 L beef consommé without madeira (see above) **5 cups**
3 medium-sized mushrooms, thinly sliced **3**
30 mL chopped green onions **2 tbsp**
4 spinach leaves **4**

1 Remove stems from the spinach and chop the leaves coarsely.

2 Bring the consommé to a boil. Add the mushrooms, green onions and spinach; cook for 1 minute. Serve immediately.

Chilled Buttermilk Soup

4 servings

INGREDIENTS

3 egg yolks 3
125 mL sugar 1/2 cup
5 mL fresh lemon juice 1 tsp
2 mL lemon zest 1/2 tsp
750 mL buttermilk 3 cups
fresh strawberries, raspberries or blueberries

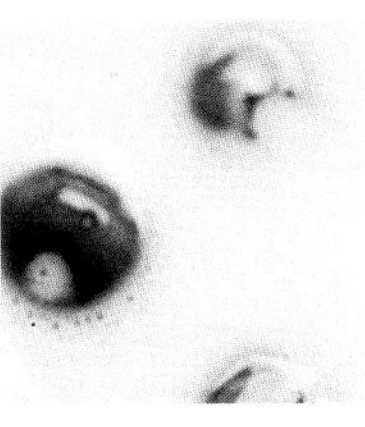

METHOD

1. Beat the egg yolks, using a whisk or electric mixer, for about 2 minutes.
2. Gradually add the sugar, beating constantly. Continue beating until the mixture forms soft peaks when dropped from the beaters or spatula.
3. Add the juice and lemon zest and beat well to blend.
4. Gradually add the buttermilk, beating gently.
5. Chill until serving. Place in a shallow soup bowl and serve with fruit, or pour into goblets.

Bouillabaisse

4 servings

The people of Marseilles claim they were the first to make bouillabaisse. There are several versions of this soup along the Mediterranean coast. Traditionally, the bouillabaisse stock was poured over pieces of dried bread and the fish and seafood were eaten as the main course.

FRANCE

INGREDIENTS

60 mL olive oil **1/4 cup**
1 leek, white part only **1**
1 small stalk celery, chopped **1**
half a chopped pepper
2 cloves garlic, finely chopped **2**
2 L cold water **8 cups**
250 mL dry white wine **1 cup**
250 mL fresh or canned tomatoes, peeled and chopped **1 cup**
5 mL salt (preferably sea salt) **1 tsp**
1 mL thyme **1/4 tsp**
1 mL fennel seeds **1/4 tsp**
1 mL saffron **1/4 tsp**
15 mL (1 sprig) fresh parsley, chopped **1 tbsp**
1 bay leaf **1**
1 kg seafood (mussels, crabs, clams, lobster, scallops, as desired) **2 lb**
1 kg firm, white-fleshed fish, in large pieces **2 lb**
croutons (optional)

METHOD

1. Heat the oil in a large pot and sauté the leek, celery and pepper for 5 minutes over medium heat. Add the garlic and sauté 1 minute, stirring constantly.
2. Add the water, white wine, tomatoes, salt, thyme, fennel seeds, saffron and bay leaf. Bring to a boil, lower the heat, cover and simmer for 30 minutes.
3. Add the seafood (if using lobster or crab, cut into serving-sized pieces) and bring to a boil again, lower the heat, cover and simmer for 8 minutes. If using smaller seafood such as shrimps, scallops and mussels, add at the same time as the fish. Add the fish and continue cooking for 5 to 10 minutes or until fish can be easily flaked with a fork.
4. Taste the stock and adjust the seasoning; serve with croutons brushed with rouille.

Rouille

2 egg yolks, at room temperature **2**
7 mL Dijon mustard **1 1/2 tsp**
190 mL olive oil, preferably virgin **3/4 cup**
3 mL saffron filaments **1/2 tsp**
5 mL hot red pepper, very finely chopped **1 tsp**
2 cloves garlic, finely chopped **2**

1. Beat the egg yolks and mustard in a small bowl, using a whisk.
2. Stir in the oil, pouring it in a thin stream and beating constantly. If you stop beating, stop adding oil.
3. Add the saffron, hot pepper and garlic; mix well until smooth texture is obtained. Place in a small bowl on the table with the basket of croutons so that guests can help themselves.

Here's a delectably creamy soup that is served either hot or cold. If it has been refrigerated and you wish to serve it hot, remove it from the refrigerator and bring to room temperature before heating it over very low heat, stirring constantly.

GREECE

Avgolemono

6 servings

INGREDIENTS

1.5 L homemade chicken stock **6 cups**

125 mL long-grain rice **1/2 cup**

5 mL salt **1 tsp**

3 eggs **3**

60 mL fresh lemon juice **1/4 cup**

METHOD

1. Bring the chicken stock to a boil and then lower the heat. Add the rice and salt. Cover and simmer for 25 to 30 minutes or until the rice is tender. Stir once or twice during this operation to ensure that the rice does not stick to the bottom of the pot.
2. Break the eggs into a medium-sized bowl when the rice is nearly done. Whisk until they turn pale yellow and slightly foamy around the edge of the bowl. Gradually stir in the lemon juice, whisking constantly.
3. When the rice is done, remove about 500 mL (2 cups) of stock and pour in a thin stream into the egg-lemon juice mixture, whisking constantly.
4. Over very low heat, return this mixture to the pot, pouring slowly and stirring constantly. Cook for 1 or 2 minutes over very low heat, stirring with a wooden spoon. The soup must not be allowed to boil.

HOLLAND

Dutch Green Pea Soup

10 servings

INGREDIENTS

60 g salted lard **2 oz**

500 g split green peas **1 lb**

3 L cold water **12 cups**

1 pork hock, about 600 g (1 1/4 lb) **1**

1 bay leaf **1**

3 leeks 2.5 cm (1 in.) in diameter, white part only, chopped **3**

1 (250 mL) small celeriac, peeled and cut into 1 cm (1/4-in.) cubes **1 (1 cup)**

1 large potato, peeled and cut into 1 cm (1/4-in.) cubes **1**

45 mL celery leaves, chopped **3 tbsp**

2 mL dried savory **1/2 tsp**

250 g smoked sausages, precooked **8 oz**

Salt and pepper to taste

METHOD

1. Place the salted lard in a small pot, cover with cold water and bring to a boil. Immediately remove from the heat, drain and rinse in cold water. Drain again.
2. Rinse the split peas in cold water and place in a large pot. Add the cold water, pork hock and salted lard. Bring to a boil and skim off any foam that forms on the surface. Add the bay leaf, cover and simmer for about 1 1/2 hours or until the meat on the pork hock separates easily from the bone and the peas have almost completely disintegrated.
3. Remove pork hock and lard; allow to cool before removing meat from bone.
4. Add the leeks, celeriac and potato to soup, cover and continue cooking for about 30 minutes or until the vegetables are tender. Stir occasionally.
5. While the vegetables are cooking, remove the meat from the pork hock and chop into small pieces. Remove the meat from the salted lard. Boil or steam the smoked sausages for about 10 minutes and cut into diagonal slices of about 1 cm (1/4 inch).
6. When the vegetables are done, add the celery leaves and savory, and cook for about 10 minutes.
7. Season with salt and pepper; add the meat and sausage slices. Reheat and serve. This soup keeps for 5 days in the refrigerator or 3 months in the freezer.

The Hungarians excel at making tasty soups with only a few ingredients, and goulash is a fine example of this. They are also world-renowned for growing and manufacturing paprika. To obtain an authentic taste, it is essential to use a delicate paprika from the Szeged or Kalocsa region.

HUNGARY

Beef Goulash

8 to 10 servings

INGREDIENTS

1 slice salted lard, diced **1**

30 mL vegetable oil **2 tbsp**

1 1/2 kg stewing beef, in 2 cm (3/4-in.) cubes **2 lb**

2 medium-sized onions, coarsely chopped **2**

1 clove garlic, finely chopped **1**

2 mL caraway seeds **1/2 tsp**

5 mL salt **1 tsp**

30 mL mild Hungarian paprika **2 tbsp**

1 L freshly boiled water **4 cups**

1 medium-sized tomato, peeled, sliced and cut into 2.5 cm (1-in.) cubes **1**

2 green peppers, coarsely chopped **2**

4 medium-sized potatoes, peeled and cut into 2 cm (3/4-in.) cubes **4** (peel at the last minute or cover with cold water to prevent discolouration)

Dumplings

1 egg **1**

45 mL flour **3 tbsp**

1 mL salt **1/4 tsp**

If you plan to freeze the soup, omit the potatoes; to serve, add freshly cooked potato cubes to the goulash when reheating.

METHOD

1. In a large pot, heat the oil and salted lard over medium heat until the lard is almost completely melted.
2. Brown the beef cubes in the fat on all sides. Set aside.
3. Sauté the onions over low heat until transparent. Remove the pot from the heat.
4. Crush the garlic, caraway seeds and salt in a small mortar and add to the pot, along with the beef cubes.
5. Sprinkle all ingredients with paprika.
6. Add the hot water, cover and simmer for 1 hour over low heat.
7. Add the tomatoes and pepper; continue cooking for another 30 minutes.
8. Add the potatoes and continue cooking for 15 to 25 minutes or until potatoes are done.
9. To make the dumplings, beat the egg in a small bowl, without foaming, and gradually add the flour and salt until the mixture is smooth. Drop by small spoonfuls (1 ml or 1/4 tsp) into the goulash and simmer for 3 minutes.
10. Serve in large bowls.

Sauerkraut Soup

6 servings

INGREDIENTS

750 mL sauerkraut **3 cups**
1.5 L beef stock **6 cups**
2 slices bacon, cut into small pieces 2
1 large onion, chopped 1
5 mL sweet Hungarian paprika **1 tsp**
2 mL caraway seeds **1/2 tsp**
15 mL flour **1 tbsp**
225 g kielbasa or smoked sausage **8 oz**
salt and pepper to taste
sour cream for garnish

METHOD

1 Place the sauerkraut in a bowl and cover with cold water. Allow to soak for 15 minutes. Rinse well under cold water and drain well. Press the sauerkraut to extract as much water as possible. Place in a pot with the beef stock and bring to a boil. Lower the heat, cover and simmer for 30 minutes.

2 While the sauerkraut is simmering, sauté the bacon pieces in a large pot until crisp. Add the onion and sauté over medium heat for 5 minutes. Sprinkle the paprika and caraway seeds over the onion and stir over low heat for 2 minutes. Sprinkle with the flour and cook for another minute over low heat, stirring constantly. Set aside the pot until the sauerkraut is done.

3 When the sauerkraut is ready, add it with its cooking juices to the vegetable/spice mixture. Add a generous pinch of pepper, cover and simmer for 15 minutes.

4 While the soup is simmering, steam or pan-fry sausages; cut into 1 cm (1/4-in.) slices. When the soup is done, add the sausage slices and simmer for 5 minutes before serving. Garnish each bowl with a small dollop of sour cream.

In Scotland, this main-course soup was traditionally prepared with mutton. Today, we are more likely to use lamb or beef.

BRITISH ISLES

Scotch Broth

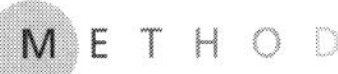

6 servings

INGREDIENTS

- **60 mL** pearl barley **1/4 cup**
- **750 g** lamb – shoulder, neck or shank, bone in **1 1/2 lb**
- **1.5 L** cold water **6 cups**
- **1** leek, green part only **1**
- **1** stalk celery, chopped **1**
- **1** medium-sized carrot, chopped **1**
- **1** medium-sized leek, chopped **1**
- **125 mL** turnip, in small cubes **1/2 cup**
- **15 mL** parsley **1 tbsp**
- salt and pepper to taste

METHOD

1. Pour the barley into a sieve and rinse under cold water. Allow to soak in cold water until needed.
2. Place the lamb in a large pot and cover with cold water. Bring to a boil, lower the heat and remove any foam that forms on the surface. Add a pinch of salt and pepper, the drained barley and the green part of the leek. Simmer for 1 hour.
3. Add the remaining vegetables and simmer for another hour. Test the lamb to see if it is done: if it is, the meat should separate easily from the bone. Remove the lamb from the pot and allow to cool for a few minutes. Remove the bones and cartilage, and cut into cubes no larger than 2.5 cm (1 in.). Return to the pot and season with salt and pepper.
4. The soup will keep for about 5 days in the refrigerator or 6 months in the freezer.

Soupe au pistou, which is usually served at the midday meal, is a classic Provençal dish that resembles Italian minestrone.

FRANCE

Soupe au pistou

6 to 8 servings

INGREDIENTS

2.5 L cold water **10 cups**

2 leeks, cut in 4 lengthwise and then into largish pieces **2**

1 onion, coarsely chopped **1**

2 medium-sized carrots, sliced **2**

2 medium-sized potatoes, peeled, cut in 4 and then into slices 0.5 cm (1/4-in.) thick **2**

Half a small turnip, cut into the same size as the potatoes **half**

1 bouquet garni (see page 15) **1**

250 mL fresh green beans cut in 1 cm (1/2-inch) lengths **1 cup (7 oz)**

2 small zucchinis, sliced in half lengthwise and cut into 0.5 cm (1/4-inch) slices **2**

250 mL elbow macaroni **1 cup**

1 can (540 mL) cooked white beans **1 can (19 oz)**

pinch each of pepper and salt to taste

pistou for garnish

METHOD

1. In a large pot, bring the water to a boil. Add the leeks, onion, carrots, potatoes and turnip, and return to a boil.
2. Lower the heat. Add the bouquet garni; cover and simmer for 30 minutes.
3. Add the green beans, zucchini and macaroni; bring to a boil, lower the heat and simmer for about 15 minutes or until the beans are tender but still slightly crunchy.
4. Carefully add the white beans, after draining and rinsing them in cold water, and simmer for 5 minutes.
5. Season and serve. Place a bowl of pistou on the table so that guests can garnish their soup.

Pistou

250 mL well-packed basil leaves **1 cup**

4 small cloves garlic, minced **4**

190 mL olive oil, preferably extra virgin **3/4 cup**

190 mL freshly grated Parmesan **3/4 cup**

1 small tomato, peeled, seeded and finely chopped **1**

2 mL salt **1/2 tsp**

1 mL pepper **1/4 tsp**

1. To prepare pistou, crush basil leaves in a mortar or with a blender or food processor while it is running.
2. Add the garlic and half the oil, mixing it in with a fork or using the machine.
3. If using a food processor or blender, pour the mixture into a small bowl. Add the remaining oil.
4. Gradually blend in the cheese with a fork and then add the tomatoes.
5. Season.

Cheddar Soup

4 servings

INGREDIENTS

45 mL butter **3 tbsp**
1 small onion, finely chopped **1**
45 mL all-purpose flour **3 tbsp**
500 mL chicken stock **2 cups**
500 mL milk **2 cups**
salt and pepper to taste
250 mL medium cheddar, grated **1 cup**
15 mL fresh parsley, chopped **1 tbsp**

METHOD

1 Melt the butter in a pot and sauté onion over low heat for 5 minutes, stirring constantly.

2 Remove from the heat and add the flour. Stir well and cook for 1 minute over low heat. Remove from the heat.

3 Gradually add the chicken stock and milk, using a whisk. Return pot to the heat and bring to a boil over medium heat, stirring constantly. Lower the heat and simmer until the mixture thickens to the texture of a cream soup.

4 Season with salt and pepper; simmer for a few minutes.

5 Add the cheese, stirring until melted, and immediately remove from the heat.

6 Garnish each bowl with chopped parsley and serve.

MICROWAVE:

1 Melt the butter at maximum power for about 1 minute. Add the onion and continue cooking at maximum power for 2 minutes. Add the flour and cook at maximum power for 1 minute. Whisk in the chicken stock and milk and cook for 20 to 30 minutes at medium power, stirring occasionally and scraping down sides of the bowl with a spatula.

2 Season and heat for 1 minute at maximum power. Remove from the oven and stir in the cheese until it is melted. Garnish with chopped parsley.

Lentil Soup

6 servings

INGREDIENTS

- **30 mL** olive or vegetable oil **2 tbsp**
- **1** large onion, finely chopped **1**
- **1** medium-sized carrot, coarsely grated **1**
- **2 mL** dried marjoram **1/2 tsp**
- **2 mL** dried thyme **1/2 tsp**
- **1.25 L** beef stock **5 cups**
- **200 g** dried brown lentils, washed and drained **1 cup**
- **500 mL** fresh tomatoes peeled and finely chopped *or* canned tomatoes chopped **2 cups**
- **60 mL (2 sprigs)** fresh parsley, chopped **1/4 cup**
- **30 mL** sherry (optional) **2 tbsp**
- salt and pepper to taste
- fresh parmesan, grated

METHOD

1. In a large pot, heat the oil and sauté the onion and carrot for a few minutes, until the onion is transparent.
2. Add the marjoram and thyme; cook for another minute.
3. Add the stock, lentils, tomatoes and parsley. Bring to a boil and simmer for about 1 hour or until the lentils are soft.
4. If using sherry, add it now and continue simmering for about 10 minutes.
5. Season with salt and pepper to taste.
6. To serve, ladle the soup into bowls and place a bowl of grated Parmesan on the table.
7. This soup keeps for 4 days in the refrigerator and also freezes well.

This is the type of hearty soup Italians are fond of. It is important to ensure that the mussels are alive: only those that are fully closed are alive. To check if an opened shell contains a live mussel, tap the shell and it should start to close up in a few seconds.

ITALY

Mussel Soup

3 servings

INGREDIENTS

30 mL olive oil **2 tbsp**

1 medium-sized onion, finely chopped **1**

1 small stalk celery with leaves, chopped **1**

1 large clove garlic **1**

30 mL fresh parsley, finely chopped **2 tbsp**

5 mL dried basil **1 tsp**

125 mL dry white wine **1/2 cup**

250 mL tomatoes, diced **1 cup**
(If using fresh tomatoes, peel and remove core)

1 kg mussels, cleaned **2 lb**

salt and pepper to taste

garlic croutons for garnish (see page 16)

1. In a large pot, heat the oil and sauté the chopped onion and celery over medium heat for 5 minutes, stirring occasionally with a wooden spoon.
2. Add the garlic, parsley and basil; cook for another minute. Add the white wine, bring to boil and reduce the liquid by one-third.
3. Add the tomatoes, bring to a boil, cover and simmer for 20 minutes, stirring occasionally.
4. While the stock is simmering, wash and debeard the mussels, discarding any that are not completely closed.
5. Add the mussels to the cooking stock; bring to a boil and cook over medium-high heat for about 5 minutes or until all mussels have opened. Stir once or twice. The soup will be done as soon as all the mussels have opened. Remove any that are still closed and discard.
6. Shell the mussels and return them to the soup. Pour into bowls over garlic croutons or serve croutons separately.

Lovers of exotic mushrooms can replace the cultivated mushrooms with oyster mushrooms or marasmes des oréades, also known as mousserons.

FRANCE

Cream of Mushroom

8 servings

INGREDIENTS

250 g butter **8 oz**

4 (500 mL) medium-sized onions, chopped **4 (2 cups)**

500 g sliced mushrooms **1 lb**

190 mL flour **3/4 cup**

1 L milk **4 cups**

1 L chicken stock **4 cups**

salt and pepper to taste

METHOD

1. Melt the butter in a large pot and sauté the onion over low heat for 10 minutes, stirring occasionally.
2. Add the sliced mushrooms and mix well. Cover and continue cooking for 5 minutes. It is normal for a fair amount of liquid to form.
3. Stir in the flour, cover and cook for 1 minute.
4. Gradually add two-thirds of the liquids, beating with a whisk, and bring to a boil. Lower the heat, and simmer for about 45 minutes, stirring occasionally with a wooden spoon. Watch closely: if the cream seems too thick, add the rest of the milk and stock.
5. Season with salt and pepper and serve. The soup will keep for 3 or 4 days in the refrigerator or 6 months in the freezer.

What began as a simple soup eaten by peasants during the Russian Revolution has become a culinary classic and is now known the world over. There are a wide variety of versions—both simple and elaborate—containing many different vegetables and meats, accompanied with piroshki stuffed with meat and kasha.

RUSSIA

Borscht

8 servings

INGREDIENTS

500 g beef brisket **1 lb**

2 slices lean salted lard, about 0.5 cm (1/4 in.) thick **2**

2 L water **8 cups**

1 large onion, finely chopped **1**

1 carrot, sliced **1**

1 stalk celery, sliced **1**

2 pinches thyme **2**

1 sprig parsley, chopped **1**

1 bay leaf **1**

500 g beets (about 6 medium) **1 lb**

500 g green cabbage, thinly sliced in lengths no more than 2.5 cm (1 in.) long **1 lb**

5 mL sugar **1 tsp**

10 mL salt **2 tsp**

15 mL red wine vinegar **1 tbsp**

Sour cream, or cream mixed with a few drops of fresh lemon juice

Chopped fresh parsley and dill for garnish (optional)

METHOD

1 Place the beef and lard slices in a large pot; add 8 cups cold water. Bring to a boil, lower the heat and skim off any foam that forms on the surface. Add the onion, carrot, celery, thyme, parsley and bay leaf; cover and simmer for 1 to 2 hours or until the meat separates easily from the bone.

2 Set aside one beet and cook the rest in water until tender, leaving the tail and some of the leaf stems intact. They can also be oven-baked, wrapped in aluminum foil.

3 When the beef is done, remove it from the pot and set aside. At this point, the stock may be allowed to cool completely and be defatted before continuing.

4 Once the stock has been defatted, if applicable, bring to a boil with the vegetables. Finely grate the remaining beet and extract the juice using a strainer, pressing well. Add to the stock along with the sliced cabbage. Bring to a boil, reduce the heat, cover and simmer for 25 minutes. In the meantime, peel the cooked beets and cut into match-sized strips.

5 Add the beets, sugar, salt and vinegar to the stock and simmer for 20 minutes.

6 Adjust seasoning as required and serve each bowl with a dollop of sour cream garnished with chopped parsley and dill. Borscht keeps for 4 to 5 days in the refrigerator or can be frozen for 6 months.

Cream of Kidney Beans with Cloves

4 servings

INGREDIENTS

15 mL olive oil **1 tbsp**

1 medium-sized onion, finely chopped **1**

1 medium-sized garlic clove, chopped **1**

400 g cooked red kidney beans or one 540 mL (19-oz) can red kidney beans, rinsed and drained **2 cups**

1 potato, peeled and diced **1**

2 cloves, crushed **2**

pinch ground white pepper

1 mL salt **1/4 tsp**

750 mL water or chicken stock **3 cups**

60 mL 35% cream **1/4 cup**

METHOD

1. In a large pot, sauté the onion and garlic over medium heat for 4 to 5 minutes. Add the beans, potato cubes, cloves and all other ingredients except the cream. Partially cover and bring to a boil. Skim off any foam that forms on the surface and simmer for 20 minutes.

2. Purée the soup in a blender or food processor and pass through a strainer.

3. Serve piping hot. Swirl in the 35% cream.

MOROCCO

Chickpea Soup with Spinach

6 to 8 servings

INGREDIENTS

15 mL olive oil 1 tbsp

3 medium-sized onions, diced 3

1 clove garlic 1

2 mL ground cumin 1/2 tsp

pinch ground white pepper

10 mL salt 2 tsp

pinch cayenne pepper

2.5 L water or chicken stock 10 cups

3 potatoes, diced (about 400 g) 3

800 g cooked chickpeas or two 540 mL (19-oz) cans chickpeas, rinsed and drained 4 cups

500 g fresh spinach, washed, stems removed and chopped 2 cups

1. In a large pot, heat the olive oil over medium heat, and cook the onions and garlic with the seasonings. Add the water and cook, covered, over low heat for 20 minutes.

2. Add the potatoes and cook until they are tender but still slightly crunchy.

3. Add the chickpeas and bring to a boil again; keep warm.

4. Garnish bowls with chopped spinach and serve the soup very hot. The spinach will cook in the hot soup.

White Beans with Pasta

4 to 6 servings

INGREDIENTS

250 g blanched smoked bacon, julienned **8 oz**
1 large onion, chopped **1**
1 clove garlic, chopped **1**
2 carrots, chopped **2**
5 mL dried oregano **1 tsp**
2 mL dried basil **1/2 tsp**
1 mL dried thyme **1/4 tsp**
10 mL paprika **2 tsp**
2 mL salt **1/2 tsp**
1 bay leaf **1**
pinch cayenne pepper
10 mL tomato paste **2 tsp**
2 L water or chicken stock **8 cups**
400 g cooked white beans or one 540 mL (19-oz) can white beans, rinsed and drained **2 cups**
300 g cooked linguine or spaghetti **11 oz**
125 mL fresh parsley **1/2 cup**

METHOD

1. In a large pot, cook the bacon strips over high heat until lightly caramelized. Remove the fat, leaving about 15 mL (1 tbsp) in the pot.
2. Add the onion, garlic, carrots and seasonings. Cook over medium heat for 5 minutes.
3. Add the tomato paste and continue cooking for another 2 minutes.
4. Add the water and bring to a boil. Simmer, partially covered, for 20 minutes.
5. Add the beans and pasta. Heat for another 3 minutes.
6. Garnish with chopped parsley.

Chicken Broth with Fava Beans and Pesto

6 to 8 servings

INGREDIENTS

500 g chicken thighs **1 lb**
2.5 L cold water **10 cups**
1 large onion, chopped **1**
2 stalks celery, chopped **2**
1 clove garlic **1**
1 mL dried thyme **1/4 tsp**
pinch ground black pepper
2 bay leaves **2**
1 clove **1**
1 mL fennel seeds **1/4 tsp**
1 mL dried tarragon **1/4 tsp**
400 g fava beans, cooked and skinned, or one 540 mL (19-oz) can fava beans, drained, skinned and rinsed **2 cups**
45 mL pesto **3 tbsp**

Pesto (about 500 mL or 2 cups)

375 mL fresh basil **1 1/2 cups**
75 mL olive oil **1/3 cup**
125 mL fresh parsley **1/2 cup**
5 mL salt **1 tsp**
125 mL fresh spinach **1/2 cup**
pinch cayenne pepper
5 cloves garlic **5**
freshly ground pepper
60 mL fresh Parmesan **1/4 cup**

Pesto

1 Place all the ingredients in a food processor and purée (3 to 5 minutes). Refrigerate.

Broth

1 Place the chicken in a large pot and add cold water.

2 Bring to a boil. Reduce heat to low and skim off any foam that forms on the surface. Add all the ingredients except the beans and the pesto. Simmer over low heat for about 1 hour.

3 Drain the chicken thighs using a strainer, saving the cooking liquid. Cut the chicken thighs into small pieces and return them to the stock. Add the beans and the pesto.

4 Reheat without allowing to boil.

This Scottish soup features the flavour of leeks. It is said to be of medieval origin: the Scots made it famous by replacing the onions with leeks. The soup is made with rice or barley, and carrots are sometimes added.

BRITISH ISLES

Cock-a-leekie

8 servings

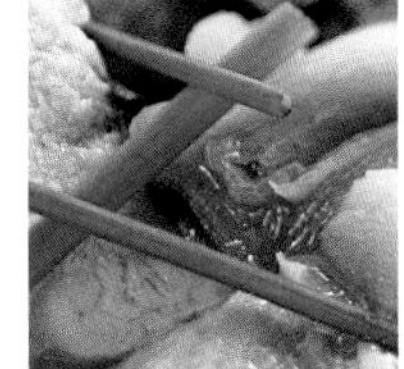

INGREDIENTS

60 mL (50 g) pearl barley **1/4 cup (2 oz)**

1 (1.5 kg) chicken **1 (3 lb)**

2.5 L cold water **10 cups**

1 leek, green part only **1**

1 bay leaf **1**

1 stalk celery, with leaves **1**

6 leeks 2.5 cm (1 in.) in diameter, white parts only, cut into 1 cm (1/2-in.) slices **6**

salt and pepper to taste

parsley for garnish

METHOD

1. Rinse the barley under cold water and soak in cold water while preparing the other ingredients.
2. Remove the chicken skin by making a cut on the underside, or ask your butcher to do it for you.
3. Place the chicken in a large pot, add water and bring to a boil. Lower the heat and skim off any foam. Add the leek greens, celery stalk, bay leaf and barley; cover and simmer for 30 minutes.
4. Remove the leek greens, celery stalk and bay leaf. Add the leek slices and cook for another 30 minutes or so.
5. Remove the chicken from the stock and allow to cool slightly. Remove the bones and cut into 5 cm (2-inch) pieces. Return the chicken pieces to the stock.
6. Serve with a garnish of fresh chopped parsley.

Any other type of cabbage may be substituted, but the cooking time may vary.

PORTUGAL

Caldo verde

6 to 8 servings

INGREDIENTS

180 mL finely chopped onion **3/4 cup**

3 cloves garlic, finely chopped **3**

375 mL potatoes, washed, peeled and chopped **1 1/2 cups**

60 mL olive oil **1/4 cup**

250 mL vinho verde **1 cup**

750 mL vegetable court bouillon (see recipe on p. 14) **3 cups**

150 g finely diced Salsichao sausage **5 oz**

paprika to taste

salt and ground black pepper to taste

375 mL finely chopped Galician cabbage **1 1/2 cups**

METHOD

1. In a large pot, heat the oil over medium heat and sauté the onion, garlic and potatoes. Add the vinho verde and reduce by two-thirds.
2. Add the court bouillon and cook over medium heat for 30 minutes.
3. Purée in a food processor at high speed until the mixture is smooth, and return to the large pot.
4. In a small skillet, sauté the sausage; drain off the fat and add to the contents of the large pot. Season with paprika, salt and pepper, and cook over low heat.
5. Add the finely chopped cabbage to the soup. Cook for 5 more minutes and serve with a thin stream of olive oil.

FRANCE

Clam and Zucchini Chowder

6 to 8 servings

INGREDIENTS

60 mL olive oil **1/4 cup**
2 garlic cloves, chopped **2**
60 mL chopped green onion **1/4 cup**
600 g medium-sized clams, cleaned **20 oz**
500 mL dry white wine **2 cups**
500 g sliced zucchini **1 lb 2 oz**
15 mL lemon zest **1 tbsp**
5 mL lime zest **1 tsp**
1 L fish stock (see recipe on p. 13) **4 cups**
125 mL heavy cream **1/2 cup**
80 mL parsley **1/3 cup**
salt to taste
ground white pepper to taste

METHOD

1. In a large pot, heat the oil over high heat and cook the garlic, green onion and clams.
2. Add the white wine and simmer, covered, for 10 minutes.
3. Remove the clams and keep warm.
4. Add the zucchini, zest, half the shelled clams and the fish stock, and cook for 30 to 40 minutes over medium heat.
5. Purée the mixture on high in a food processor and continue cooking over low heat.
6. Add the cream, parsley and seasoning. Cook for another five minutes.
7. Serve garnished with the remaining unshelled clams.

PORTUGAL

Guinea Fowl Soup with Mint and Watercress

4 to 6 servings

INGREDIENTS

125 mL finely diced carrots **1/2 cup**
125 mL sliced green beans **1/2 cup**
125 g julienned green pepper **4 oz.**
125 mL finely diced tomato **1/2 cup**
240 g diced guinea fowl meat **8 oz**
45 mL olive oil **3 tbsp**
1 L clear poultry stock *or* chicken bouillon **4 cups**
salt to taste
ground black pepper to taste
45 mL finely chopped mint leaves **3 tbsp**
125 mL finely chopped watercress **1/2 cup**

This soup may also be lightly creamed.

METHOD

1. Heat the oil in a large pot and sear the guinea fowl over high heat.
2. Lower the heat and add all the vegetables; cook for 1 to 2 minutes.
3. Add the poultry stock and mint, and season.
4. Simmer for 45 minutes.
5. Add the watercress 5 minutes before serving.

Minestrone

8 to 10 servings

INGREDIENTS

1 slice salted lard **1**

15 mL olive oil **1 tbsp**

1 medium-sized onion, chopped **1**

2 carrots, finely diced **2**

125 mL turnip, finely diced **1/2 cup**

2 stalks celery, chopped **2**

1 medium-sized leek, halved and sliced **1**

250 mL green cabbage, chopped **1 cup**

250 mL large green pepper, chopped **1 cup**

2 cloves garlic **2**

750 mL fresh or canned tomatoes, chopped **3 cups**

125 mL uncooked macaroni **1/2 cup**

90 mL rice **1/3 cup**

1.5 L beef stock **6 cups**

175 mL cooked white beans **2/3 cup** *or* **60 mL** dried white beans, before cooking **1/4 cup**

175 mL fresh green beans, cut into 1 cm (1/2-inch) lengths **2/3 cup**

175 mL fresh or frozen green peas **2/3 cup**

Garnish

1 small sprig basil, finely chopped **1**

1 small sprig parsley, finely chopped **1**

grated parmesan

METHOD

1. Place the lard in a small pot, cover with cold water and bring to a boil. Remove from the heat immediately, drain and rinse in cold water. Cut into small cubes.
2. In a large pot, heat the olive oil and add the lard cubes. Sauté over medium heat until the lard cubes are crisp, stirring occasionally.
3. Add the onion, carrots, turnip, celery, leek, cabbage and pepper; sauté for 5 minutes, stirring constantly.
4. Add the garlic, tomatoes, rice and beef stock; bring to a boil, lower the heat and simmer for 30 minutes.
5. Add the green beans, white beans and pasta; cook for about 25 minutes or until pasta is done.
6. Season with salt and pepper.
7. Mix the basil and parsley in a small bowl and garnish each soup bowl when serving. Place a bowl of grated Parmesan on the table so that guests can sprinkle it on their soup.

Stone Soup

8 servings

1 pig's ear 1

150 g diced smoked bacon 5 oz

180 mL onion 3/4 cup

3 cloves garlic 3

200 g black chorizo, julienned 7 oz

200 g chorizo *or* other Portuguese sausage 7 oz

270 mL (1/2 can) red kidney beans, rinsed and drained 9.5 oz

2 bay leaves 2

salt to taste

ground black pepper to taste

750 mL diced potato 3 cups

250 mL diced carrot 1 cup

125 mL diced yellow turnip 1/2 cup

125 mL diced tomato 1/2 cup

30 mL chopped coriander 2 tbsp

1 In a medium-sized saucepan, bring the water to a boil and poach the pig's ear for 15 minutes.

2 Peel the onions and garlic, chop and place in a large pot. Add the pig's ear, diced bacon, both kinds of chorizo, kidney beans and bay leaves. Season.

3 Cover with cold water, bring to a boil and simmer for 45 minutes.

4 Remove the meat and bacon from the pot; set aside.

5 Add the vegetables to the soup, adjust seasonings, and simmer for 30 minutes until the vegetables are done.

6 Place the meat and sausages in terrines, and cover with the soup. Garnish with coriander and add a clean stone to the soup before serving.

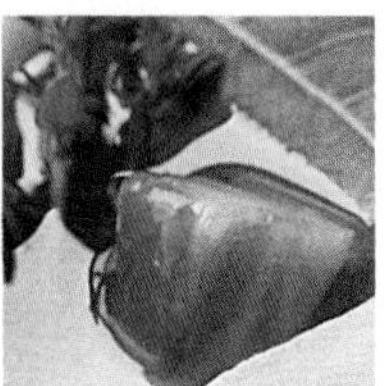

Gumbo with Greens

6 to **8** servings

A meatless version of this dish was traditionally served on Friday, the day on which Catholics abstain from meat. If one or more of these greens is unavailable, replace with another or double the quantity of one listed in the ingredients. The list of ingredients may seem long, but the taste of this gumbo makes the effort worthwhile.

UNITED STATES

INGREDIENTS

- 1 bunch spinach 1
- 1 bunch parsley 1
- 1 bunch watercress 1
- 1 bunch Swiss chard 1
- 1 bunch mustard greens 1
- 1 bunch green onions 1
- 1 small head cabbage 1
- 1 large bay leaf 1
- 2 mL dried thyme 1/2 tsp
- 2 mL dried basil 1/2 tsp
- 2 mL dried oregano 1/2 tsp
- 1 mL pepper 1/4 tsp
- 1 mL cayenne 1/4 tsp
- 1 mL ground cloves 1/4 tsp
- 10 mL salt 2 tsp
- 2 L chicken stock 8 cups
- 1 to 1.25 L cold water for cooking the greens 4 to 5 cups
- 500 g lean pork, cut into 1-cm (1/2-in.) cubes 1 lb
- 250 g lean smoked ham,cut into 1-cm (1/2-in.) cubes 8 oz
- 1 kielbasa or garlic sausage,cut into small cubes 1
- 5 mL Cajun-Creole seasoning mix 1 tsp
- 45 mL vegetable oil 3 tbsp
- 125 mL vegetable oil 1/2 cup
- 125 mL flour 1/2 cup
- 1 large onion, chopped 1
- 1 small green pepper, chopped 1
- 2 large cloves garlic, minced 2
- 2 mL sugar 1/2 tsp
- hot cooked white rice
- 2 green onions, chopped 2
- 45 mL chopped parsley 3 tbsp

METHOD

1. Wash all the greens except the cabbage, remove stems and any large ribs. Chop coarsely. Remove the core and finely chop the cabbage.
2. Place the greens and cabbage in a large pot, and add the bay leaf, thyme, basil, oregano, pepper, cayenne, cloves, salt and chicken stock. Add the cold water, bring to a boil, reduce the heat, cover and simmer while you complete the next steps.
3. Mix the pork, ham and kielbasa cubes with Cajun-Creole seasoning mix. Heat 45 mL (3 tbsp) vegetable oil in a large, deep cast-iron skillet and sauté the cubes of meat until browned on all sides. Remove the cubes from the skillet with a slotted spoon, to leave as much cooking grease as possible in the skillet. Add the meat cubes to the greens.
4. Heat 125 mL (1/2 cup) oil over low heat, whisk in the flour and cook over low heat for 20 to 30 minutes, stirring constantly until the roux is the colour of peanut butter. Add the onion, green pepper and garlic, and cook for 5 minutes over medium heat. Add this mixture to the saucepan with the greens, along with the sugar. Simmer for 1 hour.
5. Adjust the seasoning and add salt, pepper and cayenne as needed. Cook for 30 minutes.
6. Serve immediately, pouring a small serving of rice in a soup bowl. Garnish each bowl with chopped green onions and parsley.

This soup may also be served cold.

Pea Soup with Mint

4 servings

INGREDIENTS

60 mL butter **1/4 cup**
4 medium onions, chopped **4**
450 g fresh *or* frozen green peas **1 lb**
625 mL poultry stock **2 1/2 cups**
2 sprigs fresh mint **2**
625 mL milk **2 1/2 cups**
salt to taste
freshly ground pepper to taste
60 mL heavy cream **1/4 cup**
8 fresh mint leaves **8**

METHOD

1 In a large pot, melt the butter over medium heat and cook the onions, without browning.

2 Add the peas, poultry stock and mint, and bring to a boil; cover and simmer until peas are tender.

3 Remove from heat. Set aside 45 mL (3 tbsp) of peas for garnish.

4 Pour the soup into a food processor, add the milk and purée until smooth.

5 Pour the soup into a clean pot, season and reheat over low heat for a few minutes.

6 Pour into bowls and garnish with the cream, mint and peas.

Crab Won Ton Soup

CHINA

serves **6 to 8**

INGREDIENTS

1 medium onion, cut into pieces 1
2 large carrots, cut into pieces 2
6 stalks celery, cut into pieces 6
1 leek, cut into pieces 1
125 mL white mushrooms, cut into pieces 1/2 cup
4 cloves garlic 4
10 mL fennel seed 2 tsp
10 mL coriander seed 2 tsp
5 mL whole black peppercorns 1 tsp
5 mL dried thyme 1 tsp
4 bay leaves 4
pinch hot pepper flakes
15 mL olive oil 1 tbsp
3 L cold water 12 cups
2.5 kg live crabs 5 lb

Won tons

15 mL butter 1 tbsp
6 leeks, white part only, finely chopped 6
chopped crab meat
2 cloves garlic 2
5 mL finely chopped fresh ginger 1 tsp
salt and pepper to taste
40 won ton wrappers 40
1 egg, beaten 1
water to cook the won tons
125 mL chopped green onions 1/2 cup

METHOD

1. In a large saucepan, sauté the vegetables, garlic and seasonings in the olive oil over moderate heat.
2. Add the water and bring to a boil. Reduce the heat to low and simmer, partially covered, 30 minutes.
3. Lower the crabs into the water. Return to a boil and simmer over low heat 8 to 10 minutes. Turn off the heat and let the crabs cool in the broth.
4. Remove the crabs and strain the broth. Refrigerate broth until ready to use.
5. Chop the crab meat and refrigerate until ready to use.

WON TONS

1. In a frying pan, heat the butter over moderate heat. Add the leeks and sauté 4 to 5 minutes.
2. Add the crab meat, garlic, ginger, salt and pepper and cook 2 minutes longer. Turn off heat and let cool.
3. To make the won tons, place 5 mL (1 tsp) crab mixture in the centre of each wrapper.
4. Lightly brush with beaten egg and firmly press the edges together.
5. In a large saucepan, bring the water to a boil and add the won tons. Cook uncovered 3 to 5 minutes, or until tender. Drain well.
6. In another saucepan, reheat the reserved crab broth and the won tons. Serve piping hot.
7. Sprinkle with green onions.

Salmon Caldillo

serves **6 to 8**

INGREDIENTS

15 mL olive oil **1 tbsp**
1 medium onion, thinly sliced 1
2 cloves garlic, chopped 2
1 can diced tomatoes (796 mL/28 oz) 1
1 mL dried thyme **1/4 tsp**
2 bay leaves 2
2 L fish stock **8 cups**
5 medium potatoes, peeled and cut into 2-cm (3/4-in.) slices 5
salt and freshly ground pepper
1 whole salmon, cut into steaks (2 kg/4 lb) 1
60 mL chopped fresh parsley **1/4 cup**
60 mL chopped cilantro **1/4 cup**

METHOD

1 In a large stockpot, heat the olive oil over moderate heat. Sauté the onion and garlic 2 to 3 minutes.

2 Add the undrained tomatoes, thyme, bay leaves and fish stock. Bring to a boil and simmer, partially covered, 4 to 5 minutes.

3 Add the potatoes, adjust the seasoning and cook 4 to 5 minutes longer, or until the potatoes are cooked but still firm.

4 Add the salmon steaks and cook 4 to 5 minutes. Do not overcook.

5 Serve piping hot with chopped parsley and cilantro.

When you make this thick, hearty soup, you'll quickly realize that it is completely different from the courtbouillon of classic French cuisine. Red snapper may be replaced by cod, haddock or catfish.

UNITED STATES

Courtbouillon

4 servings

INGREDIENTS

Preparing the fish

500 mL water 2 cups
1 bay leaf 1
pinch dried thyme
3 whole allspice 3
15 mL freshly squeezed lemon juice 1 tbsp
4 red snapper fillets, 50 g (8 oz) each 4

Preparation

80 mL vegetable oil 1/3 cup
125 mL flour 1/2 cup
2 medium onions, chopped 2
1 small green pepper, chopped 1
1 large sprig celery, chopped 1
2 cloves garlic, minced 2
500 mL fresh or canned tomatoes, chopped 2 cups
15 mL red tomato ketchup 1 tbsp
160 mL dry red wine 2/3 cup
2 mL freshly ground black pepper 1/2 tsp
1 mL cayenne 1/4 tsp
5 mL salt 1 tsp
pinch sugar
3 green onions, finely sliced 3
60 mL chopped fresh parsley 1/4 cup

METHOD

1 Place the water, bay leaf, thyme, whole allspice and lemon juice in a medium-sized pot. Bring to a boil, cover and cook over medium heat for 5 minutes. Add the red snapper fillets and simmer over very low heat for 10 to 15 minutes until the fish is opaque in the centre. Remove the fillets from the broth and set aside. Measure the broth and add enough water to make 500 mL (2 cups) of liquid.

2 In a large, deep pot, heat the oil and gradually whisk in the flour. Cook over low heat, stirring frequently until the roux is the colour of a hazelnut shell. Remove the pot from the heat as soon as the roux is ready and add the onions, green pepper and celery immediately. Cook over low heat for 5 minutes, stirring constantly. Add the garlic and cook for another minute.

3 Stir in the tomatoes, ketchup, red wine, cooking broth from the fish, pepper, cayenne, salt and sugar. Mix well, bring to a boil, cover and simmer for 30 minutes, stirring occasionally.

4 Break the fish into pieces and add to the mixture, along with the green onions and parsley. Heat for a few minutes. Avoid stirring to prevent the fish from flaking.

5 Adjust the seasonings and serve.

Main courses

Main courses are the main attraction of a good meal. When possible, cooks of yore would traditionally serve meat as the main course for its taste and nourishment, enhanced with cooking juices or a more sophisticated sauce. Today, seafood, pasta and legume recipes are also enjoyed as main courses. Of course, some meats aren't available in every part of the world. Some cultures may eat mutton, while others enjoy tuna or poultry, legumes only or grains only. No matter the availability of these products, however, the main course is intended to fill the stomach, satisfy the appetite, allow the organism to rebuild its strength and the gourmet to indulge his taste buds.

The recipes that follow cover a wide range of diets and are inspired from the most popular dishes the world over. They call on diversified, at times specialized, ingredients that are nonetheless easy enough to unearth. Obviously, some of the recipes are easier to make than others depending on the seasonal availability of ingredients. Since the freshness and quality of foods almost always guarantee a succulent main course, a good cook's main challenge lies in finding them. The vast culinary array offered in this chapter has been selected to help you satisfy the hungriest appetites and most refined palates, and even surprise the fussiest eaters with an exotic or totally original dish!

PORTUGAL

4 servings

Algarve-style Roast Loin of Lamb

It is preferable to have the loin deboned by a butcher.

INGREDIENTS

1 lamb loin roast, deboned (with whole fillets) 1

300 g lamb cubes 10 oz

80 mL heavy cream 1/3 cup

80 mL egg white 1/3 cup

4 chestnuts 4

500 mL brown beef stock (see recipe on p. 12) 2 cups

6 figs 6

5 mL ground almonds 1 tsp

5 mL salt 1 tsp

7.5 mL freshly ground black pepper 1 1/2 tsp

2 mL chopped fresh rosemary 1/2 tsp

2 mL chopped fresh thyme 1/2 tsp

5 mL chopped fresh Italian parsley 1 tsp

METHOD

1 Place the chestnuts in a small saucepan, add the beef stock and bring to a boil.

2 When the stock has come to a boil, lower the heat to medium and cook for 10 minutes.

3 Remove the chestnuts from the stock and allow to cool. Remove the skin and set aside.

4 Debone the lamb loin and remove the two fillets. Refrigerate.

5 In a food processor, place the lamb cubes, egg white, chestnuts, ground almonds, salt, pepper and herbs, and blend well.

6 Add the cream and blend until the mixture is very smooth.

7 Pour the mixture into a bowl and add the flesh of the figs, cut into pieces. Mix with a spoon.

8 Place the lamb loin on a work surface, fat side down. Stuff the centre with the mixture. Bring the two outer sides of the meat toward the centre and attach with string.

9 Preheat the oven to 160°C (325°F).

10 In a large skillet, heat the oil and sear the meat on all sides. Place in an ovenproof dish and cook until the temperature in the centre of the meat reaches 50°C (125°F), about 25 minutes.

11 Remove from the oven and let sit for 5 minutes before serving.

Guinea Fowl Jambonneaux

The supremes can also be braised in the oven at 180°C (350°F) for 30 to 40 minutes.

2 servings

INGREDIENTS

2 supremes of guinea fowl, with skin 2
60 mL finely chopped black olives **1/4 cup**
10 mL chopped savory **2 tsp**
5 mL chopped thyme **1 tsp**
salt to taste
15 mL olive oil **1 tbsp**
500 mL clear poultry stock *or* chicken stock **2 cups**

METHOD

1. In a small bowl, combine the olives, herbs, salt.
2. On a cutting board, flatten the supremes, skin side down, and cut into papillons.
3. Garnish the supremes with the pili-pili, olive and herb mixture.
4. Roll the suprêmes and attach them with strings so that they retain the shape of a small ham.
5. In a medium-sized skillet, heat the olive oil over high heat and sear the jambonneaux on all sides.
6. Add the poultry stock, reduce the heat to medium high and cook, covered, for 12 to 14 minutes.

Rack of Wild Boar with Juniper Berries

4 to 6 servings

The wild boar may be replaced by pork.

INGREDIENTS

- 1 rack of wild boar *or* pork, trimmed 1
- 750 mL dry red wine 3 cups
- 45 mL juniper berries 3 tbsp
- 3 bay leaves 3
- 4 sprigs fresh thyme 4
- 60 mL fresh chopped sage 4 tbsp
- 125 mL chopped Spanish onion 1/2 cup
- 80 mL chopped carrot 1/3 cup
- 125 mL chopped celery 1/2 cup
- 10 black peppercorns 10
- 125 mL crushed blueberries (fresh *or* frozen) 1/2 cup
- salt to taste
- ground black pepper to taste
- 30 mL olive oil 2 tbsp
- 625 mL demi-glace (see recipe on p. 18) 2 1/2 cups

METHOD

1. In a large glass bowl, combine the wine, juniper berries, bay leaves, thyme, sage, onion, carrot, celery, peppercorns and blueberries.
2. Add the wild boar to the marinade and refrigerate for 6 to 8 hours.
3. Preheat the oven to 180°C (350°F).
4. In a large skillet, heat half the oil over high heat and sear the meat on all sides.
5. Season the rack of wild boar and shape it into a crown, bones up and facing inward. Attach with string.
6. Cook in the oven until the temperature in the centre of the meat reaches 55°C (130°F).
7. Meanwhile, pour the marinade into a medium-sized saucepan and reduce by three-quarters over medium heat. Add the demi-glace and reduce by one-half.
8. Strain the sauce through a chinois and keep warm.
9. Remove the string from the crown, slice and serve with the sauce.

Confit of Rabbit in Filo

1 serving

INGREDIENTS

- **500 mL** goose *or* duck fat **2 cups**
- **180 g** rabbit meat **6 oz**
- **30 mL** chopped carrot **2 tbsp**
- **30 mL** chopped onion **2 tbsp**
- **30 mL** chopped celeriac **2 tbsp**
- **30 mL** chopped leek **2 tbsp**
- **2** sprigs fresh thyme **2**
- **1** sprig fresh rosemary **1**
- **4** sprigs fresh parsley **4**
- **1 mL** coarse salt **1/4 tsp**
- **2 mL** freshly ground pepper **1/2 tsp**
- **80 mL** butter **1/3 cup**
- pinch saffron
- **2** sheets filo dough **2**

METHOD

1. In an ovenproof earthenware dish, place the goose fat, rabbit meat, carrot, onion, celeriac, leek, pepper, salt and herbs. Cook at 100°C (200°F) for 2 hours.
2. Remove the rabbit and goose fat; keep warm.
3. Increase the oven temperature to 180°C (350°F).
4. In a small saucepan, melt the butter and add the saffron.
5. Spread out a sheet of filo and brush it with the saffron butter. Place a second sheet of filo on top and brush with saffron butter.
6. Cut the filo into 12 equal rectangles.
7. Place the rectangles of filo on a cookie sheet and place in the oven.
8. Remove them from the oven as soon as they begin to turn golden, about 30 seconds.
9. On a plate, place 2 rectangles one on top of another so that the corners do not match up, and add one quarter of the rabbit confit. Repeat the operation to obtain two layers of confit. Finish off with 2 rectangles of filo.

Quail Duo on a Bed of Lentils

4 to 6 servings

INGREDIENTS

1.5 kg quail, deboned **3 lb**

30 mL olive oil **2 tbsp**

500 g red onions, sliced **1 lb**

2 kg kale, sliced **2 lb**

500 g red apples, peeled and diced **1 lb**

400 mL small brown lentils, cooked, or one 540 mL (19-oz) can brown lentils, rinsed and drained **2 cups**

125 mL cider vinegar **1/2 cup**

salt and pepper

60 mL fresh parsley, chopped **1/4 cup**

Marinade

60 mL olive oil **1/4 cup**

5 mL dried basil **1 tsp**

2 mL dried thyme **1/2 tsp**

15 mL Worcestershire sauce **1 tbsp**

30 mL Calvados **2 tbsp**

pinch cayenne pepper

salt and pepper

METHOD

MARINADE

1. In a large bowl, mix all the marinade ingredients. Place the quail in the marinade and refrigerate for at least 2 hours.

QUAIL DUO

1. In a large nonstick skillet, fry the quail over high heat for 3 minutes per side or until the meat is no longer pink on the inside. Remove from heat and keep warm.
2. To the same skillet, add the olive oil and cook the onions for 2 to 3 minutes over medium heat. Add the kale and cook for 5 minutes. Add the apples and lentils, and cook for another 3 minutes over high heat.
3. Deglaze with 60 mL (1/4 cup) cider vinegar, season with salt and pepper and cook for another 2 minutes. Remove from heat and sprinkle with parsley.
4. Serve the lentil and cabbage mixture in the middle of the plates, with the quail arranged on top and drizzled with the remaining cider vinegar.

Chicken Supremes Stuffed with Clams

2 servings

If there is not enough liquid in the pot, add 125 mL (1/2 cup) of water or chicken stock.

INGREDIENTS

2 chicken supremes **2**
30 mL olive oil **2 tbsp**
10 fresh clams **10**
30 mL finely chopped onion **2 tbsp**
30 mL finely chopped leek **2 tbsp**
15 mL finely chopped green onion **1 tbsp**
salt to taste
ground white pepper to taste
180 mL dry white wine **3/4 cup**

METHOD

1. Thoroughly wash the clams under cold running water.
2. Heat 15 mL (1 tbsp) olive oil in a medium-sized pot.
3. Cook the onion, leek and green onion until the onion is translucent but not browned.
4. Add the clams, white wine; cook, covered, for 10 minutes over medium heat.
5. Remove the pot from the heat and shell the clams. Reserve the cooking liquid.
6. Chop the clams and vegetables, and place in a bowl; season.
7. Using a knife with a thin blade, make a 2.5 cm (1-in.) incision 10 to 13 cm (4 to 5 in.) lengthwise through the centre of the supreme, cutting in about halfway. Fill the cavity with the clam and vegetable mixture.
8. In a medium-sized skillet, heat the rest of the olive oil over high heat, and sear the stuffed supremes.
9. Remove the supremes from the skillet, season and continue cooking in the pot containing the cooking liquid from the clams. Cook, covered, over medium heat for 12 to 15 minutes.

Pan-fried Shrimps and Lima Beans with Hot Pepper Oil

4 to 6 servings

INGREDIENTS

45 mL hot pepper oil (see recipe below) **3 tbsp**
700 g large shrimps **1 1/2 lb**
125 mL chopped green onion **1/2 cup**
125 mL chopped green pepper **1/2 cup**
125 mL chopped red pepper **1/2 cup**
400 mL large cooked lima beans, or one 540 mL (19-oz) can lima beans, rinsed and drained **2 cups**
salt and pepper
30 mL balsamic vinegar **2 tbsp**
125 mL chopped fresh parsley **1/2 cup**

Hot Pepper Oil

250 mL olive oil **1 cup**
375 mL chopped red pepper **1 1/2 cups**
3 cloves garlic, chopped **3**
1/2 jalapeño pepper, chopped **1/2**
2 mL ground annato or paprika **1/2 tsp**
2 mL dried thyme **1/2 tsp**
pinch ground black pepper
1 bay leaf **1**

METHOD

Hot Pepper Oil

1. In a saucepan, heat 30 mL (2 tbsp) olive oil over high heat. Add the red pepper and cook until caramelized (3 minutes).
2. Add the garlic, jalapeño pepper and spices; cook for another minute. Reduce heat to low, pour in the remaining oil and simmer, uncovered, for 15 minutes.
3. Remove from heat, cool and filter through a strainer. Keep at room temperature.

Pan-fried Shrimps

1. In a large skillet, heat the pepper oil over high heat. Cook the shrimps for 2 to 3 minutes or until done. Remove from skillet and keep warm.
2. In the same skillet, sauté the green onion, and red and green pepper for 3 minutes over medium heat.
3. Add the beans, parsley, salt and pepper to taste, and continue cooking for 2 to 3 minutes or until the cooking liquid has evaporated. Deglaze with balsamic vinegar. Remove from heat.
4. Place the bean and pepper mixture on the plates, add the shrimps and pour over the remaining pepper oil.

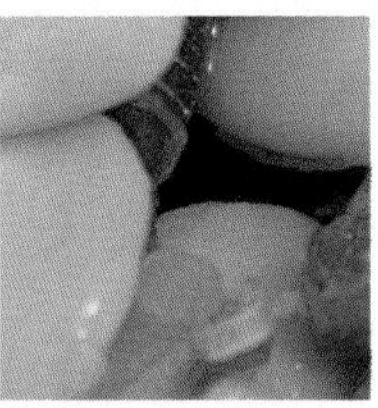

ITALY

Fried Sardines with Concassé of Lupini

4 to 6 servings

INGREDIENTS

- **2** eggs **2**
- **500 mL** milk **2 cups**
- **250 mL** flour **1 cup**
- **1 kg** fresh sardine fillets **2 lb**
- **250 mL** shelled almonds, coarsely chopped **1 cup**
- **500 mL** vegetable oil **2 cups**

Concassé

- **15 mL** olive oil **1 tbsp**
- **125 mL** chopped onion **1/2 cup**
- **2** cloves garlic, chopped **2**
- **400 mL** cooked lupini, skinned, or one 540 mL (19-oz) can lupini, rinsed, skinned and drained **2 cups**
- **60 mL** white wine **1/4 cup**
- **375 mL** fresh tomatoes, seeded and chopped **1 1/2 cups**
- pinch salt
- pinch brown sugar
- pinch cayenne pepper
- freshly ground pepper
- **10** leaves fresh basil, chopped **10**

METHOD

1. In a medium-sized bowl, beat the eggs and milk.
2. Dredge the sardine fillets in the flour and dip one by one in the egg and milk mixture. Remove from the mixture, drain and roll in the almonds.
3. In a skillet, heat the oil over high heat 180°C (425°F) measured with a thermometer and fry the fillets for about 3 minutes.
4. Remove from the skillet, drain on paper towels and keep warm.

CONCASSÉ

1. In a large skillet, heat the oil and sauté the onion, garlic and lupini over medium heat for 3 minutes.
2. Deglaze with white wine and add the tomatoes and seasoning. Bring to a boil, reduce the heat and simmer, uncovered, for 2 minutes.
3. Remove from heat and add the chopped basil.
4. Divide the concassé among the plates and top with very hot sardines.

Chicken Kebabs

2 servings

INGREDIENTS

2 chicken breasts, cut into large cubes 2
500 mL white wine 2 cups
45 mL olive oil 3 tbsp
4 cloves garlic 4
1 bay leaf 1
2 sprigs fresh thyme 2
125 mL sliced onion 1/2 cup
6 black peppercorns 6

METHOD

1. Oven-roast the garlic in the olive oil in a small earthenware container at 200°C (400°F) for 40 minutes.
2. Remove the garlic from the oil, reserve.
3. In a large bowl, combine the chicken, wine, crushed garlic cloves, herbs, onion and pepper. Marinate for 6 to 8 hours, stirring occasionally.
4. Remove and drain the chicken; thread onto skewers.
5. Preheat the barbecue to medium or use the oven broiler. Season and place the kebabs on the barbecue grill or under the broiler. Cook each side for 4 to 5 minutes until the chicken is done in the centre.

Skate Wings with Sautéed Bean Sprouts

4 to 6 servings

INGREDIENTS

1.5 kg cleaned skate wings, bone in 3 lb

Marinade

125 mL chopped fresh lemon grass 1/2 cup
60 mL olive oil 1/4 cup
30 mL curry powder 2 tbsp
juice of half a lemon
15 mL fish sauce 1 tbsp
15 mL sesame oil 1 tbsp

Sauté

15 mL olive oil 1 tbsp
60 g julienned red onion 1/4 cup
60 g julienned carrot 1/4 cup
60 g julienned red pepper 1/4 cup
1 can (375 mL/16-oz) baby corn, drained 1
500 g bean sprouts 1 lb
250 mL coarsely chopped watercress 1 cup
30 mL black bean and garlic sauce 2 tbsp
125 mL water or fish stock 1/2 cup
salt and freshly ground pepper
60 mL chopped fresh coriander 1/4 cup
or 2 mL dried coriander 1/2 tsp
60 mL chopped green onion 1/4 cup
60 mL sesame seeds 1/4 cup

METHOD

Marinade

1. In a large bowl, combine all the marinade ingredients and mix well. Add the skate and marinate for 1 hour in the refrigerator.

Sauté

1. Heat a large nonstick skillet and cook the skate 3 to 4 minutes per side until the bone separates easily from the flesh. Remove from the skillet and keep warm.
2. In the same skillet, add the olive oil and sauté the julienned onion, carrot and red pepper for 2 to 3 minutes over medium heat.
3. Add the baby corn, bean sprouts, watercress and bean sauce. Continue cooking for 2 minutes.
4. Add water, season and heat thoroughly for 1 minute. Remove from heat.
5. Place the vegetable and bean sprout mixture on the plates, garnish with coriander, green onion and sesame seeds.

SPAIN

Clams with Spicy Chorizo

4 servings

INGREDIENTS

15 mL olive oil **1 tbsp**
230 g julienned chorizo **1/2 lb**
180 mL finely chopped onion **3/4 cup**
3 cloves garlic, thinly sliced **3**
60 mL chopped green onion **4 tbsp**
90 mL chopped fennel **1/4 cup**
pinch cayenne pepper
2.5 mL ground black pepper **1/2 tsp**
sea salt to taste
1 L shrimp stock (see recipe on p. 13) **4 cups**
48 fresh medium clams **48**
4 large Italian tomatoes, diced **4**
3 sprigs thyme 3
80 mL chopped parsley **1/3 cup**

METHOD

1. In a large pot, heat the oil over medium heat and add the chorizo. Cook until browned.
2. Lower the heat and cook the onion, garlic, green onion and fennel, without browning, for 3 to 5 minutes.
3. Season with salt, pepper and cayenne; add the shrimp stock, tomatoes, thyme, parsley and the clams.
4. Cover and cook for 5 to 7 minutes over high heat, stirring occasionally.

Grilled Pork Chops with Green Split Pea Purée

CANADA

4 to 6 servings

INGREDIENTS

60 mL olive oil **1/4 cup**
15 mL Worcestershire sauce **1 tbsp**
10 mL dried oregano **2 tsp**
5 mL paprika **1 tsp**
salt and freshly ground pepper
1 kg pork chops **2 lb**

Green Split Pea Purée

15 mL olive oil **1 tbsp**
1 clove garlic, chopped **1**
30 mL chopped green onion **2 tbsp**
800 g cooked green split peas **4 cups**
125 mL 35% cream **1/2 cup**
salt and pepper
60 g butter, cubed **2 oz**

Mustard Sauce

15 mL olive oil **1 tbsp**
15 mL chopped green onion **1 tbsp**
125 mL 35% cream **1/2 cup**
500 mL water or chicken stock **2 cups**
salt and pepper
15 mL cornstarch **1 tbsp**
45 mL water **3 tbsp**
30 mL mustard seeds **2 tbsp**
2 mL Dijon mustard **1/2 tsp**

METHOD

Marinade

1. In a large bowl, blend the oil, Worcestershire sauce and spices. Place the pork chops in the marinade and refrigerate for 1 hour in the refrigerator.

Green Split Pea Purée

1. In a 2 L (8-cup) pot, heat the olive oil over medium heat; cook garlic and green onion for 2 minutes.
2. Add the green peas and 35% cream. Season and boil, uncovered, for 2 minutes. Remove from heat.
3. Purée in a food processor and pass through a strainer. Add the butter gradually, blending gently. Keep warm.

Mustard Sauce

1. In a 2 L (8-cup) pot, heat the olive oil over medium heat and cook the green onions for 2 minutes.
2. Pour in the cream and stock. Bring to a boil, season, lower the heat and simmer, uncovered, for 2 minutes.
3. In a small bowl, mix the cornstarch with 45 mL (3 tbsp) cold water.
4. Pour the cornstarch into the mixture in a stream, whisking constantly, over low heat. Boil for 1 minute, stirring constantly. Remove from heat.
5. Add both mustards, whisking vigorously. Keep warm.

Grilled Pork Chops

1. Preheat the barbecue or the oven broiler to medium heat. Place the pork chops on the barbecue grill or broiling pan. Cook for 4 to 5 minutes per side until the meat is no longer pink inside.
2. Arrange the pork chops on the plates next to the purée and top with mustard sauce.

Veal Medallions with Small Red Beans and Duxelles

4 to 6 servings

INGREDIENTS

1 kg larded veal medallions, in fillets about 2.5 cm (1 in.) thick and 6 to 7 cm (2 1/2 in.) in diameter **2 lb**

Marinade

60 mL olive oil **1/4 cup**

30 mL dried tarragon **2 tbsp**

5 mL paprika **1 tsp**

15 mL Worcestershire sauce **1 tbsp**

salt and pepper

Small Red Beans

15 mL olive oil **1 tbsp**

125 mL chopped green onion **1/2 cup**

2 cloves garlic **2**

400 g cooked small red beans or one 540 mL (19-oz) can red beans, rinsed and drained **2 cups**

Duxelles

250 mL 35% cream **1 cup**

salt and pepper

60 mL fresh parsley **1/4 cup**

Duxelles

350 g mushrooms, cleaned **12 oz**

2 green onions **2**

10 mL butter **2 tsp**

salt and pepper

METHOD

MARINADE

1. In a large bowl, mix all the marinade ingredients. Place the veal medallions in the marinade and refrigerate for at least 1 hour.

DUXELLES

1. In a food processor, finely chop the mushrooms and green onions.
2. In a skillet, heat the butter over medium heat and add the chopped mushroom mixture. Season with salt and pepper. Cook over low heat, uncovered, for about 10 minutes or until cooking liquid has evaporated. Set aside.

MEDALLIONS

1. In a nonstick skillet, cook the medallions for 2 minutes per side or until the meat is no longer pink in the middle. Remove from heat and keep warm.
2. In the same skillet, heat the olive oil. Sauté the green onion, garlic and red beans for 3 minutes. Add the duxelles and cream.
3. Season and bring to a boil. Boil for 2 minutes or until the cream has thickened. Remove from heat and sprinkle with parsley.
4. Serve the veal medallions with the bean and duxelle mixture.

PORTUGAL

Cod and Mussels with Cream Sauce

4 servings

INGREDIENTS

400 g cod fillets **14 oz**
48 fresh mussels **48**
60 mL chopped green onion **4 tbsp**
15 mL butter **1 tbsp**
5 mL chopped garlic **1 tsp**
60 mL chopped red onion **4 tbsp**
500 mL dry white wine **2 cups**
80 mL chopped Italian parsley **1/3 cup**
30 mL chopped coriander **2 tbsp**
125 mL heavy cream **1/2 cup**
60 g olive oil **1/4 cup**
200 g julienned potatoes **7 oz**
5 mL thyme **1 tsp**
1 bay leaf **1**
2 mL paprika **1/2 tsp**
salt to taste
ground black pepper to taste

METHOD

1. In a large pot, sauté the green onion, onion and garlic in the butter. Add the mussels and wine; cover and simmer over medium heat for 10 minutes.
2. Remove the mussels and leave the cooking liquid in the pot. Keep the mussels warm. Place the cod fillets in the pot and cook, covered, over low heat for about 10 minutes.
3. Meanwhile, cook the julienned potatoes in the olive oil over medium heat; add the bay leaf, thyme and paprika; season with salt and pepper to taste.
4. When the cod fillets are done, remove from the pot and add the cream, parsley and coriander to the cooking liquid. Reduce by one-half.
5. Serve the cod over the julienned potatoes with the cream sauce and mussels.

Tournedos with Mixed Bean Ratatouille

4 to 6 servings

INGREDIENTS

Mixed Bean Ratatouille

- **15 mL** olive oil **1 tbsp**
- **175 mL** chopped onion **3/4 cup**
- **1** clove garlic, chopped **1**
- **15 mL** tomato paste **1 tbsp**
- **796 mL** diced tomatoes **26 oz**
- **400 g** cooked mixed beans or one 540 mL (19-oz) can mixed beans, rinsed and drained **2 cups**
- **1 mL** dried thyme **1/4 tsp**
- **2 mL** dried oregano **1/2 tsp**
- **2 mL** dried basil **1/2 tsp**
- pinch brown sugar
- salt and pepper

Tournedos

- **1 kg** beef fillets (medallions) **2 lb**
- **15 mL** olive oil **1 tbsp**
- **30 mL** green onion, chopped **2 tbsp**
- **1 mL** dried thyme **1/4 tsp**
- **2 mL** dried oregano **1/2 tsp**
- pinch freshly ground black pepper
- **250 mL** dry red wine **1 cup**
- **125 g** butter, cubed **4 oz**
- salt and pepper

METHOD

Mixed Bean Ratatouille

1. In a 2 L (8-cup) saucepan, heat the olive oil and cook the onion, garlic and tomato paste over low heat for 3 minutes.
2. Add the tomatoes and their juice, beans, spices, sugar, salt and pepper, and simmer over low heat, uncovered, for 15 minutes or until the tomato liquid has been slightly reduced. Remove from heat and keep warm.

Tournedos

1. In a large nonstick skillet, cook the tournedos for 2 to 3 minutes per side over high heat or according to preference. Transfer to another container and keep warm.
2. To the same skillet, add the olive oil and cook the green onion with the spices for 2 minutes. Deglaze the skillet with red wine, bring to a boil and reduce by half over high heat.
3. Remove from heat and gradually whisk in the butter cubes. Adjust the seasoning and keep warm.
4. Serve the ratatouille with the tournedos on top and drizzle with the red wine sauce.

Rack of Lamb in Minted Cornmeal Crust

2 servings

INGREDIENTS

2 racks of lamb, trimmed 2
15 mL olive oil 1 tbsp
125 mL cornmeal 1/2 cup
250 mL brown beef stock (see recipe on p. 12) 1 cup
50 g almond pieces 1 3/4 oz
30 mL prepared mustard 2 tbsp
30 mL chopped fresh mint 2 tbsp
250 mL balsamic vinegar 1 cup
60 mL finely chopped green onion 4 tbsp
salt to taste
freshly ground pepper to taste

METHOD

1. Pour the balsamic vinegar into a small saucepan and add the chopped green onion. Reduce over low heat until only 60 mL (4 tbsp) of liquid remain.
2. Bring the beef stock to a boil in a small saucepan and add the cornmeal.
3. Reduce over medium-high heat, stirring constantly until cornmeal is tender.
4. Remove from the heat and place in a medium-sized bowl. Preheat the oven to 190°C (400°F).
5. In the bowl, combine the mint, almonds, mustard, cornmeal, the reduced balsamic vinegar and green onion. Season.
6. In a large skillet, heat the oil over high heat. Sear the lamb in the skillet, remove and season.
7. Cover the racks of lamb with the cornmeal mixture, pressing it to ensure it adheres to the meat.
8. Place the racks of lamb on an ovenproof sheet and cook to the desired degree of doneness.
9. Remove from the oven and let sit 1 to 2 minutes before serving.

Lobster Medallions with Mung Beans

4 to 6 servings

INGREDIENTS

1 kg lobster tails **2 lb**
2 L water **8 cups**
pinch salt

Marinade

30 mL olive oil **2 tbsp**
10 mL Dijon mustard **2 tsp**
1 clove garlic, chopped **1**
5 mL ground allspice **1 tsp**
2 mL dried thyme **1/2 tsp**
10 mL dried basil **2 tsp**
pinch cayenne pepper
freshly ground pepper

Mung Beans

15 mL olive oil **1 tbsp**
15 mL chopped green onion **1 tbsp**
1 clove garlic, chopped **1**
125 mL chopped red pepper **1/2 cup**
125 mL chopped yellow pepper **1/2 cup**
250 g sliced Shiitake or oyster mushrooms **1 cup**
500 g cooked mung beans **2 cups**
60 mL soy sauce **1/4 cup**
250 mL 35% cream **1 cup**
salt and pepper
60 mL chopped fresh parsley **1/4 cup**

1. In a large pot, bring 2 L (8 cups) of salted water to a boil. Immerse the lobster tails in the water. Once the water has returned to a boil, cook the lobster tails for 5 minutes, Remove from the water and allow to cool. Remove meat from the shell.

MARINADE

1. Cut the lobster meat into medallions of about 1 cm (1/2 in.). In a bowl, blend all the ingredients and place the medallions on top of the mixture. Marinate for 12 hours in the refrigerator.

MUNG BEANS

1. In a 2 L (8-cup) saucepan, heat the olive oil over high heat and cook the green onion, garlic and peppers for 2 to 3 minutes. Add the mushrooms and continue cooking for 2 minutes. Add the beans and cook for another 2 minutes.
2. Deglaze with the soy sauce; pour in the 35% cream, season and bring to a boil. Lower heat to medium and reduce the sauce for 2 to 3 minutes. Remove from heat, sprinkle with parsley and keep warm.

SERVING

1. In a nonstick skillet, heat the medallions over medium heat for 1 for 2 minutes per side. Arrange the bean and mushroom mixture on the plates and top with the medallions.

Grilled Salmon with Green Lentils

FRANCE

4 to 6 servings

INGREDIENTS

1 kg skinned salmon fillets **2 lb**
30 mL coriander oil **2 tbsp**
pinch salt
freshly ground pepper

Coriander Oil

125 mL olive oil **1/2 cup**
60 mL fresh coriander, chopped **1/4 cup**
juice of half a lemon
1/2 clove garlic, chopped **1/2**
pinch cayenne pepper
pinch salt
freshly ground pepper

Semolina

250 mL medium semolina **1 cup**
10 mL curry powder **2 tsp**
30 mL olive oil **2 tbsp**
250 mL hot water or hot vegetable stock **1 cup**
1 clove garlic, chopped **1**
60 mL green onions, chopped **1/4 cup**
30 mL dried tomatoes in oil, drained and chopped **2 tbsp**
250 g cooked green lentils **1 cup**
pinch cayenne pepper
pinch salt
freshly ground pepper

METHOD

1. Brush the salmon fillets with coriander oil; season with salt and pepper.
2. Grill the salmon for 3 to 4 minutes per side on a very hot barbecue or under the broiler.
3. Keep warm.

Coriander Oil

1. Using a blender or food processor, blend all ingredients for 3 minutes. Strain through a sieve. Set aside at room temperature.

Semolina

1. In a large bowl, thoroughly blend the semolina, curry powder and 15 mL (1 tbsp) olive oil. Add the hot water or vegetable stock.
2. Stir, cover with plastic wrap and leave at room temperature for 1 hour.
3. Uncover and fluff the semolina with a fork. Refrigerate.

Green Lentils

1. In a medium-sized skillet, heat the remaining olive oil over high heat and sauté the garlic, green onions and dried tomatoes for 2 minutes.
2. Add the lentils and seasonings. Continue cooking over medium heat for another 2 or 3 minutes, until the lentils are dry. Remove from heat and allow to cool.
3. In a large salad bowl, mix the semolina and lentils; serve hot or cold. If serving hot, reheat in the microwave.
4. Place the semolina and lentil mixture in the middle of the plates and arrange the salmon over top. Drizzle with the remaining coriander oil.

Leg of Wild Boar with Mousseline of Yellow Split Peas

CANADA

4 to 6 servings

INGREDIENTS

Marinade

1 clove garlic, chopped 1
5 mL paprika 1 tsp
2 mL dried thyme 1/2 tsp
5 mL dried tarragon 1 tsp
500 mL dry red wine 2 cups

Leg of Wild Boar

1 kg leg of wild boar, boned and fat removed, cut into 2.5 cm (1-inch) pieces 2 lb
60 mL brown sugar 1/4 cup
250 g fresh cranberries, washed 1/2 lb
30 mL balsamic vinegar 2 tbsp
500 mL water 2 cups
60 g butter, cubed 2 oz

Mousseline

15 mL olive oil 1 tbsp
1 clove garlic 1
30 mL chopped green onions 2 tbsp
800 g yellow split peas, cooked 4 cups
150 mL 35% cream 2/3 cup
salt and pepper
60 g butter, cubed 2 oz

Marinade

1 In a medium-sized bowl, mix the garlic, spices and 250 mL (1 cup) red wine. Add the boar cubes and marinate for 12 hours in the refrigerator.

Leg of Wild Boar

1 Pour the red wine and sugar into a 2 L (8-cup) saucepan. Boil over high heat, uncovered, for 2 minutes. Add the cranberries and lower the heat to minimum; cook for 5 minutes. Cranberries should still be crunchy. Remove the cranberries and set aside.

2 Over high heat, reduce the syrup, uncovered, for 3 to 5 minutes or until it begins to caramelize. Stop the caramelization by adding vinegar and water. Bring to a boil, uncovered, and reduce by half and remove from heat.

3 Gradually whisk in the butter and add the cranberries. Keep warm.

4 Remove the boar cubes from the marinade and drain well.

5 In a very hot, nonstick pan, cook the boar for about 5 minutes or to desired degree of doneness. Season with salt and pepper. Remove from heat and keep warm.

Mousseline

1 In a 2 L (8-cup) saucepan, heat the oil over medium heat and cook the garlic and green onions for 2 minutes.

2 Add the yellow split peas and cream. Season and cook, uncovered, for 2 minutes. Remove from heat.

3 Using a food processor, purée and pass through a strainer. Add the butter little by little, stirring gently. Keep warm.

4 Pile the mousseline in the middle of the plates and arrange the boar cubes around the edge. Cover with cranberry sauce.

PORTUGAL

Quails Stuffed with Escargots

1 serving

Serve with sautéed pearl onions, carrots and mushrooms.

INGREDIENTS

- **2** quails **2**
- **15 mL** butter **1 tbsp**
- **115 g** canned escargots, rinsed and drained **3 2/3 oz**
- **60 mL** chopped green onions **1/4 cup**
- **15 mL** finely chopped leek **1 tbsp**
- **60 mL** chopped onion **1/4 cup**
- **60 mL** port **1/4 cup**
- **60 mL** poultry glaze **1/4 cup**
- **15 mL** chopped parsley **1 tbsp**
- salt to taste
- ground black pepper to taste
- **15 mL** olive oil **1 tbsp**

METHOD

1. Debone the quails from the inside and refrigerate.
2. In a small saucepan, cook the green onions, leek and onion in the butter, without browning, over low heat.
3. Season, add the port and reduce by one-quarter over low heat.
4. Add the poultry glaze and reduce by another quarter, until thick, for about 2 to 3 minutes.
5. Remove from the heat, stuff the quail and tie the legs with string to hold in the stuffing.
6. Preheat the oven to 190°C (375°F).
7. Heat the olive oil over high heat in a medium-sized skillet and sear the quails on all sides.
8. Place the quails in an ovenproof dish and bake for 15 to 20 minutes.

How to debone a quail

Using a knife with a thin blade, follow the steps illustrated below, taking care not to pierce the skin.

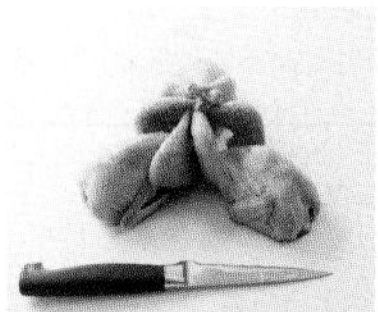

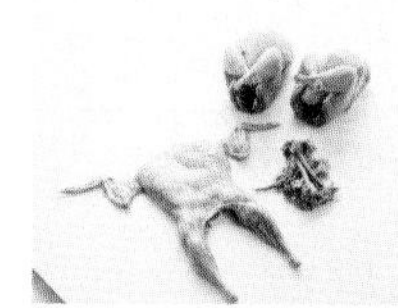

Lamb Chops with Provençal-style Chickpeas

4 to 6 servings

INGREDIENTS

1.5 kg lamb chops 3 lb

Marinade

30 mL olive oil 2 tbsp
1 clove garlic, chopped 1
15 mL Dijon mustard 1 tbsp
2 mL dried thyme 1/2 tsp
5 mL oregano 1 tsp
5 mL basil 1 tsp
10 mL paprika 2 tsp
pinch ground white pepper
pinch cayenne pepper
salt and freshly ground pepper

Provençal-style Chickpeas

15 mL olive oil 1 tbsp
175 mL chopped onion 3/4 cup
100 g mushrooms, minced 3 1/2 oz
2 cloves garlic, chopped 2
400 g cooked chickpeas or one 540 mL (19-oz) can chickpeas, rinsed and drained 2 cups
60 mL pastis 1/4 cup
250 mL fresh tomatoes, seeded and chopped 1 cup
60 mL parsley 1/4 cup

METHOD

Marinade

1 In a large bowl, blend all the ingredients of the marinade, add the lamb chops and marinate for 1 hour in the refrigerator.

Provençal-style Chickpeas

1 In a large nonstick skillet, sear the chops for 3 minutes per side, or according to preference. Remove from heat and keep warm.

2 To the same pan, add the olive oil and, over medium heat, sauté the onion for 3 to 5 minutes until caramelized.

3 Add the mushrooms and garlic; cook for 2 minutes. Add the chickpeas and the tomatoes and cook for another 2 minutes over high heat.

4 Deglaze with the pastis and cook for 2 minutes. Remove from heat and sprinkle with parsley.

5 Arrange the chickpea mixture on the plates and place the chops on top.

Any other anise-flavoured liqueur can be substituted for the pastis.

Turkey Paupiettes with Lima Beans

THAILAND

4 to 6 servings

INGREDIENTS

180 mL sliced carrots **3/4 cup**
180 mL sliced zucchini **3/4 cup**
180 mL sliced daikon* **3/4 cup**
1 kg flattened turkey cutlets **2 lb**
24 toothpicks **24**

Marinade

60 mL soy sauce **1/4 cup**
30 mL honey **2 tbsp**
60 mL vegetable oil **1/4 cup**
60 mL hoisin sauce **1/4 cup**
30 mL sesame oil **2 tbsp**

Lima Beans with Nectarines

15 mL olive oil **1 tbsp**
500 g pitted nectarines **1 lb**
2 mL brown sugar **1/2 tsp**
60 mL chopped green onion **1/4 cup**
1 clove garlic, chopped **1**
400 g cooked lima beans or one 540 mL (19-oz) can lima beans, rinsed and drained **2 cups**
salt and pepper
juice of half a lime
125 mL chicken stock or water **1/2 cup**
60 g diced butter **2 oz**
60 mL chopped fresh coriander **1/4 cup**
or **2 mL** dried coriander **1/2 tsp**

**Daikon is also known as "Japanese radish."*

Marinade

1. In a large bowl, whisk together all the liquid ingredients. Add the turkey cutlets and marinate for 6 hours in the refrigerator.

Paupiettes

1. In a salad bowl, mix the carrots, zucchini and daikon. Set aside at room temperature.
2. Remove the meat from the marinade, drain well and lay flat on a work surface.
3. Portion out the vegetable mixture in the middle of the cutlets, roll and fasten with 2 toothpicks. Refrigerate.

Lima Beans with Nectarines

1. In a large, very hot nonstick skillet, cook the paupiettes for 4 to 5 minutes or until the meat is no longer pink in the centre. Remove from heat and keep warm.
2. To the same pan, heat the olive oil over high heat and add the nectarines and sugar; cook for 2 minutes until golden. Transfer to another container and keep warm.
3. In the same pan, sauté the green onion and garlic for 1 minute. Add the beans, season and continue cooking for 2 to 3 more minutes over high heat. Deglaze with the lime juice, pour in the chicken stock and bring to a boil.
4. Remove from heat. Gradually add the butter, stirring gently. Sprinkle with chopped coriander.

It is easier and faster to replace the whole trout with fillets.

PORTUGAL

Trout with Port Sauce

1 serving

INGREDIENTS

1 trout **1**
30 mL melted butter **2 tbsp**
4 parisienne potatoes **4**
15 mL butter **1 tbsp**
60 g julienned leek **2 oz**
30 g julienned carrot **1 oz**
30 g julienned yellow pepper **1 oz**
60 g tomato, scooped out and julienned **2 oz**
salt to taste
ground white pepper to taste
125 mL port sauce (see recipe on p. 17) **1/2 cup**

METHOD

1. Preheat the oven to 180°C (350°F).
2. Cook the potatoes in the salted water; set aside and keep warm.
3. Wash the trout and remove fins.
4. Gut the trout from the back, remove backbone and wash under running water; set aside.
5. In a small skillet, sauté the julienned vegetables in 15 mL (1 tbsp) butter; keep warm.
6. Place the trout on a buttered baking sheet, brush the inside with the melted butter season.
7. Bake the trout in the oven for about 10 minutes.
8. Cover the bottom of the plate with the port sauce, place the trout on the sauce, garnish with the potatoes and place the vegetables on the fish.

Magrets of Duck with Kiwis and Snow Peas

CHINA

4 to 6 servings

INGREDIENTS

1 kg duck cutlets **2 lb**

Marinade

60 mL honey **1/4 cup**

60 mL soy sauce **1/4 cup**

250 mL orange juice **1 cup**

15 mL chopped ginger **1 tbsp**

1 clove garlic, chopped **1**

Kiwis and Snow Peas

30 mL chopped green onion **2 tbsp**

125 mL sliced red pepper **1/2 cup**

175 mL sliced carrot **3/4 cup**

500 g snow peas, cleaned, blanched but still crisp **1 lb**

1 can baby corn (450 mL/6-oz), drained **1**

10 mL brown sugar **2 tsp**

30 mL rice vinegar **2 tbsp**

175 mL chicken stock or water **3/4 cup**

30 mL butter **2 tbsp**

salt and pepper

4 kiwis, peeled and puréed **4**

METHOD

Marinade

1. In a large bowl, whisk together all ingredients. Add the duck and marinate for 6 hours in the refrigerator.

Kiwis and Snow Peas

1. Preheat the oven to 240°C (475°F).
2. Heat a nonstick skillet over high heat. Place the cutlets skin side down and cook for 3 minutes. Turn and cook for another 2 to 3 minutes.
3. Remove the cutlets and place in an oven-proof dish, skin side up. Bake the cutlets for 5 minutes in a 240°C (475°F) oven. Remove from heat and keep warm.
4. Discard the excess cooking fat, saving about 15 mL (1 tbsp). Add green onion, pepper and carrot and cook over high heat for 2 minutes.
5. Add the snow peas, baby corn and sugar, and cook for 2 to 3 more minutes. Deglaze with rice vinegar. Remove the vegetables from the skillet and keep warm.
6. Add the stock to the skillet, bring to a boil, add salt and pepper, and reduce the heat. Gradually whisk in the butter and the kiwi.
7. Thinly slice the cutlets and place on the plates. Serve with the snow pea mixture and top with kiwi sauce.

Veal Chop Malvasia

1 serving

INGREDIENTS

- 1 veal rib chop 1
- 2 garlic cloves, crushed 2
- 1 bay leaf 1
- 30 mL finely chopped marjoram 2 tbsp
- 15 mL chopped parsley 1 tbsp
- 5 mL cumin seeds 1 tsp
- 5 mL coriander seeds 1 tsp
- 250 mL Madeira *or* sherry 1 cup
- 10 black peppercorns 10
- 5 green peppercorns 5
- 5 pink peppercorns 5
- salt to taste
- 15 mL olive oil 1 tbsp
- 125 mL demi-glace (see recipe on p. 18) 1/2 cup

METHOD

1. In a glass bowl, combine the garlic, bay leaf, marjoram, parsley, cumin, coriander, Madeira, peppercorns and salt.
2. Marinate the veal in this mixture for 8 hours in the refrigerator, turning it 4 to 6 times.
3. Remove the chop, strain the marinade and pour into a small saucepan.
4. Preheat the oven to 180°C (350°F).
5. Heat the oil and sear the veal chop, and transfer it to the oven for 10 to 20 minutes until desired degree of doneness.
6. Meanwhile, reduce the marinade by one-quarter over medium heat and add the demi-glace.
7. Cook for 2 to 3 minutes over low heat, and serve with the veal.

FRANCE

Scallops with Pigeon Peas and Coulis

4 to 6 servings

INGREDIENTS

15 mL olive oil **1 tbsp**

700 g large scallops, halved lengthwise **1 1/2 lb**

10 mL unsalted butter **2 tsp**

1 clove garlic **1**

175 mL oyster mushrooms **3/4 cup**

500 g cooked pigeon peas **2 cups**

salt and pepper

60 mL fresh parsley, chopped **1/4 cup**

Black Olive Coulis

15 mL olive oil **1 tbsp**

400 g black olives, pitted and drained **14 oz**

15 mL chopped green onion **1 tbsp**

pinch fennel seed

pinch dried thyme

pinch salt

pinch cayenne pepper

1 bay leaf **1**

freshly ground pepper

125 mL water or vegetable stock **1/2 cup**

METHOD

Black Olive Coulis

1 In a medium-sized saucepan, heat the olive oil and cook all the ingredients for the coulis over low heat for 5 minutes.

2 Add water or vegetable stock and bring to a boil over high heat. Reduce the heat, cover and simmer for 20 minutes. Remove from heat and allow to cool for 10 minutes.

3 Purée in a food processor or blender. Serve hot or cold.

Scallops

1 In a large skillet, sear the scallops in very hot olive oil for 1 minute per side. They must not be overcooked.

2 Remove from the skillet and keep warm.

3 In the same skillet, add the butter and sauté the garlic and oyster mushrooms for 2 to 3 minutes.

4 Add the pigeon peas, season and cook for another 3 minutes over medium heat. Remove from heat and sprinkle with parsley.

5 Place the pea and mushroom mixture in the middle of the plates and pile the scallops around the periphery to form a crown. Top with the hot black olive coulis.

Pork with Clams

4 servings

INGREDIENTS

675 g pork cubes **1 1/2 lb**
250 mL white wine **1 cup**
5 mL paprika **1 tsp**
2.5 mL cumin **1/2 tsp**
salt to taste
ground black pepper to taste
2 bay leaves **2**
1 clove **1**
3 garlic cloves, chopped **3**
900 g cleaned fresh clams **2 lb**
80 mL olive oil **1/3 cup**
125 mL chopped red onion **1/2 cup**
80 mL chopped green onion **1/3 cup**
250 mL finely diced tomatoes **1 cup**
30 mL olive oil **2 tbsp**

METHOD

1. In a glass bowl, combine the paprika, cumin, salt, pepper, bay leaves, clove, garlic and wine. Add the pork cubes and marinate for 8 to 12 hours in the refrigerator, stirring occasionally.
2. Drain the pork and save the marinade.
3. In a large pot, heat the oil over high heat and sauté the clams, onion, green onion tomato. Add the marinade and cook, covered, over medium-low heat.
4. In a large skillet, heat 30 mL (2 tbsp) of olive oil over high heat and sear the pork cubes in small batches.
5. Add the pork to the pot and cook over low heat for 10 to 12 minutes, stirring occasionally.
6. Remove the pork and clams. Serve with the vegetable mixture remaining in the pot.

Braised Rabbit with Black Beans

4 to 6 servings

INGREDIENTS

60 mL olive oil **1/4 cup**

2 kg rabbit, cut into large pieces **4 lb**

250 mL chopped onion **1 cup**

250 g chopped carrot **5 1/2 oz**

250 g chopped celery **5 1/2 oz**

2 cloves garlic, chopped **2**

500 mL chicken stock or water **2 cups**

salt and pepper

800 g cooked black beans or two 540 mL (19-oz) cans black beans, rinsed and drained **4 cups**

Marinade

250 mL dry white wine **1 cup**

5 mL ground fennel seeds **1 tsp**

5 mL crushed coriander seeds **1 tsp**

5 mL ground anise seeds **1 tsp**

5 mL ground cardamom seeds **1 tsp**

5 mL ground caraway seeds **1 tsp**

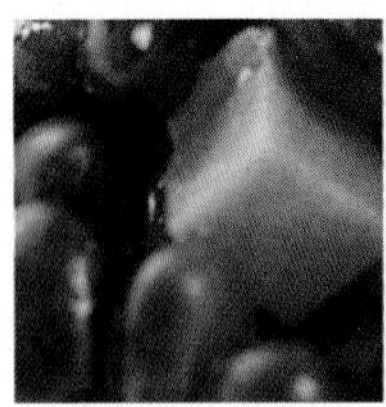

METHOD

Marinade

1 In a large bowl, mix all the marinade ingredients. Place the rabbit pieces in the marinade and refrigerate for at least 6 hours.

Braised Rabbit

1 Preheat the oven to 220°C (425°F).

2 In a large skillet, heat the olive oil over high heat and sear the meat 3 minutes per side. Remove the meat and place in a large ovenproof casserole dish.

3 Add the vegetables and garlic to the casserole dish. Pour in the chicken stock and add salt and pepper. Cover and bake in the oven for 1 hour at 220°C (425°F).

4 Uncover the dish and lower the oven temperature to 180°C (350°F). Bake for another 30 minutes. Baste the rabbit pieces with cooking juices every 15 minutes. Remove the dish from the oven, remove the meat and keep warm.

5 Pour the vegetables and cooking liquid into a 4 L (16-cup) casserole dish, defat the liquid and add the black beans. Simmer over low heat, half-covered, for 30 minutes.

6 Pour the bean and vegetable mixture into deep plates, and place the rabbit meat around it; drizzle with the cooking juices.

Use the sauce sparingly as it has a very strong flavour.

ENGLAND

Filet Mignon with Lemon Mustard Sauce

1 serving

INGREDIENTS

240 g filet mignon **8 oz**
15 mL butter **1 tbsp**
salt to taste
freshly ground pepper to taste
90 mL milk **6 tbsp**
15 mL potato *or* corn starch **1 tbsp**
30 mL prepared mustard **2 tbsp**
45 mL heavy cream **3 tbsp**
5 mL lemon zest **1 tsp**

METHOD

1. Preheat the oven to 190°C (375°F).
2. In a small skillet, heat the butter over high heat and sear the meat. Season.
3. Place the filet mignon on a baking sheet and cook in the oven for 10 to 20 minutes until desired degree of doneness.
4. Five minutes before it is done, mix the milk and potato starch in a small container, and pour into a small saucepan.
5. Whisk in the mustard, stirring well.
6. Add the lemon zest and cream; reduce over low heat until desired consistency is obtained. Serve with the filet mignon.

Snapper with Citrus Fruit and Polenta

serves **4 to 6**

INGREDIENTS

Polenta

1 L milk 4 cups
salt and freshly ground pepper
250 mL cornmeal 1 cup
60 mL unsalted butter 1/4 cup
60 mL grated Parmesan cheese 1/4 cup
60 mL chopped fresh rosemary 1/4 cup

Fish and Dressing

3 medium oranges 3
2 medium pink grapefruit 2
3 clementines 3
1 lime 1
125 mL olive oil 1/2 cup
1 kg snapper fillets, scaled 2 lb
salt and freshly ground pepper

Polenta

1. Bring the milk to a boil in a 3-L (12-cup) stockpot. Stir in salt and pepper. Add the cornmeal gradually and cook over low heat 25 to 30 minutes, stirring constantly with a wooden spoon. Add the butter, Parmesan cheese and rosemary. Mix well and pour into a 25 cm x 10 cm (10 in. x 4 in.) pan lined with plastic wrap. Refrigerate 24 hours.
2. Cut the polenta into squares or diamonds and brown over moderate heat in a non-stick frying pan 2 to 3 minutes on each side.

Fish and Dressing

1. Over a bowl to catch the juice, use a knife to remove all the peel and white skin of the citrus fruits, so that the flesh is exposed.
2. Separate into sections and refrigerate with the juice until ready to use.
3. Heat 30 mL (2 tbsp) olive oil in a large frying pan over moderate heat and cook the snapper 3 to 5 minutes, skin side down. Remove from pan and keep warm. Pour the remaining olive oil into the same pan and warm over low heat. Add the fruit and the juice.
4. Add salt and pepper and beat vigorously. Heat 1 to 2 minutes without boiling. Remove from heat and keep warm.
5. Place the polenta and the snapper on individual plates and drizzle with the olive oil citrus dressing.

Blackened Red Snapper

4 servings

A word of warning! This cooking method produces delicious fish, but it is strongly recommended that you not attempt it in your kitchen. It's best prepared outdoors on a gas barbecue. Remember to cover the handle of your skillet to prevent burns. Chef Paul Prud'homme, Louisiana's culinary ambassador, devised this new method in the 1980s. Red snapper may be replaced by salmon, swordfish or tuna.

INGREDIENTS

300 g butter **12 oz**
4 small ovenproof dishes 4
4 red snapper fillets, 2 cm (3/4 in.) thick, about 250 g (8 oz) each 4
Cajun-Creole seasoning mix

1. Melt the butter in a skillet and pour 5 mL (1 tbsp) into each of the small ovenproof dishes. Place the dishes in a warm oven while you proceed with the other steps.
2. Heat a large cast-iron skillet on a gas barbecue for about 10 minutes until the bottom of the skillet turns white.
3. When the skillet is nearly ready, lightly season the red snapper fillets with Cajun-Creole seasoning mix, dip in the melted butter, drain and place in the hot skillet. The fillets should be cooked singly or a maximum of two at a time. Immediately pour a small spoonful of butter onto the fish. Cook for 2 minutes, turn and cook for another 2 minutes or so, until the fish is opaque in the centre.
4. Remove the fish fillet from the skillet and place it in one of the small dishes warming in the oven. Repeat the procedure for the other fillets. Serve immediately.

Baked Quails with Dried Cranberries

4 servings

FRANCE

INGREDIENTS

4 quails (200 g – 7 to 8 oz each) 4
OR
8 quails (100 g – 3 to 4 oz each) 8
45 mL butter **3 tbsp**
45 mL chopped shallots **3 tbsp**
5 mL minced garlic **1 tsp**
5 mL crushed juniper berries **1 tsp**
5 mL flour **1 tsp**
30 mL cognac or brandy **2 tbsp**
375 mL brown chicken stock **1 1/2 cups**
250 mL carrots cut in julienne **1 cup**
125 mL dried cranberries **1/2 cup**
4 (or 8) small sprigs of fresh thyme **4 (or 8)**
salt and freshly ground pepper
aluminum foil

METHOD

1. Salt and pepper the quails, both inside and out. Place a small sprig of thyme inside the cavity. Truss.
2. In a skillet, sauté the quails with half the butter until browned on all sides. Place them in a casserole or a saucepan and set aside.
3. In the same skillet, sauté the shallots and garlic in butter, and add the crushed juniper berries.
4. Add the flour, mix well and deglaze with the cognac, then add the brown stock and reduce by a third.
5. Top the quails with the julienne of carrots and the dried cranberries.
6. Cover the casserole with aluminum foil, fold down over the outsides, and cover with the casserole cover (this double cover provides better sealing).
7. Bake at 180°C (350°F) in the oven for approximately 30 to 40 minutes.

Serve with puréed potatoes Florentine, rice or pasta.

Quails with Figs and Green Grapes

4 servings

METHOD

1. Peel and halve the grapes and marinate overnight in the sherry and half the sugar.
2. Drain the grapes and set aside.
3. Clean out the insides of the quails, and truss the legs and wings to the body.
4. Preheat the oven to 220°C (425°F).
5. Heat the oil over high heat in a large skillet and sear the meat on all sides; bake in the oven for 7 minutes.
6. Remove the quails from the oven and keep warm.
7. Place the figs in a small casserole dish and bake in the oven for 4 minutes; remove and keep warm.
8. In a small saucepan over low heat, caramelize the remaining sugar with the Portuguese herbs and spices along with one-quarter of the grape marinade.
9. Pour the sherry vinegar into the caramelized mixture and add the quail stock. Bring to a boil and reduce by one-half.
10. Drain and add the rest of the grapes to the sauce and cook for 2 or 3 minutes over medium heat.
11. Arrange the quails on a serving platter; garnish with figs and pour the sauce over.

INGREDIENTS

60 mL olive oil **1/4 cup**

4 quails **4**

200 g seedless green grapes **7 oz**

250 mL sherry *or* Madeira **1 cup**

125 mL sugar **1/2 cup**

15 mL Portuguese herbs and spices (see recipe on p. 31) **1 tbsp**

60 mL sherry vinegar *or* white wine vinegar **1/4 cup**

250 mL brown chicken stock (see recipe on p. 11) **1 cup**

12 fresh figs **12**

Supreme of Pheasant (or Guinea Fowl) with Pears, en papillote

AUSTRIA

8 to 10 servings

INGREDIENTS

- 4 pheasant breasts, boned, skin removed 4
- **45 mL** butter **3 tbsp**
- **60 mL** sliced shallots **1/4 cup**
- **5 mL** flour **1 tsp**
- **125 mL** white wine **1/2 cup**
- **125 mL** brown chicken stock **1/2 cup**
- **45 mL** grated pear (choose a firm pear) **3 tbsp**
- 1 pear, cored, not peeled, cut into 8 thin slices (2 per breast) 1
- **15 mL** freshly chopped ginger **1 tbsp**
- **15 mL** fresh chopped parsley **1 tbsp**
- salt and freshly ground pepper
- parchment paper or aluminum foil

METHOD

1. Salt and pepper the breasts, then sauté them in butter (30 ml - 2 tbsp) in a heavy skillet, colouring both sides lightly. Set aside.
2. In the same skillet, sweat the shallots, add the flour, then deglaze with the white wine and the brown chicken stock, then add the grated pear. Let reduce by half.
3. Add the pear slices, ginger and parsley, and let simmer for 1 or 2 minutes, turning the pear slices. Set aside.
4. Prepare the papillotes (1 per breast) with the parchment paper or the aluminum foil (see illustration). Brush the interior with the rest of the melted butter, and place one breast in each papillote. Top with the shallot, ginger, parsley and grated pear mixture, and drizzle the reduced juice over the breasts. Place the pear slices (2 per breast) on top and close the papillotes.
5. Bake in a preheated 180°C (350°F) oven for 8 to 10 minutes. Serve as is, straight from the oven. Each guest opens up her own papillote in order to enjoy the escaping aroma, a telltale sign of the flavour to come from the breasts.

Note: Cooking time for breasts (chicken, pheasant, guinea fowl) must always be short (8 to 12 minutes) in order to preserve their juices. This recipe can also be used with chicken.

Salmon Sukiyaki

serves **4 to 6**

INGREDIENTS

750 g salmon fillet, without the skin **1 1/2 lb**
30 mL olive oil **2 tbsp**
500 mL julienned carrot **2 cups**
60 mL thinly sliced white mushrooms **1/4 cup**
60 mL julienned red pepper **1/4 cup**
60 mL julienned red onion **1/4 cup**
250 mL cooked vermicelli **1 cup**
2 mL dried basil **1/2 tsp**
1 mL fresh pepper paste **1/4 tsp**
1 clove garlic, chopped **1**
2 mL chopped fresh ginger **1/2 tsp**
pinch sugar
freshly ground pepper
125 mL soy sauce **1/2 cup**
45 mL sake **3 tbsp**
60 mL thinly sliced green onion **1/4 cup**

1. Preheat oven to 240°C (475°F).
2. Cut the salmon into very thin strips (about 0.5 cm/1/4 in.) Refrigerate until ready to use.
3. Heat the olive oil in a large ovenproof frying pan over high heat and sauté the vegetables, vermicelli, basil, pepper paste, garlic, ginger, sugar and pepper 2 to 3 minutes. Remove from heat.
4. Top with the salmon strips and bake 1 to 2 minutes. Remove from oven and drizzle with soy sauce and sake. Sprinkle with green onion and serve immediately.

Scampi Fricassée à la Marseillaise

serves **4 to 6**

INGREDIENTS

- **30 mL** olive oil **2 tbsp**
- **36** large scampi, shelled **36**
- **60 mL** Pastis **1/4 cup**
- **30 mL** unsalted butter **2 tbsp**
- **2** shallots, finely chopped **2**
- **3** medium fennel bulbs **3**
- **1** clove garlic, chopped **1**
- **375 mL** fish stock **1 1/2 cups**
- **125 mL** 35% cream **1/2 cup**
- salt and freshly ground pepper
- **60 mL** seeded and chopped tomato **1/4 cup**
- **60 mL** chopped fresh parsley **1/4 cup**

METHOD

1. Heat the olive oil in a large frying pan over high heat and sear the scampi 1 to 2 minutes.
2. Deglaze with Pastis and flambé. Remove scampi from pan and keep warm.
3. Add the butter, shallots, fennel and garlic to the same pan and cook over moderate heat 2 to 3 minutes. Add the fish stock and cream. Bring to a boil and reduce, uncovered, 1 to 2 minutes. Adjust the seasoning and remove from heat.
4. Garnish with tomatoes and parsley.
5. Serve immediately with scampi on individual plates.

Duck with Rosemary Honey

2 to 4 servings

A butter-based sauce should never be overheated; this would cause it to separate and thereby ruin the sauce.

INGREDIENTS

3 kg duck **7 lb**
15 mL diced carrot **1 tbsp**
15 mL diced onion **1 tbsp**
15 mL diced celery **1 tbsp**
125 mL white wine **1/2 cup**
duck giblets
125 mL water **1/2 cup**
60 mL butter **1/4 cup**
juice of 2 lemons
30 mL honey **2 tbsp**
1 sprig rosemary **1**
salt to taste
ground black pepper to taste

METHOD

1. In a small saucepan, heat the honey with the rosemary for a few minutes. Remove from heat and leave to steep for 24 hours.
2. In a saucepan, cook the carrot, onion and celery over medium heat in 30 ml (2 tbsp) butter. Add the duck giblets and cook over medium heat, until the giblets are golden.
3. Add the water and wine, and cook for 30 minutes over medium heat.
4. Strain through a chinois and set aside the cooking liquid; keep warm.
5. Preheat the oven to 160°C (325°F).
6. Season the duck.
7. Place the duck in a roasting pan and bake in the oven until a thermometer inserted into the breast reaches 55°C (130°F), about 40 minutes.
8. Remove the duck and degrease the roasting pan; deglaze with the lemon juice.
9. Add the honey to the roasting pan and reduce by three-quarters; add 60 ml (1/4 cup) cooking liquid. Remove from the heat and add the rest of the butter.
10. Place on a serving platter and serve with the sauce.

Mexican Pan-Fried Sea Bream

serves **4 to 6**

INGREDIENTS

30 mL olive oil **2 tbsp**
15 mL lime juice **1 tbsp**
1 clove garlic, chopped **1**
2 mL ground cumin **1/2 tsp**
2 mL chili powder **1/2 tsp**
5 mL dried oregano **1 tsp**
pinch cayenne pepper
salt and freshly ground pepper
1 kg sea bream fillets, scaled **2 lb**
Jicama Salsa
60 mL cilantro **1/4 cup**

Jicama Salsa

2 medium jicamas, cut into strips **2**
1 medium red onion, thinly sliced **1**
60 mL thinly sliced red pepper **1/4 cup**
60 mL thinly sliced orange pepper **1/4 cup**
60 mL thinly sliced green onion **1/4 cup**
30 mL lime juice **2 tbsp**
60 mL chopped cilantro **1/4 cup**
60 mL chopped fresh mint **1/4 cup**
5 mL chopped fresh ginger **1 tsp**
15 mL olive oil **1 tbsp**
10 mL brown sugar **2 tsp**
1 small jalapeño pepper, thinly sliced (optional) **1**
salt and freshly ground pepper

1. Mix the olive oil, lime juice, garlic and seasonings in a bowl.
2. Brush the sea bream fillets with marinade and refrigerate 1 hour.
3. Heat a non-stick frying pan and cook the fish skin side down 2 to 3 minutes. Serve immediately with Jicama Salsa.
4. Garnish with cilantro.

JICAMA SALSA

1. Combine all the ingredients in a large bowl and refrigerate at least 1 hour.

This is one of the most popular Cajun dishes. Its complex taste belies the fact that it is actually made with only a few ingredients. The secret is in the method used to make the roux before cooking the vegetables. The shrimp can be replaced by crawfish tails or small cubes of raw chicken. If chicken is used, the cooking time must be doubled once the chicken is added to the skillet.

UNITED STATES

Shrimp Étouffée

4 servings

INGREDIENTS

60 mL butter **1/4 cup**
60 mL flour **1/4 cup**
2 large onions, chopped **2**
1 red pepper, chopped **1**
1 green pepper, chopped **1**
625 mL cold water **2 1/2 cups**
30 mL butter **2 tbsp**
1 kg uncooked, peeled shrimps **2 lb**
salt and cayenne

METHOD

1. Melt the butter in a large cast-iron skillet without browning. Remove the skillet from the heat and gradually whisk in the flour. Return the skillet to the stove and cook the roux over low heat, stirring constantly until it is the colour of peanut butter.
2. As soon as the desired colour is obtained, add the onions and peppers; continue cooking over low heat, stirring constantly for 5 minutes. Remove the skillet from the heat.
3. Gradually stir in the water, bring to a boil, reduce the heat and simmer until the sauce thickens, stirring occasionally.
4. While the sauce is simmering, melt 30 mL (2 tbsp) butter over low heat in a second skillet. Add the shrimps and cook over low heat for 10 minutes, stirring occasionally. This step can be done before making the sauce.
5. Add the shrimps to the sauce and simmer for 10 minutes over very low heat.
6. Season with salt and cayenne and serve with white rice.

PORTUGAL

Spiny Lobster with Pili-pili

2 servings

INGREDIENTS

4 spiny lobster tails, size 11/19 4
300 g diced tomato 10 1/2 oz
180 mL thinly sliced onion 3/4 cup
100 g almond pieces 3 1/2 oz
75 g walnut pieces 2 1/2 oz
75 g pine nuts 2 1/2 oz
300 mL butter 1 1/4 cups
250 mL Madeira *or* sherry 1 cup
3 L fish stock (see recipe on p. 13) 12 cups
45 mL pili-pili (see recipe on p. 31) 3 tbsp

1 Preheat the oven to 150°C (300°F)

2 In a roasting pan, place 125 mL (1/2 cup) butter, along with the tomato, onion, almonds, walnuts and pine nuts. Simmer in the oven, covered, for 30 minutes.

3 Add the Madeira and fish stock; place the lobster tails in the roasting pan and return to the oven, covered, for 20 to 30 minutes.

4 Meanwhile, mix the pili-pili with the rest of the butter and melt in small ramekins.

5 Serve the lobster tails with the melted butter and pili-pili.

Turkey osso buco (rounds) with olives and red beans

ROMANIA

4 servings

INGREDIENTS

1 kg turkey leg (drumstick and thigh) cut in rounds (osso buco) (2-3 pieces or 250 g per person) **2 lb**

30 mL flour (to dredge the rounds) **2 tbsp**

30 mL vegetable oil **2 tbsp**

325 mL chopped onions **1 1/2 cups**

5 mL minced garlic **1 tsp**

125 mL red wine **1/2 cup**

5 mL flour **1 tsp**

15 mL tomato paste **1 tbsp**

750 mL fresh tomatoes, cubed **3 cups**

250 mL carrots, cubed **1 cup**

5 mL fresh thyme **1 tsp**

2 bay leaves **2**

30 mL fresh chopped parsley **2 tbsp**

salt and pepper

125 mL sliced black olives (rinsed in water) **1/2 cup**

125 mL canned red beans, rinsed and drained **1/2 cup**

METHOD

1 Season the rounds and dredge them in the flour.

2 In a heavy saucepan, sauté them in the oil and brown well.

3 Remove from the saucepan and set aside.

4 In the same saucepan, brown the onions and garlic. Deglaze with the red wine and let reduce.

5 Add the flour, tomato paste, bay leaf, thyme, salt and pepper. Stir well. Add the cubed tomatoes with their juice and mix well. Bring to a boil and return the rounds to the mixture to cook on low heat. Add the carrots and let simmer for 60 to 75 minutes.

6 Compensate for any evaporation by adding a bit of water or chicken stock.

The rounds must be well cooked, but not so much that they fall apart. The sauce must be smooth without being thick.
At the end of cooking, add the red beans, black olives and the chopped parsley.

Surf and Turf Chowder

serves **4 to 6**

INGREDIENTS

30 mL olive oil **2 tbsp**
500 g chicken thighs without the skin **1 lb**
125 g chorizo, thinly sliced **1/4 lb**
1 medium onion, thinly sliced **1**
2 cloves garlic, chopped **2**
1 mL dried thyme **1/4 tsp**
2 mL dried oregano **1/2 tsp**
2 bay leaves **2**
125 mL white wine **1/2 cup**
1/2 can diced tomatoes, drained (796 mL/28 oz) **1/2**
750 mL fish stock **3 cups**
36 fresh mussels, cleaned **36**
36 fresh clams, cleaned **36**
18 large shrimp, shelled **18**
60 mL chopped fresh parsley **1/4 cup**
60 mL chopped cilantro **1/4 cup**
60 mL thinly sliced green onion **1/4 cup**

METHOD

1. Heat the olive oil in a large saucepan over high heat and brown the chicken 2 to 3 minutes. Add the chorizo, onion, garlic and seasonings and cook 2 to 3 minutes longer.
2. Deglaze with white wine.
3. Add the tomatoes and the fish stock and bring to a boil. Cover and cook over low heat 30 minutes, or until the chicken is no longer pink.
4. Add the mussels, clams and shrimp and cook, covered, 3 to 5 minutes longer.
5. Serve piping hot in deep dishes. Sprinkle with parsley, cilantro and green onions.

FRANCE

Herbed Halibut with Broccoli Purée

serves **4 to 6**

INGREDIENTS

30 mL unsalted butter **2 tbsp**
1 medium onion, cut into pieces 1
2 leeks, washed and coarsely chopped 2
1 clove garlic, chopped 1
1 mL dried thyme **1/4 tsp**
1 mL dried tarragon **1/4 tsp**
1 mL dried marjoram **1/4 tsp**
2 mL dried basil **1/2 tsp**
2 mL dried chervil **1/2 tsp**
1 mL coriander seed **1/4 tsp**
1 mL aniseed **1/4 tsp**
pinch cayenne pepper
250 mL fish stock **1 cup**
1 kg halibut fillets without the skin, cut into 6 pieces **2 lb**
salt and freshly ground pepper
250 mL 35% cream **1 cup**
3 L water **12 cups**
30 mL salt **2 tbsp**
2 medium heads broccoli, coarsely chopped 2
60 mL walnut oil **1/4 cup**
60 mL chopped chives **1/4 cup**

METHOD

1 Melt the butter in a large saucepan over moderate heat. Add the onion, leeks, garlic and seasonings. Cook 2 to 3 minutes.

2 Add the fish stock and bring to a boil.

3 Add the halibut to the saucepan with the salt and pepper. Cover and cook over low heat 3 to 5 minutes. Remove halibut from pan and keep warm.

4 Add cream to saucepan and bring to a boil. Reduce, uncovered, 2 to 3 minutes.

5 Blend in a food processor or blender 2 to 3 minutes. Strain and keep warm.

6 Bring the water to a boil in a large saucepan with 30 mL (2 tbsp) salt. Add the broccoli and cook, uncovered, 6 to 8 minutes, or until tender.

7 Drain well and purée in a food processor, adding the walnut oil gradually.

8 Place the broccoli purée on individual plates, top with the halibut, drizzle with sauce and sprinkle with chives.

6 to 8 servings

Portuguese-style Stuffed Turkey

To prepare a sauce, degrease the cooking liquid. Cook over high heat, add 15 mL (1 tbsp) cornstarch and 30 mL (2 tbsp) water. Stir constantly until the sauce reaches the desired thickness. Season with salt and pepper to taste.

INGREDIENTS

3 to 5 kg young turkey **6 to 10 lb**
125 mL thinly sliced onions **1/2 cup**
60 mL melted butter **4 tbsp**
turkey giblets
500 g potatoes **1 lb**
1 egg **1**
20 chopped black olives **20**
60 mL chopped parsley **1/4 cup**
nutmeg to taste
salt to taste
ground white pepper to taste
500 mL water **2 cups**

METHOD

1. Peel, wash, cut and cook the potatoes in salted water for about 40 minutes.
2. Remove from the heat, drain and mash; set aside at room temperature.
3. Chop the giblets into small pieces.
4. Heat a large skillet and cook the giblets and onions in the butter over low heat until tender.
5. Meanwhile, add the egg, olives and parsley to the potatoes. When the giblets are done, add them to the mixture, season and stir well.
6. Allow the stuffing to cool.
7. Preheat the oven to 230°C (450°F).
8. Lightly season the inside of the turkey and stuff with the mixture.
9. Place the turkey in a roasting pan, add the water and place in the oven for about 40 minutes to brown it. Lower the oven temperature to 180°C (350°F) and continue cooking until a meat thermometer inserted into the thigh reads 80°C (170°F), about 2 to 3 hours.
10. Remove from the oven and let sit for a few minutes before serving.

Sweet Scallops with Vegetable Chow Mein

serves **4 to 6**

INGREDIENTS

5 mL crushed fennel seed **1 tsp**
5 mL crushed coriander seed **1 tsp**
5 mL crushed aniseed **1 tsp**
5 mL crushed cardamom seeds **1 tsp**
5 mL crushed caraway seeds **1 tsp**
1 kg large, fresh scallops **2 lb**
15 mL olive oil **1 tbsp**
salt and freshly ground pepper
10 mL sesame oil **2 tsp**
60 mL thinly sliced red onion **1/4 cup**
60 mL thinly sliced red pepper **1/4 cup**
60 mL thinly sliced green pepper **1/4 cup**
60 mL thinly sliced carrot **1/4 cup**
60 mL thinly sliced broccoli **1/4 cup**
60 mL thinly sliced cauliflower **1/4 cup**
60 mL thinly sliced celery **1/4 cup**
750 g bean sprouts **1 1/2 lb**
15 mL hoisin sauce **1 tbsp**
30 mL oyster sauce **2 tbsp**
125 mL fish stock **1/2 cup**
30 mL sesame seeds **2 tbsp**

METHOD

1. Toast the spices in a small frying pan without oil over low heat 2 to 3 minutes, or until they release their aroma. Remove from heat, transfer to a large bowl and let cool.
2. Add the scallops and the olive oil. Mix well and marinate 1 hour in the refrigerator.
3. Sear the scallops in a large non-stick frying pan 1 minute on each side. Add salt and pepper. Remove from pan and keep warm. Add the sesame oil to the same pan and sauté all the vegetables except the bean sprouts over high heat 2 to 3 minutes.
4. Add the bean sprouts, hoisin sauce, oyster sauce and fish stock. Adjust the seasoning. Heat through, 1 to 2 minutes.
5. Remove from heat. Place the chow mein in the centre of individual plates. Arrange the scallops around the edge and sprinkle with sesame seeds.

Sautéed chicken supreme with endives

BELGIUM

Makes **4** portions

INGREDIENTS

4 chicken breasts (110 g – 3 1/2 oz each) boned, skin removed 4

15 mL butter **1 tbsp**

500 mL endives **2 cups**

1 lemon juice 1

100 g Swiss Gruyère cheese **4 slices**

pinch sugar

pinch paprika

salt and freshly ground pepper

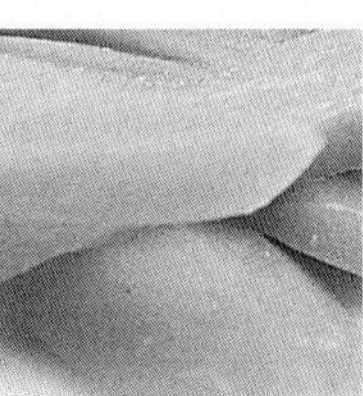

METHOD

1. Season the breasts and sauté them in butter in a skillet for 2 to 3 minutes each side.
2. Brown lightly, remove and set aside.
3. Trim the endives, remove the centre and wash them, then slice fine diagonally. Add the lemon juice.
4. In the same skillet, sauté the endives in butter without colouring, but with enough heat to remove the excess cooking liquid (4 to 5 minutes). Drain if necessary.
5. Lightly season and add the pinch of sugar. Set aside the semi-cooked endives. Spread them on the breasts and cover each breast with a slice of cheese. Sprinkle with a little paprika.
6. Place in a preheated oven at 180°C (350°F) to finish cooking and browning (approximately 10 minutes). Serve immediately with or without reduced cooking juices.

Note: Endives may be replaced by finely sliced leeks (white and green parts). In this case, the leeks must be slightly more cooked than the endives. Calculate 125 g or 1 1/2 cups of finely sliced leeks.

Pork is considered a delicacy throughout Louisiana. It has a place of honour on menus in Cajun and Creole restaurants and is always available as part of the table d'hôte.

UNITED STATES

Pork Loin

6 to **8** servings

INGREDIENTS

2 kg pork loin, bone-in if possible **4 lb**
6 garlic cloves, peeled and halved **6**
salt
cayenne
15 mL cracked black peppercorns **1 tbsp**
oil
60 mL flour **1/4 cup**
1 medium onion, chopped **1**
1/4 green pepper, finely chopped **1/4**
500 mL cold water **2 cups**
2 green onions, finely chopped **2**

METHOD

1 Preheat the oven to 180°C (350°F) and place the rack in the lower part of the oven. Using a small knife, make 12 cuts in the fat and fleshy parts of the pork loin. Insert the halved garlic cloves into the cuts. Season lightly with salt and cayenne.

2 With the palm of the hand, press the cracked black peppercorns into the surface of the meat. Place the pork loin in a large, deep cast-iron pot and add just enough water to cover. Bake in the oven for one hour, uncovered. Baste the loin with the cooking juices and return to the oven for another 2 hours, basting every 15 minutes. If needed, add a little water to the bottom of the pot to prevent the residue from burning.

3 Remove the pork loin from the pot, cover with aluminum foil and let sit.

4 Measure the cooking fat produced from the pork loin and add enough oil to make 60 mL (1/4 cup) of fat. Pour into another deep cast-iron pot and gradually whisk in the flour. Cook over very low heat, stirring constantly with a wooden spatula until the roux is the colour of a hazelnut shell. Add the onion and green pepper, and cook for 10 minutes over low heat, stirring occasionally.

5 Add a small amount of water to the pot in which the pork loin was cooked and scrape the bottom; add enough water to the residue to make 500 mL (2 cups). Gradually stir the cold water into the roux; bring to a boil, reduce the heat and simmer until the sauce thickens. Season with salt and cayenne. Stir in the green onions.

6 Slice the pork loin, place a few slices in each plate and top with sauce. Serve with puréed sweet potatoes.

Braised Partridge with Garden Vegetables

2 servings

Virtually all types of poultry can be used in this recipe.

INGREDIENTS

4 supremes of partridge 4
15 mL butter 1 tbsp
6 miniature potatoes 6
8 miniature carrots 8
10 pearl onions 10
150 mL celeriac, cut into pieces 2/3 cup
1 leek 1
160 mL canned chickpeas, rinsed and drained 6 oz
750 mL brown chicken stock (see recipe on p. 11) 3 cups
2 sprigs thyme 2
15 mL chopped chives 1 tbsp
salt to taste
4 black peppercorns 4

METHOD

1. Preheat the oven to 160°C (325°F).
2. Slice the white part of the leek into six 1 cm (1/2-in.) rounds.
3. In a skillet, heat the butter over high heat and sear the supremes on all sides. Place the supremes in a medium-sized casserole dish.
4. Add the vegetables and chickpeas to the casserole, along with the herbs, salt and pepper.
5. Add the brown poultry stock and bake in the oven for 1 1/2 to 2 hours.

Magret of duck or goose, with peaches and peppercorns

AUSTRIA

4 servings

INGREDIENTS

4 x 200 g duck or goose cutlets **4 x 7-8 oz**

15 mL oil **1 tbsp**

15 mL crushed mixture of 3 peppers (white, black, green) **1 tbsp**

30 mL butter **2 tbsp**

45 mL chopped shallots **3 tbsp**

5 mL flour **1 tsp**

30 mL gin or vodka **2 tbsp**

125 mL peach syrup **1/2 cup**

500 mL brown chicken stock **2 cups**

4 tinned peach halves, cut in slices **4**

salt

METHOD

1. Remove fat from legs, but keep as much of the skin on as possible. Make criss-cross incisions in the skin to allow the fat to escape.
2. Oil the cutlets, and pepper all sides with part of the crushed pepper mixture. Cover with plastic wrap and leave at room temperature for 1 to 2 hours, before cooking.
3. During this time, prepare the sauce: In a saucepan, sweat the shallot and remaining pepper mixture in butter, then add the flour and mix well.
4. Deglaze with gin (or vodka) and the peach syrup, add the brown stock and mix well.
5. Let simmer and reduce for 30-35 minutes to obtain the desired smoothness.
6. Verify the seasoning. Strain through a fine sieve, and keep warm.
7. Salt the cutlets and sauté in butter in a skillet for 2 or 3 minutes each side, beginning with the skin side down.
8. Place in the oven and bake at 120°C (250°F) for 6 to 8 minutes.
9. Slice or serve whole, and arrange the peach garnish attractively around the cutlets, covering with the sauce, or serve over a bed of peach slices and sauce.

Note: The duck magret is served medium or medium-rare. This recipe can also be used for pheasant and guinea fowl supremes.

Several pepper combinations are available, including mixtures with pink peppercorns, which is not really a pepper.

Veal Kidneys with Black-eyed Peas

4 to 6 servings

INGREDIENTS

1 kg veal kidneys, fat removed and cut into 2.5 cm (1-in.) cubes 2 lb

Marinade

60 mL olive oil 1/4 cup

15 mL Dijon mustard 1 tbsp

5 mL oregano 1 tsp

2 mL thyme 1/2 tsp

5 mL chili powder 1 tsp

freshly ground pepper

8 to 12 wooden skewers 8 to 12

Cumin-flavoured Black-eyed Peas

15 mL olive oil 1 tbsp

180 mL chopped onion 3/4 cup

125 mL chopped carrot 1/2 cup

125 mL chopped mushrooms 1/2 cup

125 mL chopped red pepper 1/2 cup

2 cloves garlic, chopped 2

2 mL cumin seeds 1/2 tsp

400 g cooked black-eyed peas or one 540 mL (19-oz) can black-eyed peas, rinsed and drained 2 cups

250 mL 35% cream 1 cup

pinch cayenne pepper

salt and pepper

60 mL chopped fresh parsley 1/4 cup

Marinade

1 In a bowl, blend all the ingredients. Add the kidney cubes. Marinate for 4 to 6 hours in the refrigerator. Thread the kidney pieces onto the skewers and refrigerate.

Black-eyed Peas

1 In a 2 L (8-cup) saucepan, heat the olive oil over high heat and sauté the onion, carrot, mushrooms, pepper, garlic and cumin for 3 minutes until caramelized.

2 Add the peas and cook for another 2 minutes. Pour in the cream, season and bring to a boil. Lower heat to minimum and simmer, uncovered, for 2 to 3 minutes.

3 Remove from heat and sprinkle with parsley. Keep warm.

4 Preheat the barbecue or the oven broiler to medium. Place the brochettes on the barbecue grill or broiler pan. Grill for about 5 minutes, turning regularly.

5 Serve the brochettes with the black-eyed peas and, if desired, homemade french fries.

Chicken fricassée with watercress and orange

SPAIN

4 servings

INGREDIENTS

- **500 g** chicken meat (leg or upper leg, skin removed, cut into large cubes) **1/2 lb**
- **45 mL** flour **3 tbsp**
- **45 mL** vegetable oil **3 tbsp**
- **375 mL** white wine veloutée sauce **1 1/2 cups**
- **125 mL** orange juice **1/2 cup**
- **1/2** bunch of watercress **1/2**
- **1** medium orange, peeled and sliced **1**
- salt and freshly ground pepper

METHOD

1. Salt, pepper, and coat the chicken cubes in the flour.
2. Heat the oil in a nonstick skillet and sauté the chicken cubes on all sides, browning lightly, then place the chicken in a heavy saucepan
3. Cover with hot veloutée sauce and bring to a boil. Reduce the heat and simmer for 30 to 40 minutes. Be careful! This sauce sticks easily.
4. Add the orange juice and stir. The sauce must be creamy without being thick. Add a bit of chicken stock if necessary.
5. Add the watercress at the last minute, and do not reheat again.

Serve over rice or pasta. Garnish with orange slices.

Turkey fillet with honey, soy and sesame seeds

CHINA

2 to 4 servings

INGREDIENTS

1 turkey fillet (350 g – 12 oz) 1
30 mL honey **2 tbsp**
15 mL soy sauce **1 tbsp**
30 mL sesame seeds **2 tbsp**
15 mL canola oil **1 tbsp**
salt and freshly ground pepper

METHOD

1. Marinate the turkey fillet in the honey and soy sauce for 24 hours in the refrigerator.
2. Drain, coat with sesame seeds, and season with salt and pepper.
3. Heat the oil in an ovenproof skillet, place the fillet in the oil and immediately place in the oven at 160°C (325°F). Bake for 12 to 15 minutes without turning. Switch oven to broil to finish last few minutes of cooking. Slice, and serve hot or cold with vegetables or a salad, red pepper coulis, or a sun-dried tomato and Dijon vinaigrette.

Note: Chicken, guinea fowl or pheasant supremes can also be used for this recipe.

Spicy Shrimp Risotto

4 to 6 servings

INGREDIENTS

15 mL lemon juice **1 tbsp**
30 mL olive oil **2 tbsp**
15 mL Worcestershire sauce **1 tbsp**
2 cloves garlic, chopped **2**
5 mL chopped fresh ginger **1 tsp**
2 mL crushed coriander seed **1/2 tsp**
2 mL crushed fennel seed **1/2 tsp**
1 mL cardamom seeds **1/4 tsp**
5 mL curry powder **1 tsp**
1 mL fresh pepper paste **1/4 tsp**
30 whole shrimp **30**
salt and freshly ground pepper
30 mL unsalted butter **2 tbsp**
60 mL thinly sliced onion **1/4 cup**
60 mL thinly sliced red pepper **1/4 cup**
60 mL thinly sliced white mushrooms **1/4 cup**
2 pinches saffron threads **2**
375 mL arborio rice, rinsed and drained **1 1/2 cups**
750 mL fish stock **3 cups**
60 mL grated Parmesan cheese **1/4 cup**
60 mL Shellfish Oil **1/4 cup**
60 mL chopped fresh parsley **1/4 cup**

METHOD

1. Whisk together the lemon juice, olive oil, Worcestershire sauce, garlic, ginger and seasonings in a large bowl. Add the shrimp, salt and pepper. Toss gently and marinate 1 hour in the refrigerator.
2. Cook the shrimp in a large non-stick frying pan over high heat 4 to 6 minutes, or until cooked. Remove from pan and keep warm.
3. Melt the butter in a medium-sized saucepan over low heat and cook the vegetables and saffron 2 to 3 minutes. Add the rice and cook 2 to 3 minutes longer.
4. Add the fish stock, adjust the seasoning and bring to a boil. Cover and cook over very low heat 20 minutes.
5. Remove from heat and add the Parmesan cheese, stirring gently.
6. Place the risotto on individual plates and top with the shrimp. Drizzle with Shellfish Oil and sprinkle with parsley.

Satay Chicken

JAPAN

4 servings

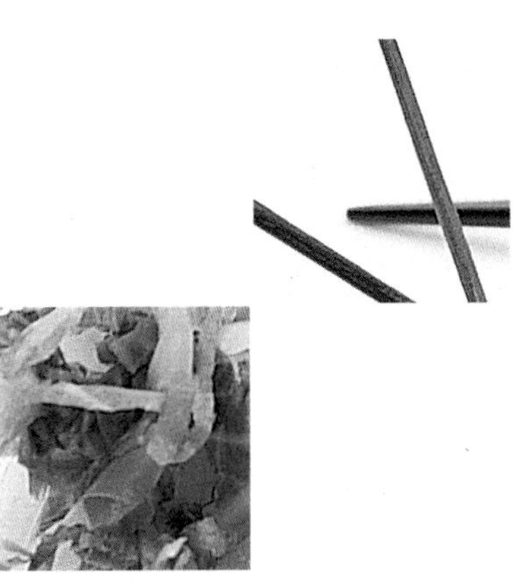

INGREDIENTS

500 g chicken leg or breast meat, bones and skin removed, cut in cubes of 2.5 cm (1 in.); allow for 6-7 cubes per brochette (100-125 g) **1 lb**

Marinade

15 mL sesame seeds **1tbsp**

15 mL canola oil **1 tbsp**

15 mL fresh chopped ginger **1 tbsp**

5 mL paprika **1 tsp**

5 mL powdered coriander **1 tsp**

15 mL honey **1 tbsp**

salt and fresh ground pepper

METHOD

1. In a bowl, mix the oil and seasonings – except the salt, which will be added just before cooking.
2. Add the poultry cubes, mix well and cover with plastic wrap.
3. Refrigerate for 2 hours.
4. If you are using wooden brochettes, soak them in water beforehand, to avoid burning during cooking.
5. Prepare the brochettes, and grill them on the barbecue or in the oven under the broiler. Take care not to overcook them.
6. Serve with a peanut, ginger and orange sauce (see recipe p. 21) over a bed of rice or couscous, to your liking.

Note: In some countries, satays are made with strips of meat threaded onto the brochettes. Chicken may be replaced by turkey. If using turkey, use only the white meat.

Blue Marlin with Mango Salsa

4 to 6 servings

INGREDIENTS

Marinade

125 mL hoisin sauce 1/2 cup

60 mL rice vinegar 1/4 cup

30 mL soy sauce 2 tbsp

10 mL Dijon mustard 2 tsp

5 mL chopped fresh ginger 1 tsp

1 clove garlic, chopped 1

pinch cayenne pepper

freshly ground pepper

1 kg blue marlin, cut into 6 pieces 2 lb

15 mL olive oil 1 tbsp

Mango Salsa

Mango Salsa

2 large mangoes, finely chopped 2

1 medium red onion, thinly sliced 1

125 mL finely chopped cilantro 1/2 cup

2 cloves garlic, chopped 2

30 mL sun-dried tomatoes in oil, drained and finely chopped 2 tbsp

30 mL rice vinegar 2 tbsp

15 mL olive oil 1 tbsp

10 mL brown sugar 2 tsp

pinch cayenne pepper

salt and freshly ground pepper

MARINADE

1 Mix the hoisin sauce, rice vinegar, soy sauce, mustard, ginger, garlic, cayenne pepper and pepper together in a bowl. Add the marlin, cover with plastic wrap and marinate 6 hours in the refrigerator.

2 Remove the fish from the marinade. Refrigerate until ready to cook.

3 Heat the olive oil in a large non-stick frying pan over high heat and cook the fish 2 to 3 minutes on each side, or to taste.

4 Serve immediately on individual plates with Mango Salsa.

MANGO SALSA

1 Mix all the ingredients together in a large bowl and refrigerate at least 1 hour.

Trout Fillets with Fresh Herbs

serves **4 to 6**

INGREDIENTS

60 mL chopped fresh tarragon **1/4 cup**
60 mL chopped fresh parsley **1/4 cup**
60 mL chopped fresh chervil **1/4 cup**
60 mL chopped fresh chives **1/4 cup**
1 kg trout fillets without the skin **2 lb**
30 mL Dijon mustard **2 tbsp**
salt and freshly ground pepper
30 mL olive oil **2 tbsp**
750 mL fettuccine, cooked al dente **3 cups**
60 mL white wine **1/4 cup**
2 small shallots, chopped **2**
250 mL fish stock **1 cup**
30 mL lemon juice **2 tbsp**
125 mL unsalted butter,
cut into small pieces **1/2 cup**

METHOD

1. Mix the fresh herbs in a small bowl and refrigerate until ready to use.
2. Brush the trout fillets with mustard and season with the chopped herbs, pressing the herbs gently into the fish.
3. Heat 15 mL (1 tbsp) olive oil in a large non-stick frying pan over high heat. Add the trout and cook 1 minute on each side. Remove from pan. Pour the remaining olive oil into the pan and sauté the fettuccine over moderate heat 3 to 5 minutes, or until piping hot. Keep warm.
4. Reduce the white wine and shallots by half in a medium-sized saucepan. Add the fish stock and the lemon juice. Reduce by half. Remove from heat and add the butter gradually, stirring gently. Adjust the seasoning. Keep warm.
5. Place the fish fillets on individual plates, add the pasta and drizzle with sauce.
6. Garnish with fresh herbs.

Grilled Salmon Tournedos with Caper Butter

4 to 6 servings

INGREDIENTS

250 mL unsalted butter **1 cup**
125 mL chopped capers **1/2 cup**
60 mL chopped fresh parsley **1/4 cup**
1 clove garlic, chopped **1**
30 mL lemon juice **2 tbsp**
1 mL Tabasco sauce **1/4 tsp**
salt and freshly ground pepper
1.5 kg peeled potatoes **3 lb**
125 mL hot milk **1/2 cup**
125 mL finely sliced fresh sorrel leaves **1/2 cup**
1 kg salmon fillet cut into 6 tournedos **2 lb**
30 mL olive oil **2 tbsp**
60 mL fresh parsley **1/4 cup**

METHOD

1. Soften the butter in a bowl with a wooden spoon. Add the capers, parsley, garlic, lemon juice, Tabasco sauce, salt and pepper and mix well.
2. Place the caper butter on a sheet of plastic wrap and shape into a 2.5-cm (1-in.) roll. Refrigerate 6 hours.
3. Cut the potatoes into 2.5-cm (1-in.) cubes and cook in boiling salted water 15 minutes, or until cooked. Drain well and force through a potato ricer. Add the milk and sorrel, adjust the seasoning and keep warm.
4. Brush the tournedos with olive oil and sprinkle with salt and pepper.
5. Grill on a very hot barbecue 3 to 4 minutes on each side, or to taste.
6. Serve immediately with sorrel mashed potatoes and caper butter.
7. Garnish with fresh parsley.

SWITZERLAND

Surprise your guests with this novel and delicious recipe. It makes an excellent centrepiece for your dining table.

Guinea fowl or pheasant casserole pie

4 servings

INGREDIENTS

1 guinea fowl or pheasant (1.5 kg – 3 lb approximate) 1

4 or 5 sprigs of fresh thyme 4 or 5

30 mL oil 2 tbsp

30 mL butter 2 tbsp

375 mL carrots cut in sticks 1 1/2 cups

375 mL onions cut in quarters 1 1/2 cups

5 mL thyme 1 tsp

375 mL water or white chicken stock 1 1/2 cups

30 mL flour 2 tbsp

30 mL water 2 tbsp

600 g commercial bread dough 20 oz

salt and freshly ground pepper

Egg wash

1 egg yolk 1

15 mL milk 1 tbsp

METHOD

1. Remove the fat from the bird, and place the sprigs of thyme in the neck cavity.
2. Truss the bird, that is, secure the wings and legs with twine to maintain their position during cooking.
3. Oil and season the fowl.
4. Place in a casserole dish large enough so that it barely juts over the edges, and sear in a very hot oven (230°C or 450°F) for 5 to 8 minutes.
5. Remove from the oven and let sit for 5 minutes.
6. In a nonstick skillet, sauté the carrots and onions in butter, and season with salt, pepper and thyme.
7. Place the vegetables in the casserole dish under the fowl, and add the stock or water.
8. Mix the 2 tbsp of flour and water in order to make a paste, and moisten the sides of the casserole dish with this paste.
9. Roll out all the bread dough evenly to the size of the casserole. Cover the casserole with this pastry, making sure you press well to seal around the rim.
10. Bake 1 hour in the oven at 160°C (325°F). Brush with the egg wash (egg yolk beaten with milk) and bring the oven temperature to 190°C (375°F). Let cook another 30 minutes. Cover with aluminium foil if the top begins to brown too much.

SERVING: Place the casserole on the table so that your guests can admire the elegance of the dish.
Remove the whole crust, cut it into pieces and place in a bread basket. Place the fowl on a carving platter to carve. Because it has absorbed the cooking flavours and poultry juices, this bread has a delicious taste, only surpassed by the bird itself!

Lobster Tails with Asparagus

4 to 6 servings

INGREDIENTS

3 L water **12 cups**
30 mL salt **2 tbsp**
1.5 kg lobster tails **3 lb**
30 mL olive oil **2 tbsp**
15 mL lemon juice **1 tbsp**
salt and freshly ground pepper
1 kg green asparagus, peeled **2 lb**
250 mL vegetable broth **1 cup**
30 mL unsalted butter **2 tbsp**

METHOD

1. Bring the water and salt to a boil in a large saucepan and add the lobster tails. After the water begins to boil once again, calculate 5 minutes and remove the tails. Let cool. Shell the tails and cut them into 1-cm (1/2-in.) slices.
2. Place the slices in a bowl and drizzle with olive oil and lemon juice. Sprinkle with salt and pepper and toss gently. Marinate 1 hour in the refrigerator.
3. Bring 3 L (12 cups) salted water to a boil in a large saucepan and add the asparagus. Cook for 7 to 8 minutes. Remove asparagus from saucepan and plunge into ice water. Drain and cut off 8-cm (3-in.) tips. Refrigerate until ready to use.
4. Bring the vegetable broth to a boil in a medium-sized saucepan. Add the asparagus and cook 1 minute.
5. Remove from heat, puree in a food processor or blender, then strain and reheat. Do not boil.
6. Turn off the heat and add the butter gradually, stirring gently. Adjust the seasoning. Keep warm.
7. Reheat the lobster and asparagus tips in a large non-stick frying pan over moderate heat 2 to 3 minutes.
8. Arrange on individual plates and drizzle with asparagus sauce.

Trout with Marguery Sauce

4 servings

INGREDIENTS

4 trout fillets, skinned, about 250 g (8 oz) each 4

Bouillon

500 mL cold water 2 cups
250 mL dry white wine 1 cup
15 mL butter 1 tbsp
2 mL salt 1/2 tsp
3 whole peppercorns 3
1 bay leaf 1
5 mL freshly squeezed lemon juice 1 tsp
1 piece lemon peel, 1 cm x 5 cm (1/2 in. x 2 in.) 1
0.5 mL cayenne 1/8 tsp
1 green onion 1
1 sprig parsley 1

Sauce

60 mL butter 1/4 cup
60 mL flour 1/4 cup
625 mL cooking liquid from fish 2 1/2 cups
2 egg yolks, lightly beaten 2
15 mL freshly squeezed lemon juice 1 tbsp
1 mL salt 1/4 tsp
500 g cooked, peeled shrimps 1 lb

METHOD

1 Add all ingredients for the bouillon to a large pot. Bring to a boil and simmer for 15 minutes.

2 Add the trout fillets to the bouillon and cook over very low heat for about 10 minutes until the fish turns opaque pink in the centre. Remove the fillets and keep warm.

3 Strain the bouillon through a sieve placed over a bowl and make the sauce. Melt the butter in a medium-sized saucepan. Remove the saucepan from the heat and gradually whisk in the flour. Return the saucepan to the stove and cook over low heat, stirring constantly for 1 minute. Remove the saucepan from the stove and whisk in the bouillon. Return the saucepan to the stove and bring to a boil, stirring constantly. Lower the heat and simmer for about 5 minutes until the sauce has thickened.

4 In a small bowl, mix the egg yolks, lemon juice and salt and gradually add to the sauce, stirring constantly. Reheat over very low heat for no more than one 1 minute.

5 Add the shrimps to the sauce and simmer over very low heat only long enough to reheat the sauce. Ladle over the cooked fillets and serve immediately.

Desserts

At last, time for the "icing on the cake" of the culinary arts – a course designed only to pamper the palate! While a dessert may contain some fibre or vitamins, its main purpose is clearly to provide pleasure, not to nourish. But just as pleasure feeds the soul, so too does a delicious dessert tantalize the gastronome who, on the occasion of a special meal, ceases to count calories in order to indulge his taste buds. While a dessert can never constitute a meal in the same way that a soup or salad can, it always crowns one. So why not exercise moderation and savour the sublime aromas, subtle flavours and unparalleled richness of the following dessert recipes?

Sugar is an ingredient that only recently emerged in foods, at least in its refined forms. The oldest sweetener used in cooking is honey. But sugar is also found in many industrially manufactured products — not only desserts. While the mass use of sugar in prepared foods can clearly lead to health problems, there is no need to be deprived of the gastronomic pleasures of a delicious dessert, eaten in moderation or on special occasions. Moreover, by preparing home-made desserts made from fresh ingredients, you can significantly limit your sugar consumption and indulge — guilt free — in the following sweet delights from the four corners of the world!

Frozen Yogurt with Honey and Cinnamon

4 to 6 servings

I N G R E D I E N T S

500 mL plain yogurt **2 cups**
125 mL honey **1/2 cup**
2 mL ground cinnamon **1/2 tsp**

M E T H O D

1 Combine all the ingredients in a large bowl.

2 Place in the freezer until the yogurt is firm. Stir vigorously several times while the yogurt is freezing.

NOTE: Yogurt with a higher fat content will yield a creamier texture. Adjust the amount of honey and cinnamon to taste.

CENTRAL AFRICA

Honey Nut Tarts

makes **10**

INGREDIENTS

10 7.5-cm (3-in.) prebaked tart shells **10**

2 eggs **2**

30 mL honey **2 tbsp**

80 mL milk or cream **1/3 cup**

30 mL flour **2 tbsp**

60 mL ground almonds **1/4 cup**

2 mL almond, orange or other extract **1/2 tsp**

160 mL nuts (walnuts, pecans, pistachios, etc.) **2/3 cup**

spices to taste (cinnamon, nutmeg, cloves)

METHOD

1. Preheat the oven to 190°C (375°F).
2. Bake the tart shells 5 to 10 minutes. Let cool.
3. Beat the eggs with the honey. Add the milk and stir in the flour mixed with the almonds.
4. Flavour with the extract of your choice and add spices to taste.
5. Fill the tart shells with the nuts and top with the liquid mixture.
6. Bake 15 to 20 minutes. Serve warm or cooled, topped with a little honey.

TUNISIA

Omelettes make great desserts. Just sweeten the mixture and fill with fresh or dried fruit. You can create your own variations based on this traditional Arab recipe.

Banana and Honey Omelette

4 servings

INGREDIENTS

6 eggs **6**

80 mL honey **1/3 cup**

60 mL 15% cream **1/4 cup**

15 mL orange zest **1 tbsp**

45 mL butter **3 tbsp**

3 ripe bananas, sliced **3**

80 mL sliced toasted almonds **1/3 cup**

METHOD

1. In a bowl, beat the eggs with the honey, cream and zest. Set aside.
2. In a non-stick skillet, melt 30 mL (2 tbsp) butter and sauté the bananas 2 to 3 minutes. Add the almonds. Set aside in a bowl.
3. Melt the remaining butter in the skillet, pour in the egg mixture and cook over low heat without stirring.
4. When the omelette is almost done, place the banana mixture in the centre, fold the omelette in half and cook for another 1 or 2 minutes. Serve immediately.

Candied Ginger Cones with Cream

4 servings

INGREDIENTS

45 mL softened unsalted butter **3 tbsp**

80 mL sugar **1/3 cup**

2 egg whites **2**

80 mL flour **1/3 cup**

30 mL chopped candied ginger **2 tbsp**

30 mL sesame seeds **2 tbsp**

250 mL 35% cream **1 cup**

30 mL icing sugar **2 tbsp**

30 mL amarula,* cognac, Tia Maria or other liqueur **2 tbsp**

METHOD

1. Preheat the oven to 200°C (400°F).
2. Cream the butter and sugar.
3. Add the egg whites one by one.
4. Stir in the flour and ginger. Work the dough only until smooth.
5. Divide the dough into 4 equal parts of about 60 mL (1/4 cup) each. On a lightly greased cookie sheet, spread out the dough using the back of a spoon to form 15-cm (6-in.) circles. Sprinkle sesame seeds over each of the circles.
6. Bake in the centre of the oven 5 to 7 minutes or until the edges turn golden brown. Remove from oven and remove the circles one by one. Place over a rolling pin or tube to give them a curved shape and then pinch the base to form a cone. Since the pastry breaks easily once it cools, it is important to handle it quickly and carefully.
7. Whip the cream. When it forms soft peaks, add the sugar and liqueur.
8. Garnish each cone with cream, using a pastry bag with a fluted tip. Serve immediately. Do not refrigerate.

* A fruit liqueur from South Africa.

NOTE: The dessert should be assembled just before it is served. The whipped cream can be made in advance, as can the cones. Store in a dry place.

Katayel

4 servings

INGREDIENTS

60 mL white flour **1/4 cup**
60 mL whole wheat flour **1/4 cup**
30 mL sugar **2 tbsp**
2 mL ground cardamom or cinnamon **1/2 tsp**
1 mL salt **1/4 tsp**
2 eggs **2**
125 mL milk **1/2 cup**
125 mL 10% cream **1/2 cup**
60 mL raisins **1/4 cup**
60 mL diced dried figs **1/4 cup**
60 mL coconut **1/4 cup**
60 mL walnut pieces **1/4 cup**
45 mL brown sugar **3 tbsp**
20 mL butter **4 tsp**
oil for frying
60 mL melted honey **1/4 cup**

METHOD

1 Combine the flours, sugar, spices and salt. Beat the eggs with the milk and cream; add to the dry ingredients. Refrigerate for about 1 hour. Set aside 30 mL (2 tbsp) batter.

2 In a bowl, mix the raisins, figs, coconut, nuts and brown sugar. Set aside.

3 Melt 5 mL (1 tsp) butter in a skillet and pour in one-quarter of the batter. Cook for about 2 minutes per side over medium heat, until the pancakes are lightly browned. Do the same with the rest of the mixture, for a total of 4 pancakes.

4 Preheat the oil in the deep fryer to 175°C (350°F).

5 Place one-quarter of the fruit mixture in the centre of each pancake. Moisten the edges of the pancakes with the remaining batter and fold over, pressing well so that the filling is sealed inside.

6 Fry the pancakes until golden brown. Serve immediately, topped with melted honey.

Kenya is one of the world's largest coffee producers. Crème brûlée was first developed in Europe: to stay true to African tradition, the cream can be replaced by coconut milk.

Coffee Crème Brûlée

6 servings

INGREDIENTS

500 mL 35% cream **2 cups**
30 mL cracked coffee beans (coarsely ground) **2 tbsp**
or 15 mL (1 tbsp) instant coffee
4 egg yolks **4**
180 mL sugar **3/4 cup**
45 mL all-purpose flour **3 tbsp**

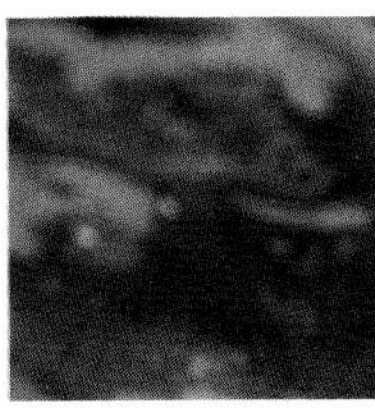

METHOD

1. Preheat the oven to 175°C (350°F).
2. Heat the cream over low heat with the coffee until it begins to steam. Strain (if using cracked coffee beans).
3. Cream the egg yolks with 125 mL (1/2 cup) sugar and stir in the flour.
4. Pour a little coffee-flavoured warm cream over the egg yolk mixture, whisking constantly. Return to the saucepan with the remaining cream and simmer, stirring with a wooden spoon until the mixture has thickened and coats the back of a spoon.
5. Fill 6 medium-sized ramekins three-quarters full with the mixture.
6. Place the ramekins in an ovenproof pan and add water until it comes halfway up the side of the ramekins. Bake in the centre of the oven until firm.
7. Remove the ramekins from the pan and let cool to room temperature before refrigerating.
8. Once cooled, sprinkle 15 mL (1 tbsp) sugar over each crème brûlée. Burn the sugar with a blowtorch or under the broiler in a preheated oven.
9. Serve immediately or refrigerate until serving, preferably the same day, so that the caramelized sugar does not liquefy.

NOTE: The crème brûlée must be cooled before the sugar on top is broiled. If a blowtorch is used, the sugar can be caramelized after Step 6.

Originally, baklava was rolled, sliced or cut into squares or diamonds, depending on the type of nuts it contained.

LEBANON

Baklava with Nuts and Citrus Fruit

6 to 8 servings

INGREDIENTS

250 mL finely chopped walnuts or pecans **1 cup**
250 mL finely chopped pistachios **1 cup**
250 mL finely chopped almonds **1 cup**
2 mL ground cinnamon **1/2 tsp**
2 mL allspice **1/2 tsp**
15 mL icing sugar **1 tbsp**
125 mL melted half-salted butter **1/2 cup**
60 mL olive oil **1/4 cup**
1 package phyllo pastry **1 package**

Syrup:
375 mL sugar **1 1/2 cups**
375 mL water **1 1/2 cups**
80 mL honey **1/3 cup**
zest and juice of 1 lemon
zest of 2 oranges
2 cloves 2
1 cinnamon stick 1

METHOD

1. Preheat the oven to 175°C (350°F).
2. Combine the nuts, spices and icing sugar. Set aside.
3. Combine the butter and oil. Set aside.

ASSEMBLING THE BAKLAVA:

1. Brush 8 sheets of phyllo with the butter mixture and place in the bottom of a lightly buttered lasagna dish.
2. Add half the nut mixture.
3. Place 4 sheets of phyllo, brushed with the butter mixture, on top of the nuts.
4. Add the remaining nuts.
5. Cover with the remaining 8 buttered sheets of phyllo. Brush the top sheet with water.
6. Cut into servings using a serrated-edge knife.
7. Bake in the centre of the oven for 45 minutes.
8. Combine the remaining ingredients for the syrup and cook over low heat for 15 minutes. Set aside.
9. Remove the cinnamon stick and cloves.
10. Pour the syrup carefully over the baklava once it is removed from the oven.
11. Let cool for 45 minutes and wait at least 1 hour before serving.

MADAGASCAR

Dark Chocolate Mousse with Candied Orange Peel

4 servings

INGREDIENTS

60 mL strong hot coffee **1/4 cup**

250 mL dark chocolate pieces **1 cup**

3 eggs, separated **3**

60 mL candied orange peel, chopped **1/4 cup**

60 mL icing sugar **1/4 cup**

125 mL 35% cream **1/2 cup**

1. Melt the chocolate in the coffee until smooth. Stir in the egg yolks one by one. Set aside.
2. Whip the egg whites into peaks and add half the sugar. Set aside.
3. Whip the cream with the remaining sugar and then fold it into the egg whites.
4. Gently fold the egg whites into the chocolate mixture.
5. Spoon the mixture into four dessert bowls. Refrigerate 2 hours before serving.

MADAGASCAR

The vanilla bean is the fruit of Vanilla plantifolia, a variety of climbing orchid. The pods are dried until they are dark brown. As it dries, the pod becomes covered in a crystalline coating of vanillin, which gives vanilla its distinctive flavour. The plant is indigenous to Mexico, but is now extensively grown on the island of Madagascar, off the coast of Africa.

Exotic Fruit Salad with Vanilla

4 to 6 servings

INGREDIENTS

VANILLA SYRUP:

125 mL water **1/2 cup**

80 mL sugar **1/3 cup**

1 vanilla bean, split **1**

juice of 1 lime

SALAD:

1 fresh pineapple **1**

2 tamarillos **2**

1 papaya **1**

2 kiwis **2**

2 blood oranges, sectioned **2**

1. In a small saucepan, heat the water with the sugar, vanilla and lime juice. Bring to a boil. Remove from heat and let cool to room temperature. Remove the vanilla bean, squeezing out any liquid.
2. Meanwhile, peel and cut up the fruit. Place in a large bowl and pour the vanilla syrup over the fruit. Refrigerate and serve chilled.

NOTE: Vanilla beans can be re-used. Simply rinse and store in the refrigerator.
A vanilla bean placed in the sugar bowl will impart a lovely subtle flavour to the sugar.

Figs are widely grown throughout the Mediterranean region.

MOROCCO

Loaded with nutrients, they can be eaten fresh or dried. Oddly enough, when we say something is "not worth a fig," it means it has little value.

Fig and Almond Rolls

6 to 8 servings

INGREDIENTS

Filling:

125 mL chopped dried figs **1/2 cup**
125 mL powdered almonds **1/2 cup**
80 mL sugar **1/3 cup**
30 mL orange-blossom water **2 tbsp**
2 mL ground cinnamon **1/2 tsp**
60 mL melted butter **1/4 cup**
1 package phyllo pastry, thawed **1 package**
icing sugar

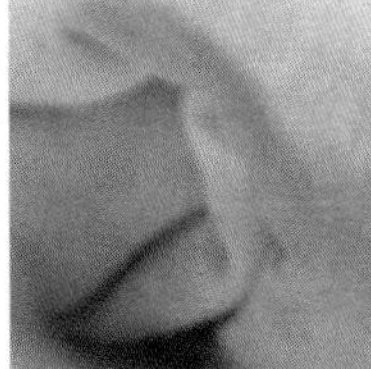

1. Preheat the oven to 175°C (350°F).
2. Mix the ingredients for the filling. Set aside.
3. Brush a phyllo sheet with the melted butter. Fold in four and place a heaping tablespoonful of filling at one end and roll the phyllo. Brush the top of the roll with butter. Continue until all the filling has been used.
4. Place the rolls on a cookie sheet and bake in the centre of the oven 25 to 35 minutes, until they are nicely golden. Serve hot or at room temperature.

NOTE: To thaw the phyllo pastry, remove from the freezer and leave at room temperature for 30 to 45 minutes.

CARIBBEAN *The Aztecs were the first to eat cacao and to appreciate its medicinal properties. They made it into a drink by mixing cacao beans with water. They named the beverage tchocoatl, meaning "bitter water."*

Hot Chocolate

4 servings

INGREDIENTS

- **1 litre** 2% milk **4 cups**
- **1** vanilla bean, split and scraped **1**
- **1** cinnamon stick **1**
- **1 mL** ground nutmeg **1/4 tsp**
- **60 mL** lightly packed brown sugar **1/4 cup**
- **60 mL** unsweetened cocoa powder **1/4 cup**
- **15 mL** cornstarch **1 tbsp**
- **1** large egg **1**
- **20 mL** smooth peanut butter (optional) **4 tsp**

METHOD

1. In a saucepan, heat the milk with the vanilla bean, cinnamon and nutmeg.
2. In a bowl, combine the brown sugar, cocoa powder, cornstarch and egg. Mix well and set aside.
3. When the milk is hot, stir in a bit of the cocoa mixture, and then add the rest.
4. Cook over low heat, stirring constantly with a wooden spoon, until the mixture thickens.
5. Remove the vanilla bean and cinnamon stick.
6. Pour the piping hot mixture into cups or café au lait bowls.
7. For a thicker hot chocolate, add 5 mL (1 tsp) peanut butter to each cup and stir well.

SUGGESTION: Frost the rims of the cups by dipping them in lemon juice and then in sugar.
Top with whipped cream for a fancier dessert.
NOTE: This hot chocolate goes well with shortbread or can even serve as a quick breakfast.

CARIBBEAN *Rum is a spirit distilled from sugar cane. At one time, imports of rum to France were banned so that it would not compete with domestic spirits distilled from wine. The only way to obtain it was on the black market. Rum is a nice complement to the flavour of pineapple and bananas.*

Oven-baked Bananas

6 servings

INGREDIENTS

- **6** ripe bananas **6**
- **60 mL** freshly squeezed lime juice **1/4 cup**
- **60 mL** dark rum **1/4 cup**
- **60 mL** unsalted butter **1/4 cup**
- **80 mL** brown sugar **1/3 cup**
- **5 mL** ground allspice **1 tsp**
- zest of **1** lime

METHOD

1. Preheat the oven to 210°C (425°F).
2. Slice the bananas in half lengthwise without peeling them and place in an ovenproof dish (skin side down).
3. In a saucepan, combine the lime juice, rum, butter, sugar, allspice and zest. Place the saucepan over high heat until the mixture comes to a boil and pour over the bananas. Bake in the oven 10 to 12 minutes.
4. Place 2 banana halves in each dish and drizzle with the cooking juices.

NOTE: Bananas oxidize quickly. They should be cooked as soon as possible after being cut.

The Spanish influence is evident in Peruvian cooking, which also reflects elements of Incan culture.

PERU

Chocolate Rum Cupcakes

6 servings

INGREDIENTS

- **4** eggs **4**
- **180 mL** sugar **3/4 cup**
- **60 mL** flour **1/4 cup**
- **60 mL** ground almonds **1/4 cup**
- **180 mL** dark chocolate, chopped into chunks **3/4 cup**
- **125 mL** unsalted butter **1/2 cup**
- **2 mL** dark rum extract **1/2 tsp**

To dust the moulds:

- **30 mL** butter **2 tbsp**
- **30 mL** flour **2 tbsp**
- **30 mL** cocoa **2 tbsp**

1. Preheat the oven to 185°C (375°F).
2. Cream the eggs with the sugar. Add the flour and almonds.
3. Melt the chocolate and butter. Stir in the rum extract.
4. Add the chocolate mixture to the egg mixture.
5. Combine the flour and cocoa.
6. Butter 6 muffin cups. Sprinkle with the cocoa mixture.
7. Divide the batter among the 6 cups.
8. Bake in the centre of the oven 12 to 15 minutes. Unmould the cupcakes and serve warm.

Peruvian Fruit Compote

INGREDIENTS

- **250 mL** water **1 cup**
- **375 mL** diced dried fruit **1 1/2 cups** (apricots, apples, figs, etc.)
- **125 mL** sugar **1/2 cup**
- 1 cinnamon stick **1**
- **5 mL** whole cloves **1 tsp**
- juice of 1 lemon
- **500 mL** fresh or canned pineapple pieces **2 cups**
- **250 mL** diced peeled pears **1 cup**
- **250 mL** diced peeled peaches **1 cup**

METHOD

1. In a saucepan, bring the water to a boil. Place the dried fruits in the boiling water to soften, and once they are plumped up, add the fresh fruit.
2. Add the sugar, spices and lemon juice.
3. Cook over low heat until the fruit is soft.
4. Serve lukewarm or chilled with the chocolate rum cupcakes.

The avocado comes from South America, where it is a favourite fruit. It can be prepared in countless ways: in salads, mousses or frozen desserts, or added to soups and stews. Since avocado oxidizes quickly, it should be prepared at the last minute or used with an acid ingredient such as lemon juice or vinegar, which delays oxidation.

BRAZIL

Avocado Cream

4 servings

INGREDIENTS

3 egg whites 3
190 mL icing sugar 3/4 cup
2 large ripe avocados 2
45 mL pineapple juice 3 tbsp
15 mL lemon juice 1 tbsp
80 mL toasted unsweetened coconut 1/3 cup

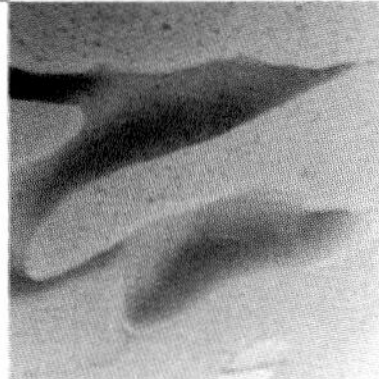

METHOD

1. Whip the egg whites into firm peaks with half the sugar. Set aside.
2. Peel and pit the avocados. Purée. Add the pineapple juice and lemon juice, along with the remaining sugar.
3. Fold the beaten egg whites into the avocado mixture with a spatula.
4. Spoon into four dessert bowls and refrigerate 1 hour.
5. Just before serving, sprinkle with grilled coconut.

NOTE: Can also be served with fresh fruit.

In Northeastern North America, maple sap is harvested in springtime and boiled down into syrup to concentrate the flavour. If it is boiled for longer, the syrup turns into taffy, butter or maple sugar. Sugar maples grow primarily in Canada, with 70% of syrup produced in the province of Quebec.

CANADA

Maple Walnut Parfait

4 servings

INGREDIENTS

4 egg yolks 4

250 mL maple syrup 1 cup

80 mL 35% cream 1/3 cup

250 mL walnut pieces 1 cup

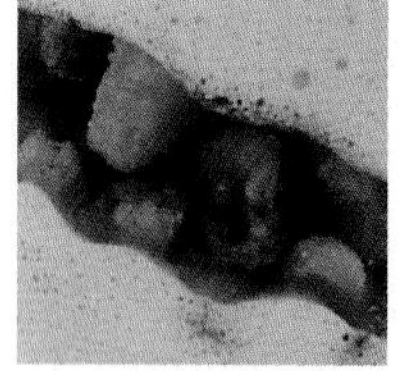

METHOD

1. In a bowl, mix the egg yolks and 180 mL (2/3 cup) maple syrup.
2. Place the bowl over a saucepan of water, heat over low and beat the mixture until a very smooth mousse is obtained. Set aside.
3. Whip the cream and add the egg yolk mixture. Set aside.
4. In a skillet, toast the nuts over low heat to crisp them up and release their fragrance. Remove from heat and drizzle with the remaining syrup. Return the mixture to the stove and continue cooking, stirring frequently until the sugar has crystallized and sticks to the nuts. Place the nuts on a cookie sheet to cool.

ASSEMBLING THE PARFAITS:

1. Just before serving, pour a small amount of mousse into 4 parfait glasses.
2. Add 30 mL (2 tbsp) nuts and another layer of mousse. Continue the procedure, ending with a layer of mousse. Serve immediately so that the nuts do not lose their crispness.

NOTE: Keep the water in the saucepan below the boiling point to prevent the eggs from curdling.

Carrot Cake

8 to 10 servings

INGREDIENTS

4 eggs **4**
250 mL sugar **1 cup**
125 mL vegetable oil **1/2 cup**
500 mL grated carrots **2 cups**
300 g crushed pineapple **10 oz**
500 mL all-purpose flour **2 cups**
10 mL baking powder **2 tsp**
10 mL baking soda **2 tsp**
10 mL ground cinnamon **2 tsp**
5 mL salt **1 tsp**
250 mL walnuts **1 cup**
250 mL golden raisins **1 cup**

Cream Cheese Icing
250 g softened cream cheese **1 8-oz package**
125 mL icing sugar **1/2 cup**
5 mL vanilla extract **1 tsp**

METHOD

1 Preheat the oven to 175°C (350°F).
2 Cream the eggs with the sugar.
3 Stir in the oil, carrots and pineapple. Set aside.
4 In a large bowl, combine the dry ingredients.
5 Stir the egg mixture into the dry ingredients. Mix until the batter is just blended.
6 Add the walnuts and raisins.
7 Pour the batter into a greased Bundt dish.
8 Bake 50 to 60 minutes, until a knife inserted in the centre comes out clean.
9 Let stand for 5 to 10 minutes before unmoulding. Place on a cooling rack.

CREAM CHEESE ICING:

1 Beat the cream cheese.
2 Add the icing sugar and vanilla extract.
3 Ice the cake once it has cooled. Slice into servings.

This dessert was inspired by a family recipe from Angelica Luna of Santiago. In Chile, this recipe is made by those who can indulge in the luxury of a bottle of wine. An inexpensive wine is normally used in this recipe.

CHILE

Apples Baked in Red Wine

6 servings

INGREDIENTS

6 baking apples (McIntosh type), peeled and halved **6**

125 mL raw sugar or brown sugar **1/2 cup**

12 drops vanilla extract **12 drops**

12 knobs of unsalted butter **12 knobs**

500 mL red wine **2 cups**

METHOD

1. Preheat the oven to 180°C (375°F).
2. Using a melon baller, remove the core from each apple half. Place the cored halves in an ovenproof dish, cut side up.
3. Place 5 mL (1 tsp) sugar and 1 drop vanilla in the centre of each apple and top with a knob of butter.
4. Pour the wine into the dish until the apples are half immersed and add the remaining sugar.
5. Bake in the centre of the oven 30 to 45 minutes, until the tops of the apples are golden and the flesh is tender. The apples will take on the colour of the wine.
6. Remove from oven and let the apples cool in the wine before serving with whipped cream or ice cream, as desired.

Commercially grown blueberries are available almost everywhere in North America, but wild blueberries pack a much bigger flavour punch. They ripen in late summer and are abundant in many areas of Eastern Canada and the Northeastern United States.

Blueberry Tart

6 to 8 servings

INGREDIENTS

1 23-cm (9-in.) precooked shortcrust pastry shell **1**
625 mL fresh or frozen blueberries **2 1/2 cups**
160 mL sugar **2/3 cup**
15 mL lemon juice **1 tbsp**
30 mL all-purpose white flour **2 tbsp**
30 mL butter **2 tbsp**
1 egg, beaten **1**

METHOD

1. In a saucepan, combine the blueberries, sugar and lemon juice. Bring to a boil over low heat.
2. Knead the butter and flour together until smooth and then stir into the blueberry mixture. Remove from heat and let cool for 20 minutes.
3. Stir in the egg.
4. Pour the mixture into the pie shell.
5. Serve cold or warm, topped with ice cream.

A dessert that combines pears from Oregon and limes from Florida.

UNITED STATES

4 servings

Poached Pears in Lime Juice

INGREDIENTS

4 ripe pears **4**
125 mL water **1/2 cup**
60 mL honey **1/4 cup**
juice and zest of **1** lime
60 mL rum **1/4 cup**
125 mL sour cream **1/2 cup**
125 mL toasted sliced almonds **1/2 cup**

METHOD

1. Peel the pears, cut in half and remove the seeds.
2. In a large skillet, combine the water, honey, lime juice and rum and bring to a boil.
3. Place the pears in the syrup, cut side down. Cover and cook over low heat 15 to 20 minutes, turning the pears from time to time.
4. After about 8 minutes, add the lime zest.
5. Remove the pears from the syrup. Set aside in a cool place.
6. Heat the syrup to concentrate the flavours. Reduce by one-half and let cool.
7. Mix the sour cream with 60 mL (1/4 cup) of the cooled syrup.
8. Serve two pear halves per portion, topped with the sour cream topping and toasted almonds.

NOTE: To ensure that the pears remain firm, do not overcook.

This refreshing summer dessert can be made up to a week in advance and fried just before serving.

MEXICO

Fried Ice Cream

4 servings

INGREDIENTS

500 mL ice cream, flavour of your choice **2 cups**
1 egg, beaten **1**
250 mL graham cracker crumbs **1 cup**
2 mL ground cinnamon **1/2 tsp**
oil for frying

METHOD

1 Form 4 balls of ice cream and freeze until very hard.

2 Roll the balls in the egg and then in the graham cracker crumbs until evenly coated. Place in the freezer for 1 hour.

3 Repeat the procedure 2 more times and freeze for 2 hours.

4 Just before serving, heat the oil to 180°C (375°F).

5 Plunge the ice cream balls into the oil for 2 minutes.

6 Remove and place the balls on paper towels. Serve immediately.

NOTE: Serve with a chocolate sauce or fresh exotic fruit.

UNITED STATES *Brownies pair beautifully with vanilla ice cream and chocolate sauce, but this dessert is sweet enough to be served on its own.*

Double Chocolate Brownies

10 servings

INGREDIENTS

160 mL unsalted butter **2/3 cup**

80 mL semisweet chocolate chips **1/3 cup**

2 eggs **2**

160 mL white or brown sugar **2/3 cup**

5 mL vanilla extract **1 tsp**

125 mL walnut or pecan pieces **1/2 cup**

125 mL cocoa powder **1/2 cup**

125 mL flour **1/2 cup**

125 mL white chocolate chips **1/2 cup**

METHOD

1. Preheat the oven to 175°C (350°F).
2. Grease and flour a 23-cm (9-in.) round cake pan or line it with parchment.
3. In the microwave, melt the butter and the chocolate chips.
4. Cream the eggs and sugar. Add the vanilla extract.
5. Add the butter and chocolate mixture. Stir well.
6. In a small bowl, combine the nuts, cocoa, flour and white chocolate chips. Add to the batter, stirring with a wooden spoon until smooth.
7. Spread the mixture evenly in the pan and bake in the centre of the oven 15 to 20 minutes. The brownies will remain moist. Serve hot, warm or cold, in squares or slices.

UNITED STATES *Thanksgiving Day takes place in early October in Canada and on November 25 in the United States, when pumpkins are in season. This is a traditional Thanksgiving dessert served on both sides of the border.*

Molasses Pumpkin Pie

8 servings

INGREDIENTS

1 23-cm (9-in.) deep-dish pie shell, unbaked **1**

2 eggs **2**

500 mL puréed pumpkin **2 cups**

80 mL molasses **1/3 cup**

60 mL brown sugar **1/4 cup**

1 mL ground ginger **1/4 tsp**

1 mL ground cloves **1/4 tsp**

2 mL ground nutmeg **1/2 tsp**

5 mL ground cinnamon **1 tsp**

250 mL 15% or 35% cream **1 cup**

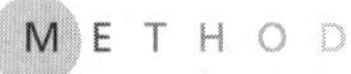

METHOD

1. Preheat the oven to 180°C (375°F).
2. Beat the eggs with the puréed pumpkin, molasses and brown sugar, ensuring that the brown sugar dissolves completely.
3. Stir in the spices and cream and mix well until smooth.
4. Pour the mixture into the pie shell. Bake in the centre of the oven 30 to 35 minutes or until the pumpkin mixture is firm. Serve warm or cold with a dollop of whipped cream, if desired.

Venezuelan cooking is among the most refined in South America, and this dessert, with its subtle pineapple flavour, is no exception.

VENEZUELA

Pineapple Flan

4 servings

INGREDIENTS

- **5** eggs **5**
- **125 mL** sugar **1/2 cup**
- **250 mL** pineapple juice **1 cup**
- **125 mL** 35% cream **1/2 cup**
- **4** fresh pineapple slices **4**
- **60 mL** sugar **1/4 cup**

METHOD

1. Preheat the oven to 175°C (350°F).
2. Cream the eggs and sugar with a whisk.
3. Gradually stir in pineapple juice and then the cream.
4. Pour the mixture into 4 medium-sized ramekins.
5. Place in an ovenproof pan and fill with water to half the height of the ramekins.
6. Bake in the centre of the oven until the flans are lightly browned on top and a knife inserted in the centre comes out clean.
7. Cool for 30 minutes at room temperature and refrigerate 2 to 3 hours before unmoulding.
8. Before serving, melt 60 mL (1/4 cup) sugar in a skillet to make the caramel. Coat the pineapple slices in the caramel and serve with the flan.
9. Slide a knife around the inside of the ramekins. Unmould the flans upside down onto plates. Top with caramelized pineapple and serve.

NOTE: It is normal for bubbles to form in the flan; they are caused by the pineapple juice used in the batter.

Cheesecake is a very dense dessert made with cream cheese. It is often topped with fresh strawberries or a fruit coulis. Many variations exist, such as chocolate and lemon cheesecake.

UNITED STATES

8 servings

Classic New York Cheesecake

INGREDIENTS

Base:

- **310 mL** graham cracker crumbs **1 1/4 cups**
- cinnamon to taste
- **60 mL** melted unsalted butter **1/4 cup**
- **60 mL** sugar **1/4 cup**

Filling:

- **500 g** softened cream cheese **2 8-oz packages**
- **250 mL** sugar **1 cup**
- **125 mL** pastry flour **1/2 cup**
- **180 mL** 35% cream **3/4 cup**
- **30 mL** lemon juice **2 tbsp**
- **5 mL** vanilla extract **1 tsp**
- **3** eggs **3**
- **180 mL** sour cream **3/4 cup**

METHOD

1. Preheat the oven to 150°C (300°F).
2. In a bowl, mix the ingredients for the base. Press into a 23-cm (9-in.) springform pan.
3. In a large bowl, beat the cream cheese, add the sugar and flour, and continue beating until the mixture is smooth.
4. Add the cream, the lemon juice and vanilla. Stir well.
5. Add the eggs one by one, beating well after each one.
6. Stir the sour cream into the mixture.
7. Pour into the springform pan and cook in the centre of the oven for about 1 1/2 hours or until the cake is firm to the touch. Turn off the oven, open the door slightly and leave the cake in the oven for 30 minutes.
8. Cool to room temperature and refrigerate for at least 3 to 4 hours before serving with your favourite topping.

NOTE: Cheesecakes often have a lighter layer on the surface; this is sour cream with sugar, which is added toward the end of the cooking time. If you wish, cover the cake with a mixture of 125 mL (1/2 cup) sour cream and 45 mL (3 tbsp) sugar after 1 hour of baking and continue with the next steps as described above.

Chinese cooking is characterized by a search for harmony. The four essential flavours—sweet, salty, sour and bitter—are often combined in the same meal. Presentation is also very important in China, in order to please the dinner guests. Cooking in the wok is an ancient method invented to economize on fuel, which was scarce. When ingredients are cut into small pieces, they cook much more quickly.

Fried Sweet Won Tons

makes **20 to 25** won tons

INGREDIENTS

430 mL chopped pitted dates **1 3/4 cups**
125 mL assorted chopped nuts
(almonds, walnuts, cashews, etc.) **1/2 cup**
zest and juice of **1** lemon
zest of **1** orange, juice as needed
1 package (250 g) thawed won ton wrappers **1 package (8 oz)**
1 egg white **1**
oil for frying
icing sugar

METHOD

1. Heat the oil in a deep fryer or wok over low heat.
2. In a bowl, mix the dates with the nuts, zests and lemon juice. Stir in the orange juice gradually if the mixture is too dry.
3. Place 1 tbsp of the mixture in the centre of a won ton wrapper. Brush the edges of the wrapper with egg white to seal them and fold into the desired shape (bundles, rolls, triangles).
4. Fry, a few at a time, in hot oil until the won tons are crisp and golden.
5. Drain and place on paper towels. Let cool.
6. Sprinkle with sugar before serving.

NOTE: Egg roll wrappers can be used instead of won tons. Since they are larger, follow the same steps but use more filling for each one.

The Jews believe that honey is the symbol of the Promised Land.

ISRAEL

Date Parosa

6 to 8 servings

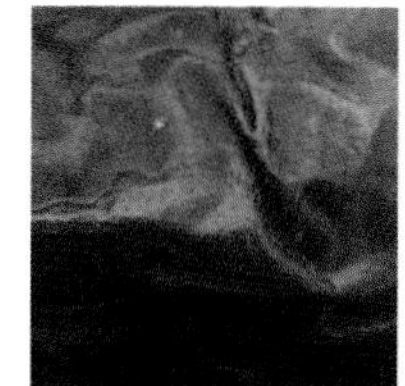

INGREDIENTS

2 eggs, separated 2
500 g cottage cheese 1 lb 2 oz
80 mL sugar 1/3 cup
2 mL cinnamon 1/2 tsp
2 mL salt 1/2 tsp
80 mL plain yogurt 1/3 cup
30 mL melted unsalted butter 2 tbsp
80 mL all-purpose flour 1/3 cup
375 mL chopped dates 1 1/2 cups

METHOD

1. Preheat the oven to 175°C (350°F).
2. In a large bowl, combine the egg yolks, cottage cheese, sugar, cinnamon and salt.
3. Add the yogurt, butter and flour. Set aside.
4. In another bowl, whip the egg whites into peaks and fold in the cottage cheese mixture with a spatula.
5. Add the dates.
6. Grease a soufflé dish and pour in the mixture.
7. Place the dish in another ovenproof dish. Fill this dish half full of water.
8. Bake 1 hour. Serve warm or chilled, with honey-sweetened yogurt.

ISRAEL

Everyday Israeli cuisine is simple. Vegetables, dairy products and fruit dominate the dinner table. The creation of the state of Israel brought a new wave of immigrants, along with their culinary traditions. This recipe is Russian or Austrian in origin.

Chilled Cherry Soup

4 servings

INGREDIENTS

250 mL plain firm yogurt or black cherry yogurt **1 cup**
45 mL or less liquid honey **3 tbsp or less**
1 284 mL can Bing cherries, drained **1 10 oz can**
60 mL cherry juice **1/4 cup**
15 mL lime juice (optional) **1 tbsp**
1 mL cinnamon **1/4 tsp**

Topping:
plain yogurt
pitted fresh cherries

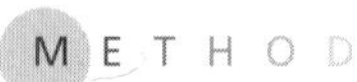
METHOD

1. In a food processor or blender, purée all the ingredients and chill for at least 3 hours.
2. Serve in deep chilled bowls.
3. Garnish each bowl with a thin stream of yogurt and some cherries.

THAILAND

Aromatic, zesty ginger is an essential condiment in Asian cooking. It was appreciated as far back as the Middle Ages. Today, we use fresh, candied or powdered ginger.

Flambéed Ginger Pineapple

4 servings

INGREDIENTS

45 mL half-salted butter **3 tbsp**
30 mL sugar **2 tbsp**
10 mL chopped fresh ginger **2 tsp**
1 fresh pineapple, sliced **1**
15 mL chopped fresh mint **1 tbsp**
60 mL dark rum **1/4 cup**

METHOD

1. In a skillet, melt the butter, add the sugar and caramelize until the mixture is amber in colour.
2. Add the ginger and pineapple. Cook both sides until golden over low heat.
3. Stir in the mint and rum. Flambé. Serve with vanilla ice cream.

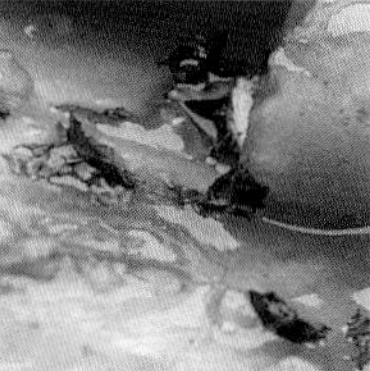

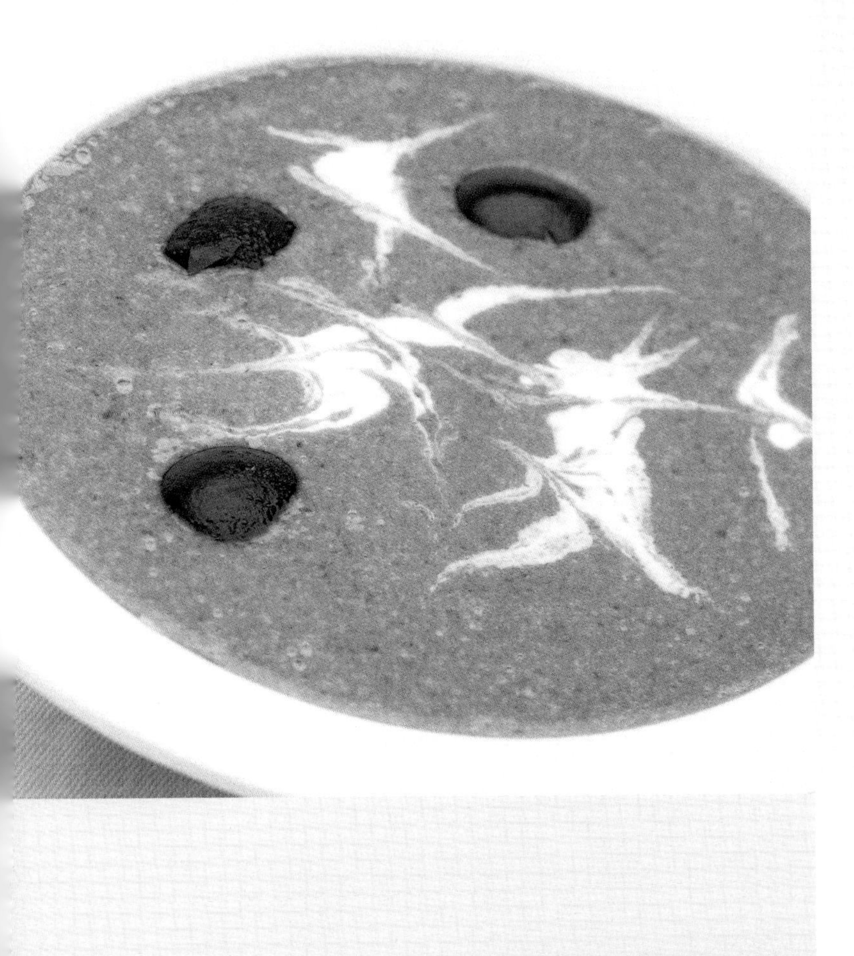

Green tea is a Chinese and Japanese specialty. There are three different varieties. In Japan, it is called shincha and it has a very deep colour.

JAPAN

Green Tea and Lime Sherbet

6 servings

INGREDIENTS

1 lime **1**
125 mL sugar **1/2 cup**
750 mL cooled green tea **3 cups**

METHOD

1. Remove the lime zest and set aside.
2. Peel the lime and finely chop the flesh.
3. Place the lime flesh in a large bowl.
4. Gradually add the sugar, then the tea, stirring well to dissolve the sugar.
5. Add the lime zest.
6. Place the bowl in the freezer until the mixture freezes. Stir vigorously a few times during the freezing process. Served well chilled in a sherbet glass or a hollowed-out lime.

Pecan pie is originally from Louisiana, the leading pecan-growing state in the U.S.

UNITED STATES

Pecan Pie

8 servings

INGREDIENTS

- **1** shortcrust pastry shell, unbaked **1**
- **4** large eggs **4**
- **310 mL** brown sugar **1 1/4 cups**
- **250 mL** corn syrup **1 cup**
- **5 mL** rum extract **1 tsp**
- **375 mL** pecan halves **1 1/2 cups**

METHOD

1. Preheat the oven to 175°C (350°F).
2. Cream the eggs with the brown sugar until the mixture is creamy and light in colour.
3. Stir in the corn syrup and rum extract.
4. Arrange the nuts on the bottom of the pastry shell and pour in the liquid mixture.
5. Bake in the centre of the oven 35 to 45 minutes. Serve with vanilla ice cream or whipped cream.

NOTE: The rum extract can be replaced by 30 to 45 mL (2 to 3 tbsp) dark rum.

One variety of rice seems to have originated in southern India and is said to have been introduced to Europe by Alexander the Great. Cardamom, dried fruit, almonds and rosewater are typical Pakistani and Indian ingredients.

PAKISTAN

Rice Pudding

4 to 6 servings

INGREDIENTS

1 L milk **4 cups**
250 mL sugar **1 cup**
1 mL ground cardamom **1/4 tsp**
1 mL ground nutmeg **1/4 tsp**
60 mL rinsed short-grain rice **1/4 cup**
1 egg **1**
60 mL sultana raisins **1/4 cup**
60 mL toasted slivered almonds **1/4 cup**
10 mL rosewater or essential oil of rose (a few drops) **2 tsp**

METHOD

1. In a saucepan, heat the milk with half the sugar and the spices.
2. Add the rice and cook in the milk, stirring with a wooden spoon, until the rice is done.
3. Beat the egg with the remaining sugar. Heat up with a little hot milk and pour into the saucepan, stirring constantly.
4. Remove the saucepan from the heat once the mixture has thickened.
5. Add the raisins, almonds and rosewater. Stir well.
6. Scoop into bowls or ramekins and let cool. Serve warm or chilled.

Ice cream flavoured with fruit and coconut is very popular in the Philippines. After the discovery of the New World, European explorers began exporting papayas to their Asian colonies.

PHILIPPINES

Papaya Ice Cream

6 to 8 servings

INGREDIENTS

2 ripe papayas 2
juice of 1 lime
375 mL milk 1 1/2 cups
2 eggs 2
80 mL sugar 1/3 cup
310 mL 35% cream 1 1/4 cups
45 mL icing sugar 3 tbsp

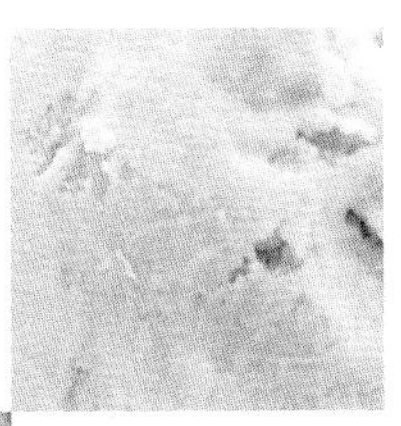

METHOD

1 In a blender, purée the peeled and seeded papaya with the lime juice. Set aside.

2 In a small saucepan, heat the milk over low heat until it begins to steam; do not bring to a boil.

3 Cream the eggs with the sugar.

4 Warm up the eggs by stirring in a few spoonfuls of warm milk.

5 Pour the egg mixture into the remaining milk, stirring with a wooden spoon.

6 Cook over low heat, stirring constantly until the mixture begins to thicken.

7 Remove from heat. Pour into a large cold bowl and let cool, stirring frequently.

8 When the mixture has cooled to room temperature, place the bowl in the freezer to cool completely.

9 Whip the cream and sugar.

10 Add the papaya purée to the whipped cream.

11 Gently fold into the egg mixture until well blended.

12 Place the mixture in the freezer until frozen firm, stirring it a few times during the process.

NOTE: Mangos, peaches or bananas can be used instead of papaya.

Sesame oil releases its full flavour when it is heated. The sesame seeds used in the following recipe can be raw, toasted or black, depending on individual tastes.

SINGAPORE

Caramelized Fried Apples with Sesame

6 servings

INGREDIENTS

Batter:

1 egg 1

160 mL cold water 2/3 cup

15 mL toasted sesame oil 1 tbsp

180 mL flour 3/4 cup

60 mL finely grated unsweetened coconut 1/4 cup

2 mL ground cinnamon 1/2 tsp

3 large cooking apples 3

oil for frying

Caramel:

430 mL sugar 1 3/4 cups

2 mL finely chopped fresh ginger 1/2 tsp

30 mL sesame seeds 2 tbsp

1. Heat the oil in a wok or deep fryer.
2. Beat the egg with the water and add the oil.
3. Blend the flour, coconut and cinnamon. Add the egg mixture all at once. Beat until the batter is smooth. Set aside.
4. Peel the apples and cut into 8 pieces.
5. Heat the sugar and ginger over low heat in a saucepan, stirring frequently, until caramelized. Take care not to burn the sugar. Add the sesame seeds.
6. Meanwhile, dip the apple slices in the batter and fry in the hot oil until the batter is golden. Drain, dip in the caramel and place the apple pieces on a greased baking sheet. CAREFUL: THEY WILL BE VERY HOT!
7. Let cool for a few minutes until the caramel hardens. Serve the same day.

NOTE: If the apples are cut in advance, place the pieces in water containing a little lemon juice or vinegar to prevent browning.

Tapioca is obtained by extracting starch from the cassava root, which is then processed into tapioca flakes and pearls. It is very popular in Asia, where it is flavoured with various ingredients.

THAILAND

Tapioca with Coconut Cream

6 servings

INGREDIENTS

310 mL tapioca **1 1/4 cups**
45 mL icing sugar **3 tbsp**
1 egg **1**
80 mL sugar **1/3 cup**
60 mL rice flour or cornstarch **1/4 cup**
375 mL thick coconut milk **1 1/2 cups**

METHOD

1. Preheat the oven to 175°C (350°F).
2. Cook the tapioca in a large amount of water until the pearls become transparent. Rinse under cold water and drain well. Sprinkle with icing sugar.
3. Spoon the tapioca into 4 medium-sized ramekins or half coconut shells.
4. Cream the egg with the sugar.
5. Whisk in the flour.
6. Gradually add the coconut milk, stirring gently.
7. Spread the coconut milk over the tapioca without stirring.
8. Place the ramekins in an ovenproof pan. Fill the pan with water halfway up the side of the ramekins.
9. Bake in the centre of the oven 15 to 20 minutes or until the coconut cream is set.

NOTE: Rinsing the tapioca thoroughly before use will make it less sticky. If you prefer tapioca cream, stir the coconut cream into the tapioca in Step 7.

Even though rice flour is always used in Vietnam, the following recipe can also be made with wheat flour.

VIETNAM

Peanut and Banana Cake

8 to 10 servings

INGREDIENTS

2 eggs **2**
125 mL brown sugar **1/2 cup**
250 mL coconut milk or 15% cream **1 cup**
4 ripe bananas, peeled and sliced **4**
410 mL flour **1 2/3 cups**
375 mL chopped unsalted peanuts **1 1/2 cups**

METHOD

1. Preheat the oven to 175°C (350°F).
2. Grease and flour a 23-cm (8-in.) cake pan, or line with parchment.
3. Cream the eggs with the brown sugar.
4. Add the coconut milk and bananas. Stir gently to avoid crushing the bananas.
5. Combine the flour with the peanuts and stir into the wet ingredients.
6. Spread the mixture in the cake pan and bake in the centre of the oven 40 to 45 minutes or until a toothpick inserted in the centre comes out clean. Serve warm or cold.

NOTE: Cashews can be used instead of peanuts.

INDIA

Indian cooking is usually very spicy. Cardamom comes from a native Indian plant; its seeds are dried and ground into powder.

Spicy Carrot Pudding

4 servings

INGREDIENTS

4 medium carrots, grated 4
875 mL milk 3 1/2 cups
pinch whole or ground saffron
pinch ground cardamom
2 pinches ground cinnamon
3 pinches ground cloves
160 mL sugar 2/3 cup
125 mL milk 1/2 cup
15 to 30 mL cornstarch 1 to 2 tbsp
1 egg, beaten 1
60 mL ground almonds 1/4 cup

METHOD

1. In a large skillet, cook the carrots in the milk with the saffron until tender.
2. Add the sugar and spices. Stir with a wooden spoon to dissolve the sugar.
3. Continue cooking until the mixture is slightly creamy, stirring frequently.
4. Dilute the cornstarch in the milk and add the egg and almonds. Add this mixture to the skillet to thicken the milk and carrot mixture until it has the texture of a pudding.
5. Adjust the consistency as needed with a tablespoon of cornstarch and correct the seasoning.
6. Serve warm or cold.

NOTE: Do not boil mixtures that contain eggs.

LAOS

Coconut, the fruit of the coconut palm, comes from southern Asia. Over the centuries, it has become indispensable, since it is not only edible but also yields oil, fuel and building materials.

Bananas with Coconut and Candied Ginger

6 servings

INGREDIENTS

6 ripe bananas 6
1 can (396 mL) thick coconut milk 1 can (14 oz.)
60 mL sugar 1/4 cup
30 mL diced candied ginger 2 tbsp
or 10 mL grated fresh ginger 2 tsp
30 mL grated coconut 2 tbsp

METHOD

1. Peel the bananas and slice in half lengthwise.
2. In a skillet, heat the coconut milk with the sugar until it begins to steam.
3. Add the ginger and bananas.
4. Cook 4 to 5 minutes over low heat until the bananas are softened.
5. Serve immediately 1 complete banana per person, drizzled with coconut milk and sprinkled with grated coconut.

NOTE: Do not overcook the bananas or they will fall apart.

PHILIPPINES

These cupcakes are known as capuchinos in the Philippines. Brandy, which is distilled from wine and aged in oak barrels, was introduced to Asia by English colonists. The word "brandy" is derived from the verb "brand," which means to burn.

Brandy Cupcakes

4 to 6 servings

INGREDIENTS

80 mL flour **1/3 cup**
2 mL baking powder **1/2 tsp**
1 mL baking soda **1/4 tsp**
30 mL ground almonds **2 tbsp**
1 egg **1**
80 mL white or brown sugar **1/3 cup**
45 mL cooled melted butter **3 tbsp**
30 mL milk **2 tbsp**
30 mL brandy **2 tbsp**
15 mL lemon zest **1 tbsp**

Syrup:

80 mL water **1/3 cup**
60 mL sugar **1/4 cup**
30 mL brandy **2 tbsp**

METHOD

1. Preheat the oven to 180°C (375°F).
2. Grease a miniature muffin tin.
3. In a large bowl, sift the flour with the baking powder and baking soda. Add the almonds. Make a well in the centre. Set aside.
4. Cream the egg with the sugar.
5. Add the butter, milk, brandy and lemon zest to the egg mixture.
6. Pour the liquid mixture into the well in the dry ingredients. Stir well.
7. Place 15 mL (1 tbsp) of mixture in each muffin cup and bake 4 to 5 minutes in the centre of the oven until the cupcakes puff up and turn golden.
8. Meanwhile, prepare the syrup: in a small saucepan, bring the water to a boil with the sugar. As soon as the sugar is well dissolved, remove the saucepan from the heat and add the brandy.
9. When the cupcakes are done, unmould them immediately and dip them in the syrup.
10. Drain on a rack. Serve warm or chilled.

The German word strudel literally means "eddy" or "whirlpool." This Viennese pastry can be made with a sweet or savoury filling.

AUSTRIA

Fruit and Cheese Strudel

6 servings

INGREDIENTS

250 g light cream cheese **1 8-oz package**
60 mL sugar **1/4 cup**
5 mL ground cinnamon **1 tsp**
15 mL all-purpose white flour **1 tbsp**
60 mL melted unsalted butter **1/4 cup**
6 sheets phyllo pastry, thawed **6 sheets**
2 apples, peeled and diced **2**
2 plums, peeled and diced **2**
80 mL raisins **1/3 cup**
30 mL milk **2 tbsp**
30 mL sugar **2 tbsp**

METHOD

1. Preheat the oven to 200°C (400°F).
2. Combine the cream cheese with the sugar, cinnamon and flour. Set aside.
3. Brush the phyllo sheets with butter and fold in half lengthwise.
4. Fill each of the 6 sheets by spreading the cream cheese mixture lengthwise down the centre.
5. Combine the fruits and arrange on top of the cream cheese.
6. Brush the edges of each phyllo sheet with melted butter, roll (like a jelly roll) and pinch the ends closed.
7. Brush the phyllo rolls with milk and sprinkle with sugar.
8. Bake in the centre of the oven 15 minutes, lower the temperature to 180°C (375°F) and bake for another 15 minutes. Serve the strudel warm with whipped cream topping.

GERMANY *Kirsch is distilled from cherries that come primarily from the Black Forest region of Germany. The cherries are first fermented in barrels before the liquid is distilled. The subtly flavoured liqueur is served as a digestive and used in baking.*

Cherries in Kirsch

6 servings

INGREDIENTS

- **500 mL** fresh or canned pitted cherries **2 cups**
- **60 mL** sugar **1/4 cup**
- **60 mL** kirsch **1/4 cup**
- **125 mL** 35% cream **1/2 cup**

or

- **250 mL** vanilla ice cream **1 cup**

METHOD

1. In a bowl, combine the cherries, sugar and kirsch.
2. Place in small sherbet or martini glasses. Top with cream.

   or

   Place scoops of ice cream in the glasses and top with the cherries.

POLAND *While rum babas are readily available in French pastry shops, they actually originated in Poland. The Polish word baba means "honest woman."*

Rum Baba Cake

8 servings

INGREDIENTS

- **125 mL** raisins **1/2 cup**
- **250 mL** water **1 cup**
- **125 mL** rum **1/2 cup**
- **160 mL** sugar **2/3 cup**
- **1 8-g envelope** yeast **1 1/4-oz envelope**
- **80 mL** lukewarm water **1/3 cup**
- **2** eggs **2**
- **15 mL** sugar **1 tbsp**
- **310 mL** flour **1 1/4 cups**
- **1 mL** salt **1/4 tsp**
- **80 mL** unsalted butter, melted and cooled **1/3 cup**

METHOD

1. In a saucepan, combine the raisins, water, rum and sugar. Bring to a boil and simmer until the raisins are plump. Remove from heat and let cool. Drain the raisins and set aside the rum syrup.
2. Meanwhile, activate the yeast in lukewarm water.
3. Beat the eggs with the sugar and gradually add the flour.
4. Add the salt and butter. Beat the batter for 3 to 4 minutes.
5. Stir in the plumped raisins.
6. Pour the batter into a greased springform pan. Keep warm until the dough has doubled in size, 30 minutes to 1 hour.
7. Meanwhile, preheat the oven to 180°C (375°F).
8. Bake the cake 25 to 30 minutes in the centre of the oven or until a knife inserted in the centre comes out clean.
9. Let stand 10 to 15 minutes before unmoulding. Cool on a rack.
10. Soak the baba in the rum syrup. Drain and serve with whipped cream.

Cranberries are traditionally served at Christmas dinner, as a side dish for roast goose and red cabbage. Here, they are featured in a nutritious, easy-to-make soufflé.

DENMARK

Healthy Cranberry Soufflé

6 to 8 servings

INGREDIENTS

300 g fresh or frozen cranberries **1 1/4 cups**
80 mL sugar **1/3 cup**
125 mL water **1/2 cup**
3 egg whites **3**
60 mL sugar **1/4 cup**
15 mL white flour **1 tbsp**

METHOD

1. In a saucepan, cook the cranberries and sugar over low heat 20 to 25 minutes.
2. Preheat the oven to 180°C (375°F).
3. Whip the egg whites into peaks and add the sugar and flour. Chill.
4. When the cranberries are cooked, pass them through a strainer or food mill to remove the seeds and skin. Let the purée cool.
5. Fold the purée into the egg whites using a spatula.
6. Pour into a large buttered soufflé dish or 8 individual ramekins (fill two-thirds full).
7. Bake in the centre of the oven 15 to 20 minutes until the soufflé has risen. Serve immediately.

Sherry is a very popular fortified wine from Andalusia in Southern Spain. It is called jerez in Spanish and xerès in French.

SPAIN

Crème Caramel with Sherry and Valencia Oranges

4 servings

- 4 Valencia oranges 4
- 5 mL grated orange zest 1 tsp
- 250 mL water 1 cup
- 250 mL sugar 1 cup
- 250 mL milk 1 cup
- 60 mL 35% cream (optional) 1/4 cup
- 2 eggs, beaten 2
- 60 mL sugar 1/4 cup
- 30 mL sherry 2 tbsp

METHOD

1. Peel the oranges, saving the peel from two of them (zest), and dice the flesh.
2. In a saucepan, dissolve the sugar in the water. Add the orange pieces and zest. Cook 20 minutes over low heat.
3. Using a slotted spoon, remove the orange pieces and zest and place in 4 medium-sized ramekins. Continue cooking the syrup until it is amber in colour. Pour over the fruit in the ramekins.
4. Meanwhile, heat the milk and cream until the mixture begins to steam. Cream the eggs with the sugar and add the sherry. When the milk is hot, whisk it into the eggs. Pour this mixture into the ramekins.
5. Place the ramekins in an ovenproof pan filled with water halfway up the side of the ramekins. Bake in the centre of the oven 25 to 30 minutes or until set (a knife inserted in the centre comes out clean). Remove the ramekins from the pan and let cool at room temperature. Chill before serving.
6. Unmould onto plates and serve.

NOTE: Valencia oranges are only available for a short while each year. They are harvested in Spain (and elsewhere) between April and July. Any other juicy, slightly sour orange can be used instead.

ENGLAND

Coffee-flavoured Queen Elizabeth Cake

10 to 12 servings

INGREDIENTS

Cake:

250 mL hot strong coffee **1 cup**
250 mL whole dates or date pieces **1 cup**
125 mL unsalted butter **1/2 cup**
125 mL brown sugar **1/2 cup**
2 eggs **2**
500 mL all-purpose flour **2 cups**
15 mL baking powder **1 tbsp**
7 mL baking soda **1 1/2 tsp**
5 mL vanilla **1 tsp**
125 mL walnut pieces **1/2 cup**

Topping:

375 mL grated coconut **1 1/2 cups**
160 mL brown sugar **2/3 cup**
80 mL unsalted butter **1/3 cup**
80 mL cream or milk **1/3 cup**

METHOD

1. Preheat the oven to 175°C (350°F).
2. Soak the dates in the hot coffee to plump them up. Let cool.
3. Cream the butter and brown sugar.
4. Add the eggs one by one, beating well after each one.
5. Combine the flour, baking powder and baking soda. Stir into the wet ingredients, alternating with the cooled coffee. Drain the dates.
6. Add the vanilla, dates and nuts and stir until smooth.
7. Spread in a 23-cm (8-in.) greased and floured cake pan.
8. Bake in the centre of the oven 40 to 45 minutes or until a knife inserted in the centre of the cake comes out clean.
9. Meanwhile, mix all the topping ingredients in a small saucepan. Bring to a boil and simmer 5 to 10 minutes.
10. Pour the topping over the cake as soon as it comes out of the oven and cool or chill completely before cutting into servings.

A far is a flan made with prunes. It is the forerunner of such Breton dishes as crepes and galettes. The prunes may be replaced by dried apricots or fresh pears.

FRANCE

Far aux pruneaux

6 to 8 servings

INGREDIENTS

375 mL pitted prunes **1 1/2 cups**

500 mL piping hot tea **2 cups**

125 mL dark rum or calvados **1/2 cup**

180 mL all-purpose white flour **3/4 cup**

250 mL icing sugar **1 cup**

4 eggs **4**

500 mL milk **2 cups**

unsalted butter

1. Preheat the oven to 180°C (350°F).
2. Soak the prunes in the tea and half the rum until well plumped, about 1 hour. Drain.
3. Cream the eggs with the sugar.
4. Gently fold in the flour with a spatula until the mixture is smooth.
5. Add the milk and remaining rum to the egg mixture.
6. Butter and flour an ovenproof dish.
7. Pour the batter into the dish and arrange the prunes on top.
8. Bake 45 minutes or until a knife inserted in the centre comes out clean. Serve warm or cold.

NOTE: Cover with aluminum foil if the top is browning too quickly.

Pudding is a perennial favourite with the British. There are many different kinds of puddings served warm and generally topped with custard cream.

ENGLAND

Fruit Pudding

6 servings

INGREDIENTS

430 mL flour **1 3/4 cups**
10 mL baking powder **2 tsp**
5 mL baking soda **1 tsp**
2 mL ground cinnamon **1/2 tsp**
1 mL ground nutmeg **1/4 tsp**
1 mL ground ginger **1/4 tsp**
1 mL ground cloves **1/4 tsp**
500 mL assorted dried or candied fruit **2 cups**
15 mL orange zest **1 tbsp**
15 mL lemon zest **1 tbsp**
80 mL softened butter **1/3 cup**
125 mL brown sugar **1/2 cup**
1 egg **1**
125 mL strong tea, cooled **1/2 cup**

METHOD

1. Preheat the oven to 200°C (400°F).
2. Grease a pudding mould or soufflé dish.
3. Sift the dry ingredients into a bowl and add the fruit and zest. Make a well in the centre and set aside.
4. In another bowl, cream the butter with the brown sugar. Add the egg and then pour in the tea.
5. Pour the liquid ingredients into the well in the dry ingredients and stir until fully blended.
6. Spread the batter in the mould and cover with aluminum foil.
7. Bake about 1 1/2 hours in a pan filled with water halfway up the side of the mould, until a toothpick inserted in the centre comes out clean.
8. Cool for at least 1 hour before unmoulding. Serve with custard cream.

We would like to thank Suzanne Daubois for explaining her traditional recipe, which inspired the following version.

Belgian Waffles

6 to 8 servings

INGREDIENTS

375 mL softened unsalted butter **1 1/2 cups**
500 mL white or brown sugar **2 cups**
8 eggs, separated **8**
5 mL vanilla or almond extract **1 tsp**
750 mL white flour **3 cups**

METHOD

1. Cream the butter and the sugar.
2. Add the egg yolks one by one and the vanilla or almond extract, beating well after each addition.
3. Sift the flour over the bowl, stirring it into the mixture.
4. Beat the egg whites into very firm peaks and fold into the mixture.
5. Refrigerate the dough overnight or at least six hours.
6. Preheat the waffle iron for a few minutes and grease as needed.
7. Place a small amount of batter in the waffle iron and cook until the waffle is crisp and golden. Repeat the process with the rest of the batter.
8. Serve hot or cold with the topping of your choice.

Quick Belgian Chocolate Sauce

INGREDIENTS

250 mL 35% cream **1 cup**
45 mL sugar **3 tbsp**
160 mL chopped dark Belgian chocolate **2/3 cup**

METHOD

1. In a small saucepan, heat the cream over low heat with the sugar until it begins to steam.
2. Add the chopped chocolate and melt completely, stirring with a whisk until smooth.
3. Serve hot with Belgian waffles or fresh fruit.

NOTE: This sauce can be made in the microwave, following the same steps.

Chestnut Chocolate Roll

FRANCE

8 to 10 servings

The chestnut is used in many sophisticated dishes, particularly regional recipes and as a side dish for a winter meal. It is used whole, frozen or preserved, puréed, creamed, ground into flour or made into jam

INGREDIENTS

Cake:

6 eggs, separated 6

2 egg yolks 2

160 mL white flour 2/3 cup

125 mL sugar 1/2 cup

80 mL melted unsalted butter, cooled 1/3 cup

Ganache:

125 mL 35% cream 1/2 cup

115 g dark chocolate pieces 1/4 lb

Chestnut butter cream:

2 egg whites 2

80 mL sugar 1/3 cup

180 mL softened unsalted butter 3/4 cup

80 mL chestnut cream or purée 1/3 cup

Syrup:

80 mL water 1/3 cup

80 mL sugar 1/3 cup

Topping:

cocoa powder

icing sugar

NOTE: Remove the cake from the refrigerator at least 30 minutes before serving so that the butter cream can soften. The butter cream, syrup and ganache can be prepared in advance and refrigerated. In this case, let the ganache and butter cream stand at room temperature 30 minutes to 1 hour before assembling the cake.

METHOD

Cake:

1. Preheat the oven to 180°C (375°F).
2. Grease and flour a 25-cm x 45-cm (10-in. x 18-in.) baking sheet.
3. Cream the 8 egg yolks with the sugar and stir in the melted butter. Sift the flour into the bowl.
4. Whip the 6 egg whites into very firm peaks and gently fold into the egg yolk mixture. Do not overstir.
5. Spread on the sheet and bake in the centre of the oven 12 to 15 minutes or until it is lightly browned and a knife inserted in the cake comes out clean.
6. Place the cake onto a damp dishtowel and roll. Let cool.

Ganache:

1. Heat the cream over low heat until it begins to steam.
2. Meanwhile, place the chocolate in a large bowl.
3. Pour the hot cream over the chocolate and stir with a whisk until the chocolate has melted completely.
4. Cool to room temperature and refrigerate 30 minutes to 1 hour before using.

Syrup:

1. In a small saucepan, bring the water and sugar to a boil. Turn off the heat and let cool. Set aside.

Butter cream:

1. Whip the egg whites into very firm peaks, adding the sugar gradually.
2. Gradually add the butter, beating well after each addition. Beat for a few minutes after all the butter has been added to obtain a very smooth butter cream.
3. Stir in the puréed chestnuts. The mixture should be used immediately while it is at room temperature.

Assembling the cake:

1. Unroll the cooled cake and brush with syrup, letting it soak in.
2. Spread the cooled ganache on the cake, followed by the butter cream.
3. Roll the cake lengthwise. Decorate the top with cocoa and sugar, in a pattern, if desired.
4. Cut into servings and chill.

Cheese and Honey Pie

8 to 10 servings

INGREDIENTS

500 mL all-purpose wholewheat flour **2 cups**
1 mL salt **1/4 tsp**
250 mL softened unsalted butter **1 cup**
30-45 mL ice water **2-3 tbsp**
flour for rolling out the dough
475 g ricotta cheese **1 lb**
125 mL liquid honey **1/2 cup**
4 large eggs **4**
15 mL ground cinnamon **1 tbsp**
30 mL liquid honey **2 tbsp**

METHOD

1 Combine the flour and salt. Gently cut in the butter with a pastry cutter or using your hands. Stir in the water. Knead until the dough is smooth and elastic. Cover and refrigerate 30 minutes.

2 Preheat the oven to 175°C (350°F).

3 Roll out the dough and place in a 25-cm (10-in.) pie plate. Prick the dough several times with a fork. Bake in the centre of the oven 10 to 12 minutes, until lightly browned. Remove and set aside. Increase the oven temperature to 180°C (375°F).

4 In a bowl, combine the cheese, honey, eggs and half the cinnamon. Pour into the pie shell. Bake 30 to 35 minutes, until the top is golden.

5 Remove from oven, brush the top of the pie with the remaining 30 mL (2 tbsp) honey and sprinkle with the rest of the cinnamon. Serve chilled.

This Italian dessert contains marsala, a fortified wine from Sicily. It can be served as is, frozen or spooned over fruit. In Italian, it is called zabaglione.

ITALY

Sabayon with Marsala

4 servings

INGREDIENTS

- **4** egg yolks **4**
- **60 mL** icing sugar **1/4 cup**
- **45 mL** marsala **3 tbsp**
- **60 mL** white wine **1/4 cup**
- **1 mL** ground cinnamon (optional) **1/4 tsp**

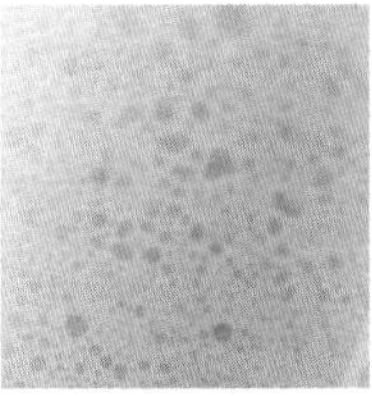

METHOD

1. In a bowl, cream the egg yolks with the sugar. Stir in the marsala, wine and cinnamon.
2. Place the bowl over a saucepan of water and, over low heat, beat the mixture until a very creamy mousse is obtained. IMPORTANT: Do not boil the water to avoid cooking the eggs.
3. Serve immediately in sherbet glasses with biscotti or butter cookies, or spoon over fresh fruit.

NOTE: Serve the sabayon immediately, since the texture changes when it is prepared in advance, and the ingredients might separate.

Tiramisu is an Italian dessert invented in the 1970s. It is made from mascarpone cheese and ladyfingers soaked in coffee. We would like to thank our dear friend Gino Cobuzzi for his delectable recipe.

ITALY

Tiramisu

8 to 10 servings

INGREDIENTS

400 g ladyfingers **12.5 oz**
475 g mascarpone cheese **15 oz**
4 eggs, separated **4**
30 mL sugar **2 tbsp**
3 cups strong coffee **3**
or 6 small cups espresso coffee, cooled
60 mL marsala **1/4 cup**
60 mL cocoa powder **1/4 cup**

METHOD

1. Whip the egg whites into firm peaks.
2. Cream the egg yolks with the sugar.
3. Add the mascarpone to the egg yolks.
4. Very gently fold in the egg whites.
5. Combine the coffee with the marsala.
6. Spread mascarpone cream on the bottom of a 23-cm to 25-cm (9-in. to 10-in.) springform pan. Arrange the ladyfingers vertically round the inside of the pan.
7. Assemble the tiramisu by alternating layers of mascarpone cream with the ladyfingers lightly soaked in the coffee mixture. Begin and end with a layer of cream.
8. Sprinkle with cocoa powder.
9. Chill 3 to 4 hours before serving. Unmould and tie with a decorative ribbon.

NOTE: Cut the rounded bottom edge off the ladyfingers so that they can be placed cut side down around the springform pan without falling over.

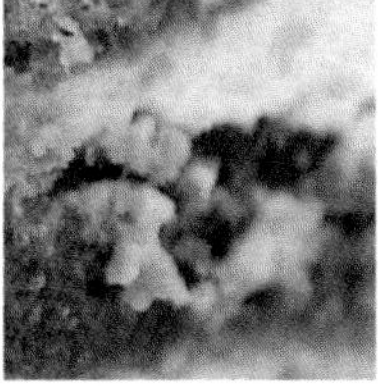

Portuguese desserts are usually made with eggs, sugar and almonds and flavoured with citrus fruits or cinnamon. Many of these recipes were developed by religious orders back when they were the only ones to have access to the ingredients. Madeira is a fortified wine that comes from a Portuguese island of the same name. Its flavour is similar to port: smooth, warm and flavourful.

PORTUGAL

Cinnamon Orange Cream with Madeira

4 servings

INGREDIENTS

560 mL milk **2 1/4 cups**

long strips of peel from **1** orange

1 cinnamon stick **1**

6 egg yolks **6**

125 mL sugar **1/2 cup**

22 mL white flour **1 1/2 tbsp**

45 mL Madeira **3 tbsp**

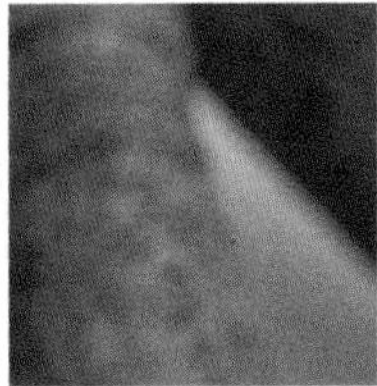

METHOD

1. Preheat the oven to 175°C (350°F).
2. In a saucepan, heat the milk with the orange peel and cinnamon stick until the milk begins to steam. Set aside.
3. Meanwhile, cream the egg yolks with the sugar.
4. Sift the flour onto the egg yolk mixture and stir in gently.
5. Add a few spoonfuls of warm milk to the egg mixture to warm it up. IMPORTANT: Stir while adding the milk to prevent the eggs from curdling.
6. Pour into the hot milk and heat over low heat until the mixture thickens, stirring constantly with a wooden spoon.
7. Remove the cinnamon stick and orange peel from the cooled milk. Add the Madeira.
8. Spoon the cream into 4 medium-sized ramekins and place them in an ovenproof pan. Pour water into the pan until it comes halfway up the side of the ramekins.
9. Continue cooking in the centre of the oven for about 15 minutes.
10. Remove from oven and let cool at room temperature. Serve warm or chilled.

NOTE: Cinnamon orange cream can also be served as a crème brûlée. Just sprinkle the tops with sugar and caramelize.

This recipe combines several typical Portuguese ingredients, including figs stuffed with almonds and port. Port comes from the Douro valley in Portugal and is exported through the town of Porto. It is the world's best-known and most popular fortified wine.

PORTUGAL

Figs with Nuts and Honey

4 to 6 servings

INGREDIENTS

500 mL red wine **2 cups**
500 mL port **2 cups**
250 mL orange juice **1 cup**
180 mL honey **3/4 cup**
1 cinnamon stick **1**
zest of **1** orange
454 g dried figs and/or apricots **1 lb**
375 mL nuts (almonds or walnuts) **1 1/2 cups**

Topping:
250 mL plain yogurt **1 cup**
30 mL brown sugar **2 tbsp**
5 mL ground cinnamon **1 tsp**

METHOD

1. Combine the liquids, cinnamon and orange zest.
2. Bring to a boil and simmer 10 minutes.
3. Cut the figs in half and stuff with 3 or 4 nut pieces.
4. Gently place the figs in the liquid and cook 45 minutes over low heat.
5. Combine the yogurt, brown sugar and cinnamon.
6. Serve the figs chilled or warm, topped with the sweetened cinnamon yogurt.

Stuffed Fruits

6 servings

INGREDIENTS

80 mL sugar **1/3 cup**
60 mL water **1/4 cup**
45 mL vodka **3 tbsp**
0.5 mL freshly ground pepper **1/8 tsp**
12 fresh or dried apricots **12**
12 dried dates or figs **12**
60 mL honey **1/4 cup**
80 mL assorted nuts **1/3 cup**
45 mL graham cracker crumbs **3 tbsp**

METHOD

1. In a saucepan, blend the sugar, water, vodka and pepper. Bring to a boil and simmer 10 minutes over low heat.
2. Remove from heat. Add the apricots and dates. Leave to plump for 15 minutes. Drain.
3. Press your finger into the centre of the apricots and cut a slit in the dates.
4. Combine the honey, nuts and graham cracker crumbs.
5. Stuff the fruits with the crumb mixture.
6. Let cool before serving with vanilla ice cream.

Vodka, the national drink of Russia, was first a traditional beverage that Poles drank at any point during the meal. A spirit distilled from potatoes, grain or beets, vodka has virtually no odour but packs a punch because of its high alcohol content.

RUSSIA

Vodka-flambéed Strawberries

4 servings

INGREDIENTS

1 L fresh strawberries, washed and hulled **4 cups**
80 mL vodka **1/3 cup**
10 mL freshly ground black pepper **2 tsp**
60 mL sugar **1/4 cup**
160 mL 35% cream **2/3 cup**
30 mL icing sugar **2 tbsp**

METHOD

1. Slice the strawberries in half and arrange in dessert bowls.
2. In a small saucepan, combine the vodka with the pepper and sugar. Heat over low heat to dissolve the sugar and warm up the alcohol.
3. Meanwhile, whip the cream with the sugar. Set aside.
4. Pour the hot vodka mixture over the strawberries and flambé.
5. Top with whipped cream and serve immediately.

Swiss chocolate is appreciated the world over. Truffles are traditionally served at Christmas. Made in various shapes and flavours, they make a lovely gift. They make a perfect dessert served with delicate cookies and coffee or as a decoration on cakes and pastries.

SWITZERLAND

Truffles

makes **30**

INGREDIENTS

250 mL 35% cream **1 cup**
250 g dark chocolate pieces **9 oz**
60 mL cocoa powder **1/4 cup**

METHOD

1. Heat the cream over low heat until it begins to steam.
2. Add the chopped chocolate and whisk until the mixture is smooth. IMPORTANT: The chocolate must be completely melted.
3. Let cool to room temperature and refrigerate for at least 2 hours until the ganache is firm.
4. Shape into balls and roll in the cocoa powder.
5. Use the truffles as a garnish or serve as is, chilled or at room temperature.

NOTE: There are many possible variations: adding a flavour extract, alcohol or liqueur to the melted chocolate, dissolving a little instant coffee in the cream or adding a pinch of spice, rolling the truffles in sugar or in chopped or ground nuts. Your imagination is the only limit!

Turkish cuisine has been influenced by both European and Asian cooking. A Turkish dessert is always served with coffee, the national beverage. The average Turk drinks 10 cups of coffee a day.

TURKEY

Pistachio Roll

8 servings

INGREDIENTS

500 mL chopped unsalted pistachios **2 cups**
80 mL sugar **1/3 cup**
7 mL ground cinnamon **1 1/2 tsp**
80 mL melted butter **1/3 cup**
45 mL olive oil **3 tbsp**
1 package phyllo pastry, thawed **1 package**

Syrup:
250 mL water **1 cup**
375 mL sugar **1 1/2 cups**
60 mL honey **1/4 cup**
2 cloves **2**
1 cinnamon stick **1**
2 mL ground nutmeg **1/2 tsp**

METHOD

1. Preheat the oven to 175°C (350°F).
2. Combine the pistachios, sugar and cinnamon.
3. Combine the butter and oil.
4. Brush a sheet of phyllo with the butter mixture and fold in half. Brush the folded sheet with butter on both sides and fold in half again.
5. Place 45 mL (3 tbsp) mixture in the centre of the phyllo.
6. Fold the ends to contain the filling and roll.
7. Repeat with the remaining phyllo sheets.
8. Place the rolls on a buttered cookie sheet and bake 30 minutes.
9. Combine all the syrup ingredients. Bring to a boil and simmer 10 minutes. Remove the cloves and cinnamon stick. Set aside.
10. After removing the rolls from the oven, dip them in the syrup. Let cool before serving.

NOTE: If the dough browns too quickly, cover with aluminum foil.

The original European recipe for clafouti is much denser than the one below, which is more like a kiwi flan baked in a crust. This is another dessert that comes from New Zealand's earliest colonists.

NEW ZEALAND

Kiwi Mint Clafouti

8 servings

INGREDIENTS

5 eggs **5**
125 mL sugar **1/2 cup**
2 mL vanilla extract **1/2 tsp**
500 mL milk **2 cups**
1 mL nutmeg **1/4 tsp**
12 kiwis **12**
60 mL flour **1/4 cup**
45 mL chopped fresh mint **3 tbsp**
1 23-cm shortcrust pastry shell (10-in.), unbaked **1**

METHOD

1. Preheat the oven to 175°C (350°F).
2. Cream the eggs with the sugar. Add the vanilla.
3. In a saucepan, heat the milk with the nutmeg until it starts to steam.
4. Meanwhile, peel the kiwis, cut into eighths and roll in the flour. Arrange the pieces in a rosette on the pie shell.
5. Slowly add the milk to the eggs, stirring constantly. Add the mint and mix well. Pour into the pie shell.
6. Bake in the centre of the oven 50 to 60 minutes or until a knife inserted in the centre comes out clean. Serve warm or chilled.

Pineapple was introduced to Britain with the discovery of the New World. The method and basic ingredients of this recipe are typical of "down under" cooking, which was strongly influenced by the Europeans who immigrated there.

NEW ZEALAND

Pineapple Custard with Fruit Topping

4 servings

INGREDIENTS

80 mL sugar **1/3 cup**
5 egg yolks **5**
60 mL flour or cornstarch **1/4 cup**
1 540-mL can crushed pineapple **1 19-oz can**
500 mL milk **2 cups**
2 mL vanilla extract **1/2 tsp**

Topping:
1 kiwi, sliced **1**
1/2 mango, cut into pieces **1/2**
1/2 papaya, cut into pieces **1/2**
60 mL toasted unsweetened coconut **1/4 cup**

METHOD

1. Cream the egg yolks with the sugar. Add the flour.
2. In a saucepan, heat the milk until it begins to steam.
3. Pour a little milk into the egg mixture to warm it up. Add the remaining milk and continue cooking 4 to 5 minutes over low heat, until the mixture thickens, without letting it boil. Add the vanilla.
4. Meanwhile, cook the pineapple with 125 mL (1/2 cup) sugar 10 to 12 minutes. Drain the pineapple.
5. Stir the pineapple into the custard.
6. Pour the mixture into a bowl and lay plastic wrap directly on the surface of the custard. Let cool for 30 minutes at room temperature. Refrigerate at least 5 to 6 hours.
7. Just before serving, whisk the custard to fluff it up.
8. Place the custard in a deep dish and top with fruit and toasted coconut.

NOTE: The custard can be used as a pie or cake filling. It can also be made with another fruit, such as mango, papaya or banana.

The kumquat, a citrus fruit, comes from China, where its name means golden orange. It is also grown in Australia. It can be eaten peel and all, and is often used in desserts, jams and marmalades, cakes and pies. It can also be candied.

AUSTRALIA

Orange and Kumquat Pie

6 to 8 servings

INGREDIENTS

- **18** kumquats **18**
- **60 mL** sugar **1/4 cup**
- **250 mL** orange juice **1 cup**
- zest of **1** orange
- **60 mL** unsalted butter **1/4 cup**
- **250 mL** sugar **1 cup**
- **6** large eggs **6**
- **30 mL** cornstarch **2 tbsp**
- **1** shortcrust or graham cracker pie shell, baked **1**

METHOD

1. Wash and thinly slice the kumquats; remove the seeds.
2. Arrange the slices in a saucepan. Cover with water, add sugar and cook over low heat for 20 minutes until the fruit is translucent and the liquid has become a thick syrup.
3. Drain and let cool. Set aside the syrup to be used to decorate the plates.
4. Meanwhile, in the top of a double boiler, blend the juice and orange zest, butter and sugar. Cook over medium heat, stirring frequently, until the sugar has dissolved.
5. In a bowl, beat the eggs. Dilute the cornstarch in 30 mL (2 tbsp) water or orange juice and then stir into the eggs. Warm up the mixture by adding a few spoonfuls of the warm orange juice mixture. Add to the mixture in the double boiler and whisk constantly until the mixture thickens, taking care to keep it from boiling.
6. Pour the mixture into the pie shell, let cool and garnish with slices of candied kumquat.

This recipe combines the culinary influences of England and the fresh products available in Australia, cottage cheese being quintessentially English and melons and coconut being easily accessible on the Australian continent. The melon can be replaced by other Australian fruit such as kiwi, papaya or passion fruit.

AUSTRALIA

Coconut Mousse

6 servings

INGREDIENTS

125 mL 35% cream **1/2 cup**
80 mL honey **1/3 cup**
2 mL vanilla extract **1/2 tsp**
2 egg whites **2**
500 mL cottage cheese **2 cups**
185 mL unsweetened toasted coconut **3/4 cup**
1 honeydew or cantaloupe, seeded and sliced **1**

METHOD

1. Whip the cream and add the honey and vanilla extract.
2. Whip the egg whites into firm peaks and fold into the whipped cream.
3. Add the cheese and coconut, stirring gently. Mix only until well blended.
4. Pour into a large bowl or 6 dessert bowls. Refrigerate.
5. Serve well chilled with melon slices.

This recipe can be time-consuming if you make the meringue shells yourself. Luckily, ready-made shells can now be purchased at the supermarket. Meringue reflects the British influence on Australian cooking.

AUSTRALIA

Pavlova

4 servings

INGREDIENTS

Chantilly:

250 mL 35% cream **1 cup**
60-80 mL icing sugar **1/4-1/3 cup**
2 mL vanilla extract **1/2 tsp**
4 storebought meringue shells **4**

Fruits:

2 kiwis, halved **2**
1 starfruit, sliced **1**
8 lychees, halved **8**
1 papaya, sliced **1**

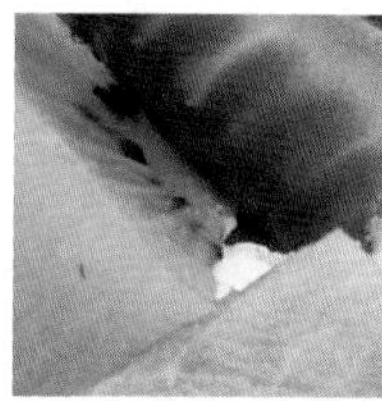

METHOD

1 Whip the cream and add the sugar and vanilla extract.

2 Fill the meringue shells with whipped cream.

3 Garnish with fruit and serve immediately.

Index

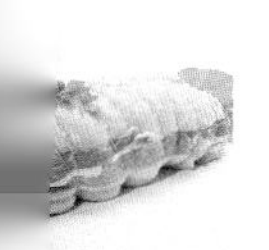      

Index

Index

Index

Index

Index

Index

Index

Notes